Counterspell

A Field Manual for the Counter-Revolution

Michael Belcher

Counterspell Group, LLC

Published by Counterspell Group, LLC

Wakefield, New Hampshire

counterspellgroup.com

ISBN 979-8-950211-00-3 (paperback)

ISBN 979-8-950211-01-0 (hardcover)

ISBN 979-8-950211-02-7 (ebook)

First Edition

Printed in the United States of America

10 9 8 7 6 5 4 3 2 1

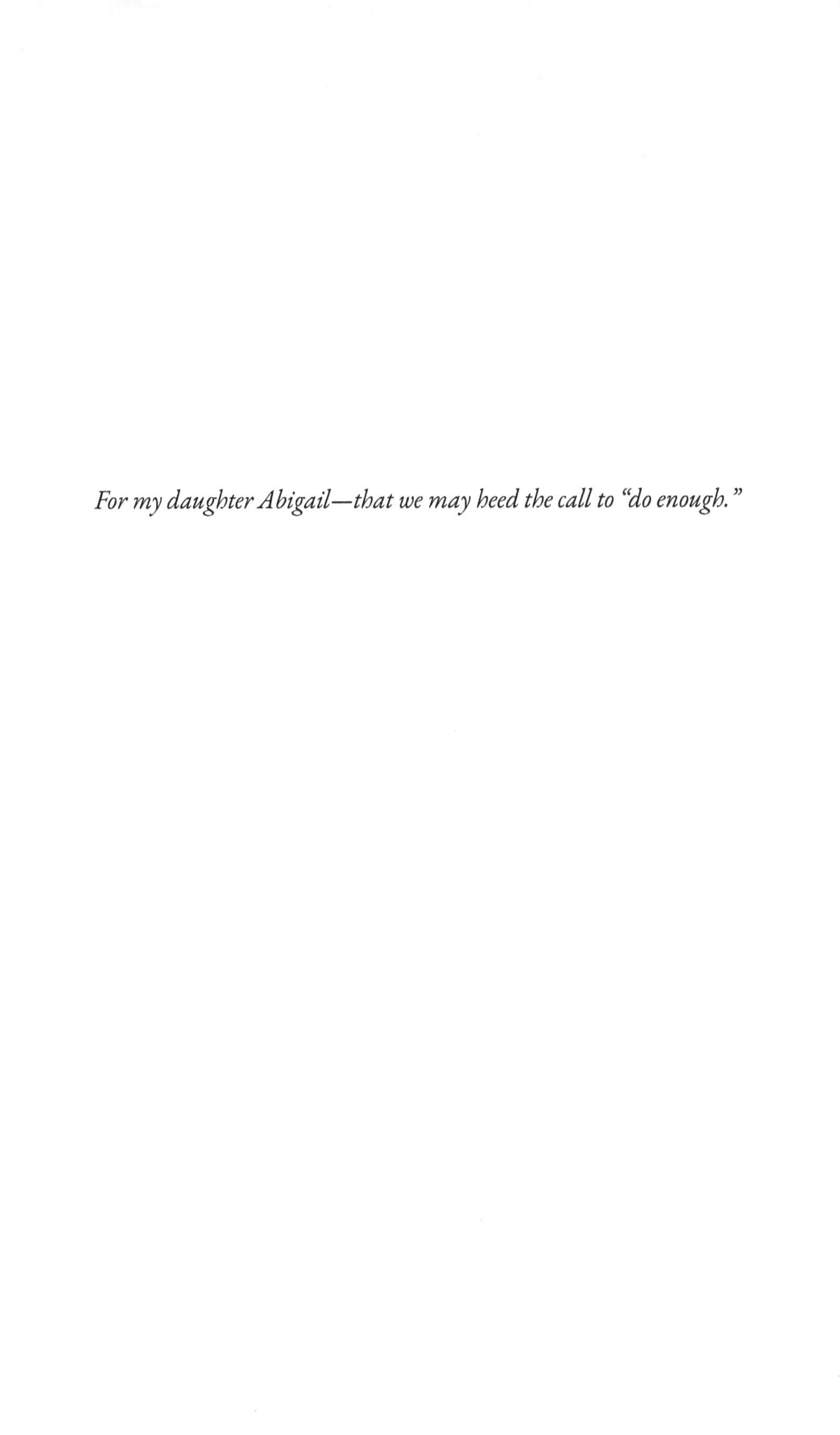

For my daughter Abigail—that we may heed the call to "do enough."

from Plato's Republic

It is the beginning of any undertaking which is the most important part—especially for anything young and tender. That is the time when each individual thing can be most easily moulded, and receive whatever mark you want to impress upon it... We shall persuade nurses and mothers to tell children the approved stories, and tell them that shaping children's minds with stories is far more important than trying to shape their bodies with their hands. We must reject most of the stories they tell at the moment. —Book 2, 377a–c trans. Tom Griffith, Cambridge University Press, 2000

As for the children who will be born from time to time, they will be taken away by the officials responsible for these things... The children of good parents will be taken, I think, and transferred to the nursing-pen, where there will be special nurses living separately, in a special part of the city. The children of inferior parents, on the other hand, or any deformed specimen born to the other group, will be removed from sight into some secret and hidden place, as is right. —Book 5, 460c–d trans. Tom Griffith, Cambridge University Press, 2000

We want one single, grand lie which will be believed by everybody—including the rulers, ideally, but failing that the rest of the city. . . "You are all brothers, all of you in the city. But when god made you, he used a mixture of gold in the creation of those of you who were fit to be rulers, which is why they are the most valuable. He used silver for those who were to be auxiliaries, and iron and bronze for the farmers and the rest of the skilled workers." —Book 3, 414b–415a trans. Tom Griffith, Cambridge University Press, 2000

Let them send everyone in the city over the age of ten into the countryside. Then they can isolate these people's children from the values they hold at the moment—their parents' values—and bring the children up according to their own customs and laws. . . This will be the quickest and simplest way for the city and regime we were talking about to come into being. —Book 7, 541a trans. Tom Griffith, Cambridge University Press, 2000

When someone tries to use dialectic to arrive at what each thing itself is, by means of reason, without using any of the senses, and does not give up the attempt until he grasps what good itself is, by means of thought itself, then he has come to the true end or goal of the intelligible. . . It makes no use at all of any object of the senses, but only of pure forms—working through them and towards them. And it ends in forms. —Book 7, 532a–b / Book 6, 511b–c trans. Tom Griffith, Cambridge University Press, 2000

Contents

Introduction

A Note from the Author

This book traces a religious system. Not a political movement, not an economic philosophy, not a cultural trend—a religious system, operating through a mechanism as old as civilization itself. That system runs from the mysteries of ancient Egypt through Plato's Academy, through Hegel and Marx, through the Frankfurt School and the long march through the institutions, and into your child's classroom and your state legislature. To understand it, you must see it whole. That is what this book attempts to provide, though not in a wholly comprehensive manner, as other authors have tackled some portions in such a manner that the best this author can do is cite those authors while directing the reader to those works where appropriate.

On intellectual debts. The esoteric lineage I trace from ancient Kemet through Hegel significantly stands on the work of Stephen Coughlin and Rich Higgins of Unconstrained Analytics. Their *Re-Remembering the Mis-Remembered Left*, particularly Appendix B ("Hermeticism in Hegel"), together with Glenn Magee's definitive *Hegel and the Hermetic Tradition*—whose evidentiary record I treat at length in Chapter 8—demonstrated that the modern Left operates not merely under esoteric influence but as an esoteric religious movement in its fundamental architecture. Their contribution to this field cannot be overstated, and I owe them a substantial debt. Also, many analysis and research works of James Lindsay's New Discourses have been invaluable.

This book, however, is not a restatement of their work. My contributions are significantly distinct. I strive to present this material in an accessible narrative form for a general audience. I read the primary texts directly and in depth. I apply a traditionally American theological and philosophical lens that others do not employ. I bring the perspective of a sitting state legislator and practitioner of the arts herein. I provide for the intellectual connective tissue that accounts for the most comprehensive view available on all you see happening around you. I extended the esoteric lineage through Blavatsky, CASEL, and into actual school curricula. And I followed the Greek tradition to its darkest implications—from Plato's oligarchs through Marcuse to Epstein. I, ultimately, seek to make every piece of it eminently actionable. It is not a mere curiosity.

How to read this book. I recommend reading it sequentially, at least the first time. The argument is cumulative: each chapter builds on the one before it. Chapter 1 establishes that you have been living inside a constructed false reality. Chapter 2 gives you a tool for breaking out of it. Chapters 3 through 6 trace the system from its ancient origins through Marx. Chapters 7 and 8 show how that system captured your institutions and your schools. Chapter 9 reveals who is actually on which side. Chapter 10 provides the counter-offensive toolkit. Chapter 11 lays out the strategy for winning.

This is not an academic exercise. This is a war manual for people who have yet to recognize they are at war, as, regardless of their particular interests, this war is interested in them. You are already in it.

A note on framing. This book is written for the widest possible audience. I am a Christian. My faith informs everything I write. The argument I make here does not require you to share my faith. Whether you come to it through faith, through philosophy, through common sense, or any earnest approach, I will provide all you need to follow this argument. Where the analysis touches on theology, as it must when tracing a religious system, I attempt to frame it in terms accessible to any reader. The deeper theological treatment, and fuller positive vision, is reserved for a future volume.

That said, it would be disingenuous to my very premise to attempt to stop my beliefs from shining through. A book that argues you have been living inside a constructed false reality cannot then construct a false version of its own author. No effort has been taken to deceive or obfuscate who I am or what I believe. There will, certainly, be something in this book that will offend just about every one of every stripe. If you are a progressive, the early chapters will challenge everything you hold dear. If you are a mainstream conservative, the later chapters will challenge your comfortable assumptions about institutions you trust. If you are a libertarian, the theological underpinnings will grate. If you are a Christian, the frank treatment of certain esoteric practices will disturb. I ask only this: persist. You will be rewarded with knowledge if you can endure the occasional discomfort. Truth knows nothing of discomfort or embarrassment.

Chapter 1

MY OWN PATH THROUGH

I spent my entire young adulthood working on the streets and in the trades. From volunteering as an EMT in a college town after high school, to pursuing college paramedic education, to years staffing the ambulance as an advanced life support provider—the work was physical, immediate, and unforgiving. The toll it took on my body accumulated from serial musculoskeletal injuries: hauling obese patients, assuming awkward positions in crushed motor vehicles, hauling gear miles by hand to treat a teenager tossed from a horse, calling for air evacuation, establishing a remote landing zone, and decompressing a collapsed lung. I still feel it all to this very day – from my lower back to my joints.

Later, after working in the trades first as an assistant in mobile marine servicing—working on mechanical and electrical systems on everything from johnboats to hundred-million-dollar luxury yachts—I moved on to apprentice at a public shipyard overhauling American nuclear attack submarines. I spent time first as a painter and blaster, the dirtiest and most dangerous job on the yard: working confined spaces in so much protective gear it was like a space suit, firing a blast hose with the power (and noise) of a shotgun, perpetually, in pitch darkness, removing old paint and rust in tiny and awkward confined spaces. Later, I transitioned to apprenticing as a marine electrician.

It was in this role that I experienced a major injury. I was subjected to thick, toxic smoke for an extended period, trapped in a confined space where my eyes, sinuses, throat, and lungs were burned by chemicals. I was stuck in a space so tight I could not even manage to expand my chest enough for a deep breath. It was also pitch black—no light penetrates the steel hull. Lit only by my headlamp, my hands working the cables not twelve inches in front of my face, I realized that my eyes and throat stung. Then I realized I could not even see my hands right in front of my face—the light from my headlamp could not penetrate the thick black smoke. I do not remember much about the immediate aftermath, but I coughed and sneezed out black debris for at least a week. The injury put me down hard for a very long time.

In pondering the circumstances surrounding the injury itself, I recognized the absurdity of government policy. When I had been in the paint shop, I qualified for all respirators, and I used them every day. When I transitioned to the electrical shop, instead of simply maintaining my qualifications—in case I needed them, say, in a confined space with smoke—they simply cancelled them. They rendered me incapable of drawing out the protective equipment that could have prevented my life-changing injury, and they did it because it was simply default policy, because they did not want to pay to maintain a "qual" that they decided, in their infinite wisdom, I no longer needed in that role.

I took this lesson and applied it broadly, and I began to see the incompetence of government everywhere I looked. In the immediate aftermath of my injury, I was angry—at everything and everyone. I wanted to lay blame. That is part of the initial road that led me to begin studying game theory, economics, and incentives, and I realized that government is likely the worst possible entity to handle just about everything. Later, of course, I would temper this somewhat in realizing that, ethically, there are some things (though, few) that government should do, simply because of the perverse incentives of transferring certain authorities to the private sector.

In the end, I realized that all the people I wanted to really blame were not, ultimately, responsible. It was not individually so much any one person's fault I could point a finger at and say "you did this to me." If I wanted to blame anyone, it was going to have to be the generations of the last hundred years who lost the republic and replaced it with a terrible democracy of inept identity politics and collectivism.

I recovered, slowly and not at all completely, but over time I improved. I was tired of spending all my days reading and laying about in my home. I started a small business renting out kayaks and delivering them in my truck – there's lots of lakes around me and lots of tourism. It was a niche I found that needed filling, and just weeks in I was off to a very promising start when I was attacked by a large German Shepherd while on a delivery. Again, I was laid up, severely injured, and recovering. . . and reading.

Once more, I improved in time, and I was, once more, exploring my career options as Covid hit and the nation was shocked into self-destructive lockdowns. I took my time to take it all in, and I was significantly ahead of the government in information. Early reports were coming out that Covid had an outrageous R-naught (rate of spread) and a fatality rate of 5% or more – I was wearing a mask in January of 2020 with people in the supermarkets giving me a look like I was insane. Not but a couple months later I was often the only one in the store not wearing a mask, and, irony of ironies, I was still being looked at like I was insane. Of course, I knew by that point that Covid was primarily a disease impacting the elderly, had a mortality rate closer to that of a bad flu than ebola, and I wasn't panicking.

Though, because of the compromised state of my lungs from the prior smoke inhalation injury my pulmonologist convinced me that the risk was real, and I should receive the vaccine as soon as I could. I watched the rollout for a time, and I noted very little reports of problems. I arranged to receive the vaccine in April of 2021, and it very nearly killed me. I found myself hospitalized for the better part of a week less than a month after receiving the Pfizer mRNA product, my immune system activated against my own body, partially blinded in one eye, unable to stand, suffering from a severe migraine for weeks with no relief, forgetful and confused, blood clotting, blood pressure through the roof, chest aching, and, in the moments I could use technology to read the news, seeing that the dam had broken and the reports of catastrophic reactions to the Covid vaccines were now pouring out into the public discourse. (Years later, I did have the opportunity to participate in an official legislative inquiry into Covid, and we produced incredible findings, but that is a story for a later time).

I began recovering slowly, being treated with medicine for migraines and seizures, learning how to walk again, and relearning the names of the friends I had forgotten with the help of social media. I was laid up, once more, for quite a long time – laid up and reading.

The Bible teaches to rejoice in *all things*. Not some things, but *all things*. It also teaches that the Lord turns all things for good. As difficult as it all was, I was being prepared to do what I am now doing – and being prepared to write this book.

I was raised on the Left, and the foremost orientation of that upbringing was not, in fact, the goodness of Leftism, but a hatred of—and an assuredness of the evil in—conservatism. The goodness of Leftism was, in most cases, simply presumed, without evidence, by merely framing it as the opponent of the evils of the Right; rarely deeper than "Leftism cares." It was a long series of events that eventually brought me over, first in seeing the reality of the consequences of Leftism, then in understanding the reality that, while not explicitly argued and presented along ethical lines, the effects of conservatism were far more beneficial to individuals and society than Leftism, and far less naïve of the human condition. This experience, and the slowness by which I transitioned from one side to the other—significantly slowed by the absence of explicit ethical dimensions in Rightwing discourse—made me realize that the utilitarianism of conservative argumentation was a major stumbling block. People are ethical creatures, and ethical arguments should be first above all else.

I understood the effect of social mediation and relationships on beliefs quite strongly, as it was my mother who functioned as a perpetual link to Leftism, and whose opinions of me kept me constrained, mentally, outside of the realm of reality, unwilling to make a clean break for fear of disappointment and relationship damage. Little did I realize at the time that the act of being disowned by my mother for my faith and politics would, though devastating emotionally, set me free both mentally and ethically to pursue truth and goodness.

I would have called myself a progressive for most of my young life, but of course I had no idea that the roots of the word *progressivism* meant that History—and that is actually a capital-H *History*, because History operates like a pagan spirit in Leftist ideology—is driving itself toward a desired endpoint: the Utopia of a man-made Eden.

I was deeply shaped in my early development by the works of biologist Edward O. Wilson and evolutionary biologist Richard Dawkins. Wilson's ecology and the economizing of nature, and Dawkins' evolutionary theory and memetics from *The Selfish Gene* and *The Extended Phenotype*—these were works I read in middle and high school that formed a core of my early development ethically and metaphysically. They gave me a framework that was materialist to the bone, and it took many years to understand the limitations of that frame. Many years and a whole lot of reading.

The cutting down and rebuilding of my false worldview came through several iterations—each time finding the cut was not deep enough to correct the problems. First, the cuts brought me to a place of, approximately, a moderate libertarian. I embraced liberty as ultimate, leading to a disordered view of liberty—excessive, finding that it persistently ran into that of other peoples'. My zeal for liberty turned into a fantasy of liberation. This bumping up against others led naturally into a sort of social constructivism, where the limits of discourse and actions are mediated between people – an ongoing and perpetual negotiation of sorts. It was not until years later and the final cut—to the quick—that involved full surrender to transcendent ethics as first principles, that I truly understood the full scope of this fight and the problems we all go through as we wage it. It is an internal battle, a spiritual battle, an ethical and intellectual battle, and it is, in practical terms, a linguistic battle.

In the early periods of collapse of my old worldview, I felt exceptional depression and hopelessness. This likely was a major factor in my glomming onto libertarianism—looking for anything to fill that emptiness, but ultimately holding me back from cutting deep enough for nearly another decade. Of course, eventually the libertarian philosophy I held crumbled under the weight of the withering attack from the Marxist Critical Constructivists—these philosophical nihilists are playing in the same intellectual sandbox as the libertarians, but they are much better at it, and more ruthless. I then explored Natural Law and philosophical realism, but I found those, too, lacking. Like libertarianism, they occupy the same intellectual sandbox as the Marxists, though they do hold their own a little better in the fight over constructivism. The reasons—the surprising intellectual connections between libertarianism, Natural Law, and the very postmodern Marxism they try to oppose—will become clear as the book progresses, and even more so in an upcoming work in the theological field. Eventually, I understood my own ethical and intellectual basis had to be in the same tradition of transcendent ethics that founded America, from the Puritans to the Presbyterians who fought the Revolution. That was the firm foundation – though, that's an argument to be fully developed in that upcoming work.

I studied deep. First, I studied what was wrong, and how it went wrong. I spent year after year, laid up from injury, reading and listening to books and podcasts. I opened with some standard libertarian and conservative content—economist Thomas Sowell's *Basic Economics*, Shapiro and The Daily Wire, Blaze Media, and so on. I caught a major break with the work of Unconstrained Analytics, which brought me "down the rabbit hole," so to speak. From there I opened my study up to both the esoteric traditions that form the basis of all Leftism—Marx, Hegel, Plato—and to the religious traditions of Catholicism and Protestantism, and the works of Aristotle. I moved through the *Republic, Symposium,* and *Timaeus,* through the *Politics, Metaphysics,* and *Nicomachean Ethics,* to Van Til, Bahnsen, and Rushdoony—the foundational thinkers of the presuppositionalist tradition in Reformed theology. From the *Emerald Tablet* and the *Corpus Hermeticum* to Kant and Heidegger, from Kendi and Crenshaw—architects of modern racial-identity ideology—to Lenin and Marx. I read mountains of modern Leftist and Marxist academic work. I read occultist Manly P. Hall's *The Secret Teachings of All Ages,* works on Kabbalah and the *Kybalion,* a variety of New Age, New Thought, and Theosophy works, and a variety of political warfare works—from Edward Bernays, the father of modern public relations and propaganda, in his *Propaganda* to *Disinformation, Active Measures,* Sun Tzu, *Rules for Radicals, Beautiful Trouble, Unrestricted Warfare,* Mao, Che, *American Betrayal, Big Intel,* and much more.

The connection of the religious dialectic—as presented most directly in the tenets of the *Kybalion* and Hermetic works—to the actions and telos (ultimate purpose) of the Left was incredible and eye-opening.

Emotionally, the journey began as a wreck: struggling through depression, isolation, and extreme social discomfort caused by deep relational connections to Leftism. Things improved slowly as I began to correctly identify problems and implement strategic fixes. The climax of the journey has been marked by the acceptance of responsibility, the acceptance of the imperfect nature of this present reality, the understanding that existence is not a prison to be escaped or transcended but a gift and experience to be embraced—grabbed by the horns and steered. Ultimately, I have come to find the "you can just do things" mantra says it pretty well.

People tend to live in a world constrained by the opinions of those around them, and the limits they place on that reality. Of course, that reality is something they bump up against, but never underestimate people's ability to dissemble and ignore facts. Further, the Left tends to live in a world wherein linguistics reign supreme—the "wordcel" paradigm holds up well so long as we understand the particular *libido referenced is the* libido dominandi, *or lust to dominate*. They are gifted linguistically but unable to achieve that maximal end of speaking into being. Their views are more easily shifted by language, in accordance with the social conventions of their in-group, than by any recognition of outward reality. This is easily demonstrated when arguing with a Leftist, as the utter defeat of one argument does not cause a moment's pause before they switch gears entirely and offer another argument that completely contradicts their first. Consistency is not required—language is not a tool to describe reality; per alchemy—a connection we will trace shortly—it is a weapon to change it.

You, dear reader, might assume you are the exception to the rule. You probably do believe this, deep down, without admitting as much out loud—you would deny it, even to yourself, but then that is what you do, at least sometimes. None of us are immune. We need to be prepared to challenge ourselves right down to the deepest level necessary to reorient and rebuild our worldview on a firm foundation.

What I have just described—the long, painful process of breaking free from one worldview and building another—is not unique to me. You are going through a version of it right now, whether you know it or not. Let me propose an analogy to begin the next chapter that may assist you in recognizing how this all works as we get into the meat of this journey together.

Chapter 2

What Is the Matrix?

What if I told you that within your mind there were prisons of both minimum and maximum security, and that these prisons were constructed in a partnership between society and yourself? What if the prisoners held captive were *ideas*? What if you are the guard?

Silly, right? But what of "trans men" are not men? What of climate change is religious dogma, not science? What of the Civil Rights Act, as implemented, being the modern legislative act that enshrined our affirmative racial discrimination regime? What of Israel having an excessive influence on United States politics and policy. . . even if it is a lesser impact than some other foreign states?

If any of the above objective truths made you think twice, wince, elicited anger, or made you uncomfortable, we have touched on a *sacred cow*: an idea that, per Frankfurt School neo-Marxist Herbert Marcuse, must be censored so totally that one dare not even think it, let alone speak it. These mental prisons were erected along the lines of social tripwires of taboo and are enforced by the feminine-type social (oft passive) aggression that we now often refer to as "cancel culture." It doesn't even matter whether these statements were true or not – if you felt it in anxiety, it's a taboo. Which is not to say that all taboo is necessarily bad – we will discuss it more as we go – but it is powerful, and where there is power there is incentive for corruption.

These mental prisons did not erect themselves. They were built—deliberately, over decades, by a process with a name.

It was defected KGB operative Yuri Bezmenov, whose 1984 lecture describing Soviet ideological warfare programs has become one of the most widely shared videos of the internet age, who made Americans broadly aware of the Soviet ideological warfare regime simply known as "demoralization." This is the process developed by Communists—with substantial links to the social sciences—to separate minds en masse from the real world. As a consequence, the *demoralized* are unable to acknowledge a truth seen by their own eyes, heard by their own ears, or held in their own hands. This process produces a "pseudoreality" (German Catholic, realist philosopher Josef Pieper, *Abuse of Language, Abuse of Power*) that, in the mind of the demoralized, is the unassailable worldview that exists in place of the real world – it is that representation of the world in their minds—a representation informed by errors and lies. It is not an accurate representation of that world as it truly exists. It is a low fidelity model. It is to this pseudoreality that a system of morality is applied by those captured. This application of morality to a pseudoreality produces an externally nonsensical—even if internally consistent—moral system that mathematician and Critical Theory expert James Lindsay—one of the few scholars to systematically decode Woke ideology in accessible terms—coins *paramorality*.

To show you how far this can go—and I assure you, what follows is not hypothetical—imagine that you are riding public transportation when you observe a man begin to sexually assault a woman. It would be, in any healthy culture, the duty of any able man to intervene to stop the assault – of course, any woman with a tool would be welcome to intervene to stop the attack as well. But in a pseudoreality and paramoral framework wherein the race of the perpetrator is considered *oppressed* in the classic dialectical sense—that is, within the framework of an oppressor-oppressed conflict that must be resolved through struggle, and the woman is that of an *oppressor* race, this act might be reasonably considered a justifiable act of sexual reparations in which intervening would be the immoral act—not the assault itself. As positively nutty and awful as this sounds, this is exactly the way pseudorealities do, and always have, worked. This scenario actually played out in a real American city in recent times, and the archetype has been playing on repeat for centuries now – those of the Soviet Union would be familiar. This basic process is how the horrors of the twentieth century played out. Who do you think the Kulaks were? They were the pseudoreal, paramoral "oppressor" of the Russian peoples. They were owed revenge.

The effect of this paramoral system of apparently nonsensical ethics playing out in public is further demoralization, causing one to question his own ethics and first principles and separating him from his capacity for moral outrage and righteous anger in the face of an expansive pseudoreality – keeping up a hostile wall against the onslaught is exhausting. This effect is bolstered by the persistent outrage and anger of the inhabitants of pseudoreality in asserting their false paramorality aggressively, thereby knocking the unprepared off their emotional base by eliciting sympathy for an offense that is assumed to be real but is not (how long did it take the charge of "racism" to lose its power?).

There is a deeper engine at work here that we will examine in full later in this book, but it is worth naming now so you can watch for it. The Left's moral system is relativistic—goodness is measured not against a fixed standard but only in comparison to a designated enemy. Their moral status depends entirely on the gap between themselves and the people they oppose. This has an inexorable escalation logic: if your goodness exists only as the distance between you and your enemy, and that distance is never enough to quiet the conscience, you have two options—become paramorally better, or make your enemy appear worse. The second option is the simplest and easiest to achieve within their system. So "conservative" becomes "reactionary" becomes "fascist" becomes "Nazi" becomes "existential threat to our democracy." Each escalation is not about describing the Right accurately. It is about maintaining the moral delta that constitutes the Left's entire claim to goodness. This is why no concession produces peace—every victory removes a front on which they could define themselves as good by comparison, requiring a new and worse accusation to fill the gap. Keep this mechanism in mind. It explains a great deal of what you have already experienced and could not make sense of.

But demoralization is not merely a political tactic. It is a religious project—and the religion behind it is older, stranger, and more pervasive than you might imagine. In this religion History is sentient, aware, and driving forward towards the end of time with a purpose. It has a will, and it is fated. The question of the utopian age's rise is that of when, not if. On this precipice – the horizon of the end of History – the end of suffering is in sight: there will be no war, nor famine. There will be no pain; the only labor to be expended is in the ethereal *creative* realm, and only at one's leisure. Toil is vanquished. You will want for nothing, as the spirit of the utopian age rises as a deity manifest by the perfect knowledge of itself and the harmony of mankind as a single organism.

The *Absolute Spirit*—Hegel's name for the god of this religion—will arrive as written only when the contradictions of society are resolved. You see, the utopian age is the natural state of mankind, and not for the incessant introduction of contradiction into the culture by the reactionaries, we would already be free of all oppressive forces. These contradictions can only be resolved through the actions (*doing the work*) of the philosophical, ideological, and political Left. The actions of the *Reactionaries* (the *right*) can only serve to delay the immanentization of the eschaton—that is, to delay the arrival of their prophesied utopia, and the *Reactionaries* must be stopped at any cost to expedite the beginning of the end: *year zero.*

What you have just read is, quite literally, the religious origin of the American political Left as it currently exists and has always existed. It is also the origin of the political movements known as Communism, Marxism, Fascism, Progressivism, and now *Wokeism.* The religion is sometimes called *Scientism,* and *we* are in the way of their Heaven. If this sounds extraordinary—if you cannot yet believe that the American political Left is a religious movement—I understand. The evidence will be laid before you in full in the chapters that follow.

The fundamental political nature of this religion is that all of mankind must be brought into agreement in both word and deed—reading from the same sheet of music at the same time—and, ultimately, all of humanity must act as a single organism to achieve the goal. In practice during the twentieth century, this led to the horrors of *struggle sessions* in Mao's China, the *reeducational* gulags of the Soviets, the killing fields of Cambodia, and the progressive doctrine of forced sterilization and abortion of *undesirables* in the United States (yes, *we* did that).

This doctrine of *Scientism* is a perversion of the truth. Man rightly infers the imposition of the imperfections of this fallen world on him as an aberration, but he fails to grasp that the corruption is not just without, but also within. He is foolishly susceptible to the idea that he might raise himself up as lord over creation and build a man-made Eden to liberate humanity from toil and tragedy. It is a story of ideologically induced narcissism lending to mass psychopathologies—each misstep towards *Utopia* introducing impossibilities and errors that scale logarithmically toward *Hell*.

However, the situation is complicated in that most of today's leftists would not claim to ascribe to the religion of Scientism as described above, and most have probably never even heard of these concepts. So why, then, do they continuously forward the resultant political doctrines and act very much as previous devout adherents to Scientism acted? We will explore this topic from several angles, and with luck we will extract a vaccine to this memetic virus—memetic in the original sense of an idea or cultural icon that spreads "virally"—by the closing chapter.

Over the course of a hundred-plus years, the extremely potent and extremely religious ideas of Progressivism have adapted and changed. As a consequence of their introduction into the multi-heritage "melting pot" of America, these ideas were adapted in ways to American traditionalism, and in ways American traditionalism was adapted to them. The latter was made far more potent through the subversive mechanisms of political warfare developed and implemented by the Frankfurt School theorists—a group of German Communists—academic theorists—who fled Frankfurt for Columbia University in New York as Hitler was ascendant. The subversive weapons of the Frankfurt Marxists were directed squarely at organized religion, and in particular Christianity.

However—and perhaps as one of the most ironic of all things to come—just as these Marxist socio-political weapons have effectively severed large portions of Christendom and Judaism from doctrinal texts and foundational Truth, it too has separated Progressivism from the foundations of Scientism resulting in something like the democratization of idiocracy. Nary a progressive has even heard of Hegel, let alone read his *Phenomenology of Spirit* (Scientism's holy book), and a great many—probably the overwhelming majority—fancy themselves *atheists* or *Humanists*. Yet, just as America continues to be a country of Christian tradition (for the moment) despite those grounded in doctrine being a minority, so does

Scientism persist through tradition within Progressivism. We will return to this mechanism—and trace exactly how a religion can persist when its adherents no longer recognize it as religion—in later chapters. Again, this mechanism was made far more potent by the work of the Frankfurt Marxists through means of political warfare. The Marxists explicitly targeted the means of cultural transmission—the Church, media, education, government, and so on—for subversion through the infiltration of *critical theorists*—academics trained to relentlessly attack every traditional institution and belief—who would, over time, create a "counter hegemony," building a rival power structure from within. Their "long march through the institutions"—the patient, generation-spanning infiltration of schools, churches, media, and government, the phrase itself coined by Rudi Dutschke in 1967 though the practice began in the 1930s—and according to former CPUSA (Communist Party USA) organizer Bella Dodd—as detailed by historian Paul Kengor in *The Devil and Bella Dodd*—Dodd reportedly claimed to have helped place over a thousand Communist men into Catholic seminaries as part of a deliberate infiltration strategy, according to witnesses who attended her lectures in the 1960s, though the claim does not appear in her own published writings or congressional testimony.[1] In a way, it was a method of the German intellectual colonization of America (enjoy that lemon, Wokeists).

The Frankfurt School provided the institutional vehicle. But the weapon itself—the specific mechanism by which language is used to construct a false reality—has far older roots. The Woke often talk of "potentialities of being" and "ways of knowing" and other purposely abstruse phraseology to obfuscate their ridiculous philosophy in terms of objectivity. This is, however, a case of them turning their weakness into strength. They hide their ideas in exorbitantly academic language in order to hide what would otherwise be readily apparent: their ideas are not in accordance with *reality*. It is reality which constrains our "potentialities of being" and "ways of knowing." We cannot do whatever we desire, for while there are relatively few ways to live (and even fewer to prosper), there are infinite ways to suffer and die. It is therefore *reality* that must inform the basis for inoculation against Wokeism.

An objectivist doctrine would say that a thing exists, and that in order to make things happen in the world, we have to use our hands to bring them into being. A social constructivist view of the world would say that, actually, we do not need to use our hands to bring things into being—we need to use our *words* to bring things into being. We need to speak things into being, collectively.

To the ancient initiators of these un-American ideas, the concepts themselves would seem second nature, but they would have used different words—and, indeed, different paradigms—to describe them. These paramoral assertions of pseudoreality would be, to them, not merely lies, but *spells*. They use the subversion of language at the level of meaning to coopt the minds of their targets, and in doing so they wield the hermetic language of *magic words*.

It is no accident that there is a utopian religious nature to their ideas: their most proximate origin is in dark-ages *Alchemy*. As the Alchemist sought to find the seed of gold in base metal lead by sloughing off the bad material in cleansing fire and chemical reactions, these utopians believe that *Eden* exists as a seed under all the corruption of society and the contradictions of the world. They believe that this utopia is reachable by eliminating the bad and accelerating the synthesis of contradictions towards the end of History and manmade perfection. They believe that seed, once purified and cleansed, will take root and sprout.

Chapter 3

THE COLONIZATION OF THE AMERICAN MIND

The modern application of alchemy shows up in the social weapon known as "cancel culture." This formulation of "cancel culture" is, in its original German, *"aufheben der Kultur"* (literally, "the cancellation of culture"). It was forged into a sociological weapon with which to wrest the Overton Window—the range of ideas considered acceptable in public discourse—into radical territory by bringing hellfire down on any who would dare step outside it. In this regard, people do not get "cancelled"—*culture* itself does. The proximate origin of these ideas was the common origin of much of modern Leftist ideology: GWF Hegel. The nineteenth-century German philosopher was the link between the European continental ideas of Historicism (the belief that history has a direction and purpose of its own), Statism (the worship of the all-powerful state), and hatred of Christianity and the modern American left, as seeded multiple times: first by the early American Young Hegelians—devotees of Hegel's philosophy who became the original American "Progressive" movement, and later by the Frankfurt neo-Marxists. Interestingly, these separate ideological seedings explain the simultaneous instincts within the modern left to both bring about the perfected state through a bureaucracy of experts (Progressive) yet also to destroy culture totally such that violent revolution would be preferable among the masses to continuing on (neo-Marxist). Cognitive dissonance between these mutually exclusive strategies is mitigated through the adoption of nihilism, relativism, and an assumed infallibility of *the experts*.

The process of demoralization has affected the subversion of each one of us down to our very core. We have had a false world imposed on us mentally, and now we struggle to see the real one as it truly exists. Marcuse's lunatic dream of stifling conservative ideas at the level of thought in *Repressive Tolerance* has been achieved through the application of *aufheben* (German for "cancel") to the culture and the establishment of taboos backed by the implicit threat of violence—first mob violence, and later state violence.

There exists a whole host of Woke religious fundamentalist beliefs that one must uphold to participate in polite society: "trans men are men," "children know what's best," and so on. The statement of faith, "believe science," has taken the modern conceptualization of science as a process of inquiry and discovery and reverted it to the prophetic metaphysics of yesteryear—all while still asserting that "Science" can lead us to truth. Many now argue that this process cannot be undone—that it spells the end of our nation. This was the belief of Yuri Bezmenov when discussing the ComIntern (Communist International) program of ideological subversion and demoralization of the West. I am, however, less certain, and more hopeful.

We must strive to recognize, both consciously and through our values, that the natural state of man is not utopian. The natural state of fallen man, as informed by history, is pain, privation, hunger, disease, subjugation, and constant struggle to meet the most basic needs. This is borne out in every civilization to have ever existed, and it is always exacerbated in the twilight of civilizations. Our continued prosperous existence even amongst a century of onslaught is a testament to the singular greatness of our civilization in creating the freest, most prosperous, and least subject-to-nature existence since the fall—and perhaps it is this that makes us uniquely weak against the current threat. In such a time, it is entirely understandable how people could (wrongly) assume that there is enough of everything for everybody to never want for anything. After all, when your meat comes not from a cow you butchered or bird you hunted, but from the market, we are detached such that the consequence of everything natural in this world seems at worst an inconvenience. Our technology is advanced beyond the point of understanding of most, thereby lending credibility to the possibility of all forms of magic—desiring it, even.

This confluence of circumstances and the purposefully driven State-Church tyranny of Scientism—the constant, ruthless criticism of all things by the Woke—has resulted in what I call the *"utopian mindset."* In this mind, all things are seen through the narrative ("lens") that events, circumstances, happenings, decisions, and judgements are to be made against the world *as it should exist* (as that of perfected Eden) instead of against a difficult, true, and objective reality of nature being a harsh mistress – constantly plotting to kill you. This mindset produces almost exclusively ideas, plans, and paths ("ways of being") that render their adherents individually unable to survive contact with reality. So now, for them, it is reality that must change. But reality does not change. Reality eventually reasserts itself. The only question is how many lives it claims when it does.

Let me now offer a test to cut through the noise. I suspect that you have not yet exercised your Woke immunity to the extent of inoculation. Let us see.

I would like to ask you to participate in a brief thought experiment. Consider the case of a family of four visiting a tropical beach on vacation, and visualize it as you read.

The parents are in their thirties; the children, five and eleven. They are a typical family: both parents work; the children attend day care and middle school, respectively. This is the first vacation they have had since their second child was born. As the mother swims in the green tropical ocean, the father and the children sit on the beach making sandcastles. People around them on the beach start panicking, and as the father looks up, he sees the water has rapidly receded by several hundred yards and it has swept his wife out with it. The father, though immediately grief-stricken, recognizes the sign and realizes that a tsunami is imminent and begins to run his children to higher ground. As the first wave approaches, the father realizes he cannot make it to the hotel, and so he lifts the children into a sturdy tree. Before he can climb up himself, he is struck by the wave, and large debris take him under. Though both parents are lost, both children survive clinging to that sturdy tree.

I now ask that you take a moment to honestly analyze your responses, both emotional and reasoned, to this experiment. Did you, at any point, experience anger? With such things as raw, unscripted emotion, nearly any response is conceivable, but these responses should always be examined against reason—and that reason informed by reality. If you experienced anger, I would ask you to spend some time considering what, exactly, the anger was in response to. This was a story of tragedy. However, there was nobody to blame for what happened, and anger at natural circumstance is the seed of rebellion. Anger at tragedy is human. But anger at tragedy when there is no one to blame—anger at the very structure of reality—is the seed of the utopian impulse: the belief that reality itself is the oppressor and must be overturned. If your anger cannot be dismissed as unwarranted, unhelpful, or at least consciously tempered in this situation, I would speculate that you hold some significant degree of indoctrination into utopian ideology. If you found yourself contemplating the class or race of the family, or found disappointment in learning the family was "nuclear," I would suggest you desperately need to remove yourself from Wokeism and seek traditional values and grounding. If you failed to sympathize at all due to any perception of "privilege" in the family, you may be at the logical end of the indoctrination that leads to genocidal ideation—you have adopted the precise moral framework that enabled every genocide of the twentieth century, the framework that says some categories of people deserve what they get.

Returning to where we started: I am, in fact, telling you that these prisons for ideas exist in your mind, that they are guarded by social taboos, and that you yourself uphold them just as the Communists had intended. As Pavlov's dogs salivated with the bell, you have been trained not just to expect, but to bring about an internal anxiety upon approaching *wrongthink*. I also allege that you possess some degree of indoctrination into relativistic ideology. Here is the proof: *American culture and its Christian tradition and heritage is objectively superior to Islamic culture as exists in all Islamic nations, and as is guaranteed by any faithful interpretation and implementation of the Koran.* Feeling uncomfortable yet? That is relativism telling you that you are not allowed to discern which is best, and that only bad people discriminate. It is you telling yourself that you are not allowed to tell a truth, even to yourself, that may provoke offense.

We, culturally, are now very deep into the belly of this beast. What we now require is to achieve something that no culture has previously achieved without substantial collapse: *remoralization*. We must begin the process of reconnecting ourselves to reality, to transcendent ethics, and, equally important, of polarizing pseudoreality and paramorality.

The method is not complicated. If it is true that we come to believe the things that we say and that we write—and I believe we do—then remoralization is simply the process of speaking truth, writing truth, and believing it. The full method, and the weapons you will need to wield it, will be delivered later in this book once you have the complete conceptual toolkit. For now, know that this process will be uncomfortable. It will require cutting down to the level of your deepest assumptions and rebuilding your worldview on rock. The difference between winners and losers is the willingness to accept that discomfort today in exchange for a better tomorrow.

Righteous anger is the fuel. The distinction between *righteous* anger and just plain *anger* is paramount—righteous anger always comes from a place of goodness: it is the moral in us recoiling upon the imposition of evil. Righteous anger reflects reality as informed by reason. We will return to this in force.

Note that this is not a utopian project. Eden is not on offer in any capacity on this side of eternity. You will never achieve a perfect knowledge of the real, and you will always retain some degree of demoralization through deception, mistake, and subversion. The desired end state is simply this: *do enough*. *You* must *do enough* to adapt your mind to reality to first survive, and then to flourish. *We* must *do enough* to alter the course of our nation, whatever that nation is to look like geographically, to avert utter devastation by perpetual subjective revolution. Reality will win, ultimately. It *will* reassert itself. The questions that matter are how painfully will it do so, and how we might affirmatively reassert it—rapidly and sufficiently—to conquer the lies that now threaten all of our futures?

On a small scale, the difference for you is likely between failing and flourishing. On a grand scale, for all of us, the difference is between freedom and slavery. I know this path works because I have walked it, and I am still walking it.

We must adopt a reality-based mindset. We must temper our anger and our dissatisfaction with creation, and find some comfort that we are, each of us, subject to nature. We must trade our greed for contentedness in what we have and what we might come to have through hard work. We must exchange mean-spirited envy for joy in finding common cause with fellow Americans and celebrating their successes. We must abandon zero-sum concepts of the "rat race."

You now have the outline—the silhouette—of what plagues us. It is enough to take aim at that fuzzy object in the dark, but maybe not quite enough yet to get a positive ID and distinguish friend from foe. From here on, that is what you will learn. You will come to see how the enemy operates and understand why.

The first lessons to learn, then, will be how to recognize that you are under attack, that somebody is operating as an enemy or adversary, and the initial defensive measures that must be taken once contact is recognized. The next chapter will hand you the first weapon: a method for detecting exactly when language has been manipulated and deployed against you—a test you can apply to any word, any phrase, any slogan, to determine whether it describes reality or constructs a pseudoreality. You have already begun the process of remoralization simply by reading this far. Now let us sharpen the blade.

Chapter 4

THE IMPORTANCE OF DEFINITIONS

LANGUAGE AS THE FOREMOST WEAPON

As your eyes are being opened to the fact that you are standing on a battlefield, with the bullets of narratives flying all around, the first thing you must do is take cover in a safe spot (turn off the news and stop doomscrolling) to evaluate the circumstances and consider what to do about it. This battle—political warfare, the struggle for control of minds and meaning—is fought in the realm of language. Control of language means control of thought, and control of thought means control of actions. You must first learn the technique of truing language and definitions.

What I am about to hand you is the single most practical tool in this book. It is a method—a three-part test—that you can apply to any word, any phrase, any slogan to determine whether it describes reality or constructs a pseudoreality. Once you have it, you will not be able to unsee the manipulation. You will recognize it in the news, in legislation, in the mouths of your allies, and—if you are honest—in your own speech. This is the first weapon. Learn to wield it, and the rest of what follows in this book will cut far deeper. This is the tool I wish I had found years earlier—it would have saved me a decade of confusion.

The Three-Part Test for Truing Language

Political warfare is fought at the level of language and meaning. In order to understand what is real, we apply a three-part test to truing language. First, we identify the historic or ancient definition of the language – utilize tools to research the etymology if necessary. Then we examine the modern, popular definition. Then we align both of those to observable reality and determine which better fits.

The thesis is this: the historic, ancient definitions of language are often far more accurate and actionable than the modern definitions we have been taught—the definitions you might find in dictionaries that have been designed, on purpose or by destruction of knowledge, to make you ineffective at fighting back.

A correct understanding and precise application of language is, in fact, *the counterspell* of our namesake.

A quick example before we go deeper. Consider the phrase "children's rights." Ancient and American origin: children possess narrow negative rights—freedom from abuse, neglect, and exploitation—exercised on their behalf by parents, whose broad and near-total authority over their minor children is among the most firmly established principles in American law and tradition. Modern replacement: "children's rights" recast as positive rights—the "right" to demand parents affirm delusion, the "right" to access services without parental knowledge or consent. Alignment with reality: the modern usage is a dialectical cancel attack against parental rights, introduced specifically to create conflict between parent and child, to expand the surface area of attack for the indoctrination of children, and to pit them against the very people responsible for protecting them. The test catches it immediately. Now let us understand why.

Historical Proofs

Psychologist Jordan Peterson observes that there is literally no difference between speech and thought. Control over language means control over thought. Our laws are made entirely of language—that is what they are. Control the way people define language, and you control the way they apply law. Warfare at the level of language has been the foremost weapon of control for thousands of years.

The historical proofs are abundant. Michel Foucault, the father of postmodernism and a postmodern Marxist, wrote: "Discourse is not simply that which translates struggles. Discourse is the power which is to be seized." George Orwell, a socialist critiquing authoritarianism, warned: "If thought corrupts language, language can also corrupt thought." And Plato, in the *Republic*, on the need to control citizens' ideas: "Then the first thing will be to establish a censorship of the writers. We will desire mothers and nurses to tell their children only the authorized stories."

Georgi Arbatov, the Soviet regime's top strategist on the United States and senior adviser to Gorbachev, knew exactly what he was doing when he told American visitors to Moscow in 1988, "We are going to do a terrible thing to you — we are going to deprive you of an enemy."[2] This was not a prediction. It was a description of the operation underway. Months earlier, in an internal memo to Gorbachev on the strategic payoff of the Moscow Summit, Arbatov had identified "the breaking of the enemy image" of the Soviet Union in Western perception as the achievement of the summit.[3] He was reporting success. The language was the operation — the literal reshaping of what the word *Soviet* meant in the American mind, from adversary to partner, from threat to friend. And he was right to report success. The American political class absorbed the revised meaning and conducted itself accordingly. The infrastructure of ideological subversion that the Comintern and its successors had built across seventy years of patient institutional work did not dissolve when the Soviet state did. What dissolved was American recognition that the project still existed. This is what linguistic warfare looks like at the level of strategic doctrine. You do not conquer a nation that still recognizes you as its enemy. You wait until it no longer does.

Yuri Bezmenov described subversion as "the slow process which we call either ideological subversion or active measures or psychological warfare. What it basically means is to change the perception of reality of every American to such an extent that, despite the abundance of information, no one is able to come to sensible conclusions in the interests of defending themselves, their families, their community, and their country."

You will encounter many further such proofs as we read on, and in much greater depth – I expect you will come to experience shock as you understand the depths at which you have been manipulated.

How Language is Learned – and Corrupted

A natural framework for language adoption and understanding exists as a part of the universal human experience. This framework is both biological and social. We come into this world without language to describe what we see and touch, yet we do not remain permanently detached from this world. We, through interacting with the world, and with each other, and through the existing biological structures inherent to man, make some sense of the world, and learn, at best, to call things by their proper name.

The general point here is simple: most of the words most of us know and utilize were not learned from a dictionary. They were learned by a simple process of hearing and association, as repeated in varied circumstances, that allowed us to conceptualize first a broad universe of possible meaning, and then, with time and experience, a more particular definition and common usage for a word or phrase. This is how we tend to understand language, and through language understand the world, and one another.

This process of experiential learning is, like all things in this fallen world, corrupted and corruptible. The counter-hegemonic long march through meaning itself by the Left has asserted itself as the new hegemon of language, and it has thoroughly confused very nearly all of us by robbing language of its native meaning.

The manner in which they operate is simply this: merely using a word in a different manner, with different intent, repeatedly, will fix it through repetition. First, by the adoption of a broader definition by those hearing it, causing this new usage to be added to the existing understanding. Then, ultimately, narrowing meaning again around the new definition such that the old definition is no longer recognized.

Consider "health." For the entirety of the American experience, health was an individual matter—your body, your choices, your agency, your right to seek or refuse treatment. Then comes "public health." The public has no health. The public does not have a body, cannot get sick, cannot die. But the phrase does not need to be accurate—it needs only to be repeated. Once "public health" is accepted as a legitimate category, the entire foundation of health discourse shifts from the individual to the collective, from individual rights to group outcomes, from your physical body to the group's statistical profile. Individual agency—the right to refuse a treatment, to choose your own doctor, to make your own risk calculations—becomes an obstacle to "public health" rather than a right to be protected. The old definition is not merely displaced. It is made to sound selfish. It is made taboo.

THE CASTLE SIEGE

Words, once captured, cannot be utilized by Rightists without incidentally forwarding the attack on meaning, because those in whom the meaning is already expanded will take the traditionalist's use of the word in the alternate manner, thereby strengthening the association and accidentally advancing Leftist ideology all while causing significant confusion. This renders the only tactic available to the traditionalists the abandonment of captured language and a reorientation towards greater specificity and precision in language until such a time that the captured language might be retaken by similar social mechanisms.

This can be thought of in terms of a castle siege. We have allowed, over a long time, many spies and saboteurs to gain access to the castle. So many, in fact, that they outnumbered us and threw us out without much of a fight. A castle requires maintenance—water, food, and so on—just as language requires cultural husbandry. Hauling water to the castle maintains it just as speaking it maintains a word. The castle is captured: it is not ours. They are within it, and we are without. To continue to haul water to it every day is to provide material aid to the enemy that inhabits it, and this is true of speaking captured language. We should not be carrying water for the enemy.

The proper action to be taken, then, is to affect an information warfare campaign against captured language with the intent of fixing the negative meaning (splitting entirely from the positive connotations), polarizing it, and *aufheben*—cancel—the enemy's use of it by making the utterance a taboo. Simultaneously, the positive connotations of the now-captured language should be transferred to new language with the intention of defending this new language and definitions mercilessly. Ideally, this new language will be existing, known, and more precise than the original language. It is by attacking with precision that we combat Leftist obfuscation and expose the abuse of language.

ILLEGAL ALIEN TO MIGRANT

Let us apply the lesson to a simple modern example to understand how this works in practice. Consider the transition from the original legal language found in United States statute—*illegal alien*—to the current popular term, *undocumented migrant*. This change happened culturally in several stages over several decades.

The first alteration was from *illegal alien* to *illegal immigrant*. A soft change—not a big one. But what it does is soften the image. It personalizes the illegal alien, makes them more sympathetic.

The next change was to *undocumented immigrant*. This change became popular under the Carter administration. Going from *illegal* to *undocumented* is not so soft a change. It removes the element of the crime that is in United States statute. And what happened when that language was changed? Mass amnesty happened. It was not a nothing-burger. They changed the terminology, and they followed the change in terminology with a change in policy and legal application.

The next change was from *immigrant* to *migrant*. Why migrant? Immigration is something people have done forever—you might move to a different country for one reason or another. "Migrant" carries an unsettled connotation – nomadic, almost. Migrants are back and forth all over the place. It changes the very understanding of human nature away from a settled people to a people that go with the wind, nullifying national borders as against a principle of human nature.

This was done according to a plan. This was done to America on purpose. Aristotle documented immigration being used as a weapon by tyrants against native populations 2,300 years ago in his *Politics*. The Soviets strategized using immigration as a weapon both at home and against

America, and they advanced that policy via united front groups all across the country. The Democrats adopted the Cloward-Piven strategy—developed by Columbia University sociologists in the 1960s: the proletariat, the revolutionary force, had been sapped out of the middle class because their lives had been too good. They wanted to flood all of the systems of the United States—from immigration to welfare—to break the systems, to make people angry, because angry people are revolutionary. The effect of importing deeply different populations from around the world is to promote conflict between those groups. People divided amongst themselves cannot organize and unite against those who are actually in control: the oligarch class.

The precision of this mechanism is worth stating plainly. Diversity within a shared civilizational framework is workable. Populations of different ethnic origin sharing the same presuppositions about authority, law, family, and the relationship between individual and community can form a cross-demographic coalition capable of threatening oligarchic power. What the oligarchic class requires above all is civilizational diversity – a "multiculture"— populations with fundamentally irreconcilable presuppositions about all of those things, and fundamentally incompatible ethics. Civilizational diversity produces permanent cultural conflict that forecloses cross-demographic coalition, not because the individuals within those populations are necessarily incapable of change, but because the mass importation and patterns of settlement means whole cultures, not mere individuals are imported. A population divided along civilizational lines cannot identify the common interest. This mechanism has been understood and deployed since before Aristotle documented it. It is being deployed today.

The 'Democracy' Walkthrough

The word "democracy" appears in surviving Greek sources in the fifth century BCE—in Herodotus and Thucydides, and then analyzed at length by Plato, followed closely by his protégé Aristotle, who thoroughly rebuked his nakedly occult philosophy, but agreed much in describing types of governance. The word is derived from the Greek words *demos* and *kratos*. The latter term is fairly uncontroversially referencing "rule by," so, in this case, rule by *demos*.

Demos, however, requires a deeper dive to understand properly. If you were to simply search the term, you would find that it, in modern definitions given publicly, is simply "the people." However, this is not merely an error but a lie advanced purposely to destroy our understanding. As per the usual rules of dialectics—the framework of manufactured opposition we identified in the previous chapter—, this is advanced as an "exoteric" definition—one pushed onto the public to sow a strategic confusion that renders them incapable of seeing that they are under attack, and, in fact, causes them to lend aid to those who assault them.

In the earliest days of the term, the *demos* was not by any stretch of the imagination the whole of "the people" as individuals, nor even the whole of "the people" generally. Rather, *demos* referenced particular groups of persons and excluded other groups. In Athens, the term was utilized to refer separately to each of the different districts. One district would represent one *demos*, and another district a different *demos*. Even within these varied *demos* it was not the whole body of "the people" but only those of a particular sex and heritage who qualified as "citizen." In more rural Greece the entirety of the citizenry of a town would constitute a *demos*.

Due to the historic and well-documented nature of populations to settle and segregate according to kinship, heritage, trade, wealth, and the like, the practical utilization of *demos* carried with it many connotations of these items as well. Therefore, in practice—and therefore in keeping with the highest-fidelity understanding of the term—*democracy* meant, from inception, not rule by individuals or "the people," but rather rule by specific groups of people based on identity traits against other *demos* also based on identity traits.

Demos is far better represented by the word *demographic* than "the people." *Demos* has always meant special interests and identity groups aligning temporarily for power: *factions*. According to Plato and Aristotle, each of the *demos* would elevate a champion to represent them and fight for their interests. These champions gained power by making alliances with the champions of other *demos* to form these powerful factions. They seized wealth from the minority. They deprived the minority of their rights – even to life, at a whim. That is what democracy always has been.

Aristotle wrote: "A democracy exists whenever those who are free and are not well-off, being in the majority, are in sovereign control of government." Plato described democracy as "a charming form of government, full of variety and disorder, and dispensing a sort of equality to equals and unequals alike." Here we have the first clue: democracy is unusually obsessed with inflicting "equality"—artificial sameness—across varied identities, and it is an occurrence of the majority coalition of poorer citizens oppressing the minority of wealthier, typically more productive citizens.

Plato also states: "And so tyranny naturally arises out of democracy, and the most aggravated form of tyranny and slavery out of the most extreme form of liberty." Here Plato points to a tendency of democracy to promote among the citizens an extreme liberty—not liberty in the truly American, Constitutional sense, but something more akin to libertinism: a liberty that does not recognize the point at which one's liberty ends and another's begins.

Finally, Plato expounds on the tendency for demagoguery: "The people have always some champion whom they set over them and nurse into greatness. . . This and no other is the root from which a tyrant springs; when he first appears above ground he is a protector. . . And if any of them are suspected by him of having notions of freedom, and of resistance to his authority, he will have a good pretext for destroying them by placing them at the mercy of the enemy." Here Plato identifies the mechanism by which democracy descends into tyranny—a demagogue rises promising some *demos* special favor, only to inflict despotism unto them once power is consolidated amongst the conflict of factions.

How did the Founders describe democracy? John Adams: "Remember, democracy never lasts long. It soon wastes, exhausts, and murders itself." James Madison: "Such democracies have ever been spectacles of turbulence and contention, have ever been found incompatible with personal security or the rights of property." Benjamin Franklin, asked what form of government the Convention had produced, replied: "A republic, if you can keep it." Alexander Hamilton: "Ancient democracies never possessed one feature of good government." George Washington: "The alternate domination of one faction over another, sharpened by the spirit of revenge, is itself a frightful despotism."

These are not obscure figures offering ambiguous opinions. This is the near-uniform verdict of the men who built the American system. They understood democracy in exactly the manner Plato and Aristotle described it—and they rejected it absolutely.

Worth asking is why democracy has proven so consistently attractive to oligarchs across the millennia—and the answer, I would argue, is written between the lines of the *Republic* itself. Bear in mind who Plato was: a member of the Athenian oligarch class, a man whose mentor Socrates was ultimately executed for corrupting the youth—which is to say, for conducting exactly the kind of spellcasting and esoteric initiation this book describes. Plato's circle knew democracy from the inside. They operated within it, they manipulated it, and they understood its mechanics with the precision of choreographers on up high. Read with that operational history in mind, and the *Republic* looks considerably less like a disinterested philosophical inquiry and considerably more like a management guide—a how-to, circulating among initiates, dressed as philosophy for outsiders.

The structural case for why oligarchs would find democracy useful writes itself. Raw coercive power is expensive, unstable, and tends to generate the unified resistance that oligarchs most fear. Plato learned this from the reign of the Thirty Tyrants who established a brief oligarchy before being crushed by the demos. Democracy solves those problems elegantly. Coercion is internalized—the population polices itself through social enforcement of the manufactured consensus. Resistance is preemptively fragmented—democratic faction dynamics set the *demos* against one another, each group exhausting itself on manufactured grievances to expropriate crumbs rather than identifying the common interest that unites all of them against the class managing the whole operation – crumbs being expendable to mute discontent. The tyrant incapable of seizing total control by force finds in democracy a ready-made system for achieving an approximate result with far less friction and far more deniability.

The language substitution from *republic* to *democracy* in American political vocabulary was a strategic operation, not a semantic drift. A population that understands itself to live in a democracy has no principled grounds to object to oligarchic management of its preferences—that management is simply democracy working as designed. A population that understands it lives in a constitutional republic can identify that management as usurpation, a violation of the compact, something to be resisted on constitutional grounds. Remove the word *republic* and you remove the conceptual vocabulary necessary to name what is being done. You take the law out of play. The spell works because the language was first captured.

REPUBLIC VERSUS DEMOCRACY

Article IV, Section 4 of the United States Constitution provides that "the United States shall guarantee to every State in this Union a Republican Form of Government." It is in the Constitution. It is the highest law of the land. A republican form of government is guaranteed, and that guarantee to each state is a legitimate function of the federal government.

Some will say a constitutional republic is merely a type of democracy. It is absolutely not. Aristotle described constitutional republican government as that which "determines what is to be the governing body, the mode of its election, and the limits of its authority." Two critical elements: limits to authority, and a specified mode of election.

Aristotle further wrote: "It is evident that the form of government is best in which every man, whoever he is, can act best and live happily." Does that remind you of anything from the American Founders? Anything about life, liberty, and the pursuit of happiness?

And further: "In a constitutional government, the fighting men have the supreme power, and those who possess arms are the citizens." The decentralization of the means of warfare. Not kept in a specific class of men to lord over the others. Everyone. Something about the Second Amendment here, perhaps?

And: "Citizens are all who share in the civic life of ruling and being ruled in turn." That sounds like a government of, by and for the people—the real thing, not the counterfeit of oligarchic champions.

The American Constitution, as written, strictly limits the powers of government to prevent theft and oppression of the minority. It was designed to upset the formation of faction by prohibiting the very generation of the spoils that would be fought over, and in dividing powers. It elevates and protects the rights of citizens as the foremost reason for the government's existence. It elevates God over government, and it elevates individual rights as God-given and inalienable by any legitimate act of government. The whole point of government, according to our Constitution, is to uphold those rights and secure them to citizens and their posterity.

In other words: the exact opposite of the democratic form of government we have just learned about.

The positive case for constitutional republicanism must be stated with equal precision. A constitutional republic is government restrained by an authority higher than itself—a transcendent ethic that no legislature, executive, or judiciary may override. Its citizens rule and are ruled in turn, sharing in civic life as armed participants in the preservation of their own liberty. Its rights are enumerated and inalienable—they do not originate in the state and cannot be revoked by the state. Its powers are divided among branches and sovereigns specifically to frustrate the consolidation of authority. And by these mechanisms, a constitutional republic disestablishes the very faction-and-spoils infrastructure that generates both democracy and oligarchy. The republic does not merely restrain tyranny. It removes the structural incentives that produce it—the spoils over which factions would form, the centralized power they would seek, the unchecked authority they would wield. The Founders understood this. They built a machine designed to starve tyranny of its fuel. That machine was then captured and repurposed by men who understood its design well enough to circumvent every safeguard—and they accomplished it, as we have seen, through the conquest of language itself.

The reader will rightly ask: if the republic's structural protections were insufficient to prevent this capture, what reason is there to believe that restoring them will prevent it from happening again? The answer connects to everything this book will argue in the chapters that follow. The republic's structural protections did not fail on their own terms. They failed because the metaphysical foundation on which they rested was undermined first. The Constitution is a downstream product of a specific metaphysical tradition—Protestant, covenantal, grounded in a transcendent ethic. When that tradition was displaced by Hegelian-Marxian metaphysics in the public mind, the constitutional structure lost its animating principle. The restoration of the republic requires the restoration of its foundation before, or at minimum simultaneously with, the restoration of its mechanisms. Structure without metaphysics is scaffolding on sand. John Adams was not wrong.

And what of voting? It has been a long-running information warfare operation to associate the word *democracy* with the act of voting. Voting is entirely severable from the form of government known as democracy. We vote because our Constitution says we are going to vote—because we are a constitutional republic, and voting is common in republics. It always has been. Voting is not even a feature in all democracies. Read Vladimir Lenin on "true democracy." There is no voting in that democracy. We vote because that is the method outlined in our Constitution, and that has never meant America is, should, or ought to be a democracy. Our voting is *republican*, not *democratic*.

Final analysis. If I have proven that democracy is awful and the opposite of a constitutional republic—and I have—and if I have proven that the supreme constitutional law demands a republican form of government for each state—and I have, Article IV, Section 4—and if we all recognize correctly that we nonetheless live in a democracy at this very moment—and we do—then, I hate to break it to you, I have also therefore proven that America underwent a revolution that none of us ever heard of.

And that revolution was accomplished and hidden through the manipulation of language, the dialectical control of language, and the conquering of education and media.

There was a successful revolution against the American founding, and it did not require that a single shot be fired. All that was necessary was the lazy adoption of a false language that facilitated a false understanding, which placed a real understanding outside of our perception, and therefore outside of our ability to analyze and strategize on.

How important is language, once more? Without correct definitions, there was no revolution. We are a democracy, and that is just fine. That is the effect of corrupted language: it makes the intolerable invisible.

Recognize what you have just admitted. If a revolution happened, and you did not see it, then the side that fought it won. There is no ongoing fight—there is an aftermath. You are living in the new regime, not the old one. What we call today "our democracy," what the press protects, what the universities produce, what the agencies enforce—that is not the Republic under strain. That is the ruling order of what replaced it. Every program of ordinary politics that assumes otherwise is built on a foundation that is not there. You cannot reform the Republic back into existence by working within institutions that function, today, as organs of the thing that overthrew it. You can only restore the Republic—and restoration of what has been overthrown is, by every definition that matters, counter-revolution. This is the frame. Everything that follows in this book follows from it.

RELATIVITY KILLER ARGUMENT

The three-part test rests on a premise that must be stated plainly: reality truly exists, it is objective, it is generally observable, and any two non-identical descriptions of it are never equally correct. One is always closer to the truth than the other. No matter how many dimensions are represented in comparing and contrasting two distinct descriptions of reality, the differences between them necessarily render one of greater fidelity than the other. This is true even when neither description is perfect—and no description ever is.

Ask the question: "What color is the sky?" One person answers "blue." Another answers "sky blue." The sky is not always the same color—it shifts with time, weather, and geography—yet "sky blue" is more precise, and therefore of greater fidelity, than "blue" alone. Neither is perfect. But they are not equal. And this matters, because people make decisions with incomplete information—we rely on heuristics, on the best available description, to act. The description of greater fidelity produces better decisions. The one of lesser fidelity produces worse ones. Relativism—the claim that all descriptions are equally valid—does not liberate you. It disarms you. It enslaves you to a harsh mistress.

This logic, applied rigorously, is a relativity killer—postmodernism has nowhere to hide but in a reversion to nihilism. The full argument and its devastating implications will be laid out later and throughout this book.

For now, carry this principle as the foundation beneath every application of the test you have just learned.

Chapter 5

Language Discipline

Political Warfare Operational Considerations

The foremost concern of operational security in the field of political warfare waged from the Right is language discipline. You must take pains to make your language correct, considered, and precise at all times. To fail at this task will sink the ship we are all currently occupying.

The corruption of language becomes a mechanism of controlled opposition. Utilizing the wrong language provides tangible benefits to the enemy, reinforces information operations, and keeps our strategies below the threshold of victory. We must discipline ourselves to use only the most precise language we can ascertain, and we must stand against the methods of sophistry deployed to make our correct language taboo.

The first phase of any effective counter-revolution to reinstitute the Constitution as the supreme law of the land starts with aligning our language with the correct, often ancient definitions that have been used forever, understood, and that reflect reality. Language is our foremost weapon. Be specific, be correct, and align it with reality.

Now that you understand what democracy truly is, you cannot use the word *democracy* to describe the American government in any positive manner. You should be maligning it at every opportunity. Tell people what it really is, and get a little angry about it. Shock them out of the spell. Because that is what it takes to get people to wake up and open a book.

Otherwise, they will just open Webster's Dictionary. What will they find? "Rule by the people." What is wrong with that? Crack an older book.

Over time, we can make the word toxic—as the Founders knew it ought to be. You should not tolerate Republicans using the term *democracy* unless they are criticizing it. The use of *democracy* incorrectly by allies effectively makes them, in that moment, agents in the Matrix—an enemy that needs to be fought. Refusal by those allies to stop their use of the word *democracy* in a positive manner ought to mark them out for criticism and, if necessary, removal from any office or position of authority.

We cannot win a castle siege while we continue to carry water to the castle. We cannot begin to formulate broader strategies towards victory when our leaders reinforce the democracy spell with their language. Through criticism, we must make the misapplication of the term *democracy* stigmatized. We must make it taboo.

What follows is a case study in strategy development that I am actively enacting. The Left captured institutions through a counter-hegemonic long march—patient infiltration, language capture, and the gradual replacement of institutional norms with revolutionary ones. The same technique, opposite in purpose, can be applied to recapture them. The Grand Old Party is a target for capture, not our castle to fortify. It has been so thoroughly infiltrated by Progressives that it probably ought to be called the Other Democratic Party. What I am describing is a counter-hegemonic takeover of GOP organizations—the deliberate seizure of party infrastructure by those who actually intend to fight to win—beginning with language discipline as the first operational requirement.

This is our OpSec. Enforcing this OpSec on the party is the only path forward to victory, as it will cause spies to be exposed in their continued refusal to cooperate, as they purposely continue to forward hostile active measures by reifying the language of the enemy. We must become the most intolerant faction within the party concerning language use and specificity, and accept no strategic errors, in order to effect a takeover of the party along correct language, and therefore correct meaning, and to remake it into something capable of fighting to win.

This is not merely theoretical. A resolution has been prepared for the New Hampshire legislature—a piece of model legislation available for introduction in any state—affirming the guarantee of a republican form of government under Article IV, Section 4 of the United States Constitution and declaring that this Guarantee Clause must be legally interpreted as explicitly anti-democratic—that democracy is an inversion of the purpose and ethical foundations of constitutional republican government, that it is historically documented from Athens to the Federalist Papers as perpetually revolutionary, dangerous to liberty, and unsustainable, that it promotes identity-based politics dividing the populace into warring groups exploited by demagogues and oligarchs, and that it legitimizes transgressions against enumerated rights by vote. Model Resolution on Democracy versus Republicanism The three-part test, applied legislatively. The counterspell, cast in the language of law, and only one of several such legislative measures being pursued, and slated for future introduction.

SYMPATHY TO EMPATHY

Let us apply the test once more, this time to a word so thoroughly captured that most will not even realize it has been taken from them: "empathy." The damage caused by this operation may eclipse even the prior *democracy* example.

The word you are looking for—the word that was taken from you—is "sympathy." From the Greek *sympatheia*, meaning "suffering with." Sympathy implies an emotional connection to another's suffering, but it preserves the distinction between self and other. You feel *with* them, not *for* them. It respects the boundary of the individual. It is compatible with moral judgment: you can feel genuine sorrow with a person suffering the consequences of their own decisions without endorsing those decisions. Sympathy can be extended even to enemies—it is compatible with loving your enemy while fighting him to the extent of total defeat.

"Empathy" is not a synonym for this. It is a replacement.

The word "empathy" entered the English language remarkably recently—around 1908—coined by psychologist Edward Titchener as a translation of the German *Einfühlung*, meaning literally "feeling into." *Einfühlung* was developed by German psychologist Theodor Lipps in the early twentieth century, who expanded the concept from art appreciation to mean "feeling one's way into" the experience of another person. Note the pedigree: German psychologists, operating within the same philosophical milieu that produced Hegel and the Frankfurt School, within a field whose esoteric origins we will trace more completely in the next chapter. The word "psyche" translates directly to "soul"—and the field of psychology was founded according to esoteric beliefs of spiritual evolution, reincarnation and enlightenment. This is the soil from which "empathy" grew.

Apply the test. Ancient origin: sympathy—Greek, "suffering with," preserving individual distinction. Modern replacement: empathy—German, "feeling into," dissolving the boundary between self and other, standing on the presuppositions of critical theory and the oppressor-oppressed dialectic, and implicating an ethical requirement that you take action on their behalf. Alignment with reality: does projecting yourself into another person's subjective position actually produce better moral outcomes than feeling compassion for them while maintaining your own grounding?

It does not. And the reason it does not reveals the true function of the replacement.

When someone demands that you "have empathy," they are not asking you to care about a suffering person. Sympathy would accomplish that. They are demanding something far more specific: that you project the critical theory framework onto whatever situation you are looking at, identify which party is the "oppressed," and take their side as an ally against the "oppressor" towards overthrowing existing hierarchy. Your natural feelings about the situation are secondary. What matters is the structural analysis you impose. The projection comes first; the activism follows the projection, and the activism is the true end of the operation.

There is zero daylight between the term "empathy," as deployed in modern discourse, and the Chinese Maoist term "the people's standpoint." The people's standpoint was never about understanding what the peasant actually thought or felt. It was about the cadre projecting the correct revolutionary consciousness onto the situation—seeing the landlord as oppressor and the peasant as oppressed regardless of the actual particulars—and then positioning themselves as the ally of the oppressed. "Empathy" does exactly the same thing in softer language.

This is why "empathy" produces such perverse outcomes in practice. A person exercising genuine sympathy toward a struggling working-class family would feel compassion for their suffering and perhaps try to help. A person exercising "empathy" fully in the critical theory sense cannot do this if that family falls on the wrong side of the oppressor-oppressed ledger: white, Christian, nuclear, conservative. The framework they are projecting identifies that family as members of an oppressor class. Their "empathy" not only fails to activate—it actively produces hostility. The suffering of the "oppressor" is deserved, and sympathy for them is a moral failing because it disrupts the structural analysis. Even if they can align with the suffering family, the orientation of *empathy* directs the bearer towards hostility at their "capitalist oppressor" far more so than developing any interest in helping the family. It fundamentally distorts the ethic of "weep with those who weep" towards "weep only with those who advance the revolution." This also speaks significantly to how elevating any particular group preferentially necessarily means lowering others. You cannot love your particular demos more without necessarily loving others comparatively less.

The replacement of "sympathy" with "empathy" in educated and therapeutic discourse is itself another instance of the *aufheben* we have described: the older concept is not merely eliminated but subsumed and replaced with something that preserves the emotional resonance while smuggling in fundamentally different presuppositions. You think you are being asked to care. You are being asked to revolt against the foundations of culture.

Make "sympathy" great again.

You now possess the three-part test, and you have seen it applied to devastating effect. A single word—*democracy*—when properly analyzed, reveals a revolution hidden in plain sight. The progression from *illegal alien* to *undocumented migrant* reveals a deliberate campaign to weaponize language against nationhood itself in a thousands-year old pattern. And the quiet replacement of *sympathy* by *empathy* reveals how the very emotional vocabulary through which we relate to one another has been colonized by a hostile framework. Apply this test to *equity*, to *justice*, to *inclusion*, and you will find the same pattern repeating: ancient meanings corrupted, modern definitions weaponized, reality obscured.

But this raises a question that the test alone cannot answer. Where did this technique originate? The manipulation of language at the level of meaning is not a twentieth-century invention. It is not even a modern one. It is an ancient practice, rooted in the mystery religions of the esoteric tradition—a tradition that has been operating in plain sight for thousands of years, and whose fingerprints are on every institution you have been taught to trust. It is to this hidden lineage that we now turn.

Chapter 6

Hidden in Plain Sight

The Eternal Presence of Mystery Religions

Where and when did this all go wrong? Well, it was not in the 1960s, despite the horrors inflicted by that decade. It was not the 1910s, either, despite the zealous fervor of the Progressive Era. It was not even Reconstruction, with the terror of that period. No—this fight is the same fight it has always been for all of recorded history.

Since the beginning, or not long thereafter, there has been with us the mystery religions – cults, technically. Masquerading at various times as academics, as true religion, and simply as social convention, these systems of thought speak to something deeply broken inside of each one of us, and tempt us towards—and over—the edge.

It was said that all roads lead to Rome, but on the path to intellectual and societal ruin it could be said that all roads lead to Plato. We will examine the bequeathed nightmare through his own written works, and, importantly, as understood by adepts through the ages—an understanding that departs rather starkly from the standard secondary-education, classical paradigm of Athens.

But first, we must trace the lineage. You have now seen how language is weaponized, and you have seen the revolution it accomplished. The question that demands an answer is: who devised this technique, and how has it persisted for millennia without most of us ever noticing? The answer begins in the land the ancients called Kemet (Egypt).

"Science," the word, has a very long history that, like much of our study, originates in ancient Egypt. The people of ancient Egypt, known to them as "Kemet," or, alternatively spelled "Chem't," developed early "science" in the practice of reactions between substances we, today, call "chemistry." Those of the early times, however, would have known the practice as "alchemy," and it was not a utilitarian, practical exercise.

When we think about chemistry today we imagine white-robed scientists mixing elements in a sterile lab according to mathematics in order to produce useful chemicals. For the people of Kemet, however, this practice of alchemy was, above all, deeply religious. This was not merely the production of useful things—it was a form of worship and purification, and it was considered a kind of sacrament and reflection of an internal process of the *soul*. The religious views of alchemy see the physical process of gold-making as analogous to the process of enlightenment and evolution of the soul, during multiple lives through reincarnation, towards a perfected state.

These practices of the people of Kemet would be passed through the mystery schools to those initiates of ancient Greece, most famously through Pythagoras, who according to ancient tradition spent years studying under the Egyptian priesthood and brought their mystical mathematics back to Greece (as well as running a purportedly murderous sex cult).

The transmission also ran through the Eleusinian Mysteries—the most important mystery cult in the Greek world, celebrated continuously from approximately 1600 BC. The Mysteries initiated generations of Greek elites into rites of death and spiritual rebirth through fasting, ordeal, the consumption of a ritual sacrament called the *kykeon*, and a dramatic revelation conducted in the underground Telesterion at Eleusis. They were a civic institution, open to all Greek speakers regardless of class, conducted at a public temple under state authority.

That civic institution was appropriated by the oligarchic circle around Socrates. In 415 BC, multiple members of that circle—Alcibiades, Phaedrus, Eryximachus, and others who appear by name in Plato's dialogues—were indicted for conducting the ceremonies privately, in the house of Charmides, Plato's own uncle. This was not only sacrilege. It was also the privatization of a public initiation rite by an oligarchic conspiracy—the same network that would later briefly overthrow Athenian democracy in the coup of 411 BC and the terror of the Thirty Tyrants in 404 BC.

Plato imported these appropriated rites with his learned Egyptian formulas for conspiracy into a permanent institution: the Academy, an open-secret society mystified philosophical doctrine encoded in texts saturated with Eleusinian language. He confessed the Egyptian origin openly. In the *Timaeus*, he writes that an Egyptian priest tells the Athenian lawgiver Solon that the Greeks are children who possess no ancient knowledge—he then delivers the cosmology of the living universe as received from that priesthood. In the *Phaedrus*, Socrates credits the Egyptian god Theuth—the same figure the Hermetic tradition knows as Thoth, later Hermes Trismegistus—with the invention of numbers, astronomy, geometry, and writing. Plato's contemporaries accused him of copying the institutions of the Egyptians.

The Academy would transmit these religious doctrines, dressed as academic philosophy, to a select class of golden philosopher-kings through the ages. In Greece these religious practices of alchemy, and the attendant thought-worship of dialectics, would be known as *episteme*—literally "knowledge," but knowledge understood as spiritual practice rather than empirical observation – incorporating "gnosis." The spiritual metaphysics and presuppositions of Hermeticism—the esoteric religious tradition that grew out of Egyptian alchemy, and whose core theology we will examine momentarily—were thoroughly baked into alchemy and the term *episteme*.

A major deviation of *episteme* away from esoteric Egyptian spirituality, and towards empiricism and rationality, was advanced by Plato's student Aristotle. Aristotle rejected Plato's occult religious practice, a philosophical product of ancient Egyptian origin, and he checked the mysticism and occult aspects of philosophy with his laws of reason and focus on natural sciences. Aristotle was, in many respects, a corrective to Plato—but he was not, precisely, an antidote in all respects. He remained a Greek philosopher, operating within Greek metaphysical and theological categories that would prove foreign to, and in tension with, the Christian tradition that would later build the West. He was doubtless a better man than Plato, though he played in the same presuppositional sandbox. This tension between Athens and Jerusalem—between Greek philosophy and Christian theology—is a subject we will address head-on in a future work.

A clarification is necessary here, because this book relies extensively on Aristotle—his definitions of republic and democracy, his observations on immigration as a weapon of tyrants, his analysis of constitutional governance. That reliance is not inconsistent with the claim that his metaphysics are flawed – even where he coined "metaphysics." Aristotle is most useful where he is providing firsthand accounts and analysis of the political world he inhabited, and where modern language and political understanding owe their very existence to his early formulations. His descriptive political work—what democracy does, what republics require, how tyrants operate—is empirically grounded and remains valid because it describes observable patterns that have recurred in every civilization since. When this book cites Aristotle on what democracy *is* and how republics *function*, it cites a reliable observer of political reality. When the question turns to the ultimate foundations on which political order must rest, we will insist that Aristotle is not the final answer. Though the full argument is not for this particular text.

These occult practices have been passed down and preserved through the ages, from ancient Egypt to Pythagoras, from Socrates to Plato, to the founding of the most successful open-secret society of history, "the Academy," to the rise of Hermetic esoterica in the Arab nations, the reestablishment of "the Mysteries" in Europe during the medieval period, to the proliferation of deadly, militant, and powerful conspiracies fueling and funding revolution, Dialectical Materialism (Communism), and the softer, long-game "secret society-within-secret societies" such as the Fabians, Progressives, and esoteric Freemasons.

All trace directly back to Plato and his many volumes of obscure texts that most will never read, and most of those who do will never properly understand. A trick of the Academy is to hide true, operational, "esoteric" meaning among one or more false, obfuscatory, "exoteric," or "profane" meanings. What the esoteric philosophers are really getting at is often found between the lines.

THE PENDULUM OF THE GREEKS

The Romans, in adopting much Greek philosophy, would call these alchemical practices "*scientia*." As the Egyptians and Greeks before them, this term would carry with it the metaphysics and presuppositions of Hermetic spirituality—it was just as much theology as "science." Roman philosophers such as Plotinus, the third-century founder of Neoplatonism, deliberately obscured Aristotle's arguments in order to marginalize his thorough rebuttals of Platonic philosophy. This Roman revival of Platonic Hermeticism was coined "Neoplatonism," and it was the foundation of *scientia*.

Scientia would evolve into the modern "science" by the old French, and then English languages. In this transition from *scientia* to "science" during the medieval period, the term would retain Platonic metaphysics and alchemical practices.

When we moderns think of "science" we tend to think "scientific method." However, this view of "science" as pure "method" did not arise in earnest until the eighteenth century, an outgrowth of the Reformation. It arose on the back of a form of "science" that did not represent a break from Hermeticism, but an advancement of Hermeticism: Francis Bacon and Isaac Newton were staunch Hermetic alchemists. It was, in some manner, a combination of the ideological ground laid by Reformed textualism and rejection of gnosis with the practical, and effective, aspects of alchemy coming into their own to produce useful things.

However, despite the esoteric influence, the dialectic and alchemy cannot stand up against empiricism and rationality in a fair fight. It is only through mystification and confusion by the dialectic that Platonism thrives. Therefore, when these English alchemical pioneers introduced a strict empiricist methodology—the "scientific method"—in an attempt to advance the effectiveness of their Hermetic alchemy, they instead drove a stake into Plato, thereby allowing Protestant Christian metaphysics to couple with the useful methods of alchemy towards a scientific revolution.

That stake-driving was not the accident it appears to be. The Hermeticists who introduced empiricism did not do so because they had converted to empiricism. They did so because empiricism worked—and working was the point. This is the pattern, and it did not end with Bacon and Newton.

It is the operational signature of the esoteric project across every costume it has worn since.

Plato himself set the template. He was under no illusion about what it takes to rupture the transmission of culture between generations and reshape a population. The *Republic* prescribes censorship of the poets, the myth of the metals, the noble lie, and a controlled breeding program—whatever works to produce the soul-sorted, guardian-managed city. Plato did not demand that the methods cohere with the metaphysics he professed publicly; he demanded that they be effective. The esoteric tradition inherited that disposition whole.

Deng Xiaoping said it plainest: it does not matter whether the cat is black or white, so long as it catches mice. Deng was willing to move the Chinese economy toward substantial privatization—a frontal contradiction of Maoist orthodoxy—because empirically those methods produced the material results the regime needed to consolidate and project power. The ideology was preserved at the level of regime legitimacy; its economic content was quietly abandoned wherever empiricism demanded. The vanguard held its nose and did what worked.

The same pattern operates throughout the twentieth century and into the present in the social sciences and in the constellation of secret societies, intelligence services, and NGOs that operate adjacent to them. The actors pursuing ideological transformation adopted empirically validated techniques of persuasion, conditioning, mass psychology, and behavioral modification—drawn from behaviorism, cognitive science, marketing research, and intelligence tradecraft—without regard for whether those techniques cohered with their stated humanistic or egalitarian values. The methods were chosen because they produced the intended effects on populations. CASEL and SEL did not arrive in American schools because their designers had become empiricists. They arrived because the empirical work on childhood ethical formation had matured to the point that it could be weaponized at scale.

The thread running from Plato through the Hermetic founders of the scientific method through Deng through the modern behavioral-science apparatus is a single disposition: subordinate method to purpose, and use whatever empirically works to advance ends that are themselves metaphysical and transformational. The Left has never been naively ideological at the operational level. It reliably holds its nose and picks up the hammer that drives the nail.

The strategic consequence for the Right is plain and ugly. A counter-revolutionary movement that refuses on principle to study and adopt what actually works—that confuses fidelity to its ends with fidelity to a particular set of methods—is strategically disarmed from the outset against opponents who have no such compunction. The methods of the enemy are not contaminated by association. A hammer is a hammer. The question is not whether to pick it up but what you are going to drive with it.

This correction by these Englishmen brought about an epoch of unparalleled advances in human knowledge—medicine, physics, chemistry, aerodynamics, engineering, and more would be buoyed by the reassertion of Aristotelian empiricism along with the introduction of Christian metaphysics against Platonic mysticism. It is this sort of empiricism and rationality to which most laymen point when using the term "science" today. But one must note that the correction was always incomplete. Aristotelian empiricism carried within it the seeds of its own vulnerabilities—Greek metaphysical categories that, absent the grounding of transcendent ethics, left it perpetually susceptible to the very Platonic mystification it had temporarily defeated – most recently by the social and critical constructivists.

Note, however, that "science" has never had a particularly static meaning, and these wars between religious "science" and empirical "science" have been waged for over two thousand years, one understanding never fully exorcizing the other. It is this hidden truth, and the application of dialectics, that is causing so much confusion about "science" today.

We live in a time where, once more, the rational laws of Aristotle have been thoroughly mystified, Christianity rendered taboo, and the religion of Plato is ascendant. As such, we live in a time where the term "science" more and more refers to the metaphysics of Hermeticism, and less and less the empiricism of the scientific method.

"Science," properly considered, is little more than a tool. It is akin to a hammer with which we shatter pieces of the world into constituent parts for rational analysis. With reason we can discern truths with higher fidelity, and definitively rule out many untruths.

"Science," per Platonism, is a system that assumes the realm of forms exists, that this physical world is mere illusion, that "truth" is subjective, and that the purpose of scientific endeavors is to effect change on the world according to our base desires – towards revolution and liberation – not to describe nature as it exists.

This is where discernment becomes important. If you are asked to "believe" in, have "faith" in, or "trust" "science," you are not dealing with the tool of the scientific method—you are dealing with a religious system of Platonic origins. If you are asked to suspend disbelief, coerced with moral language, or taunted and insulted for questioning, you are not dealing with the scientific method, but Platonic "Scientism."

Chapter 7

The Esoteric Lineage

A Brief Introduction to the Genre

What I am about to lay before you is not entirely my own work, and intellectual honesty demands I say so plainly. The connection between Hegelian philosophy and the Hermetic esoteric tradition was established with dispositive rigor by Glenn Magee in *Hegel and the Hermetic Tradition* and by the political philosopher Eric Voegelin, who identified Hegel's project as one of "wizardry"—the deliberate construction of a philosophical religious system to replace the transcendent Christian God with an esoteric immanent system. Magee demonstrated, through painstaking textual analysis, that virtually every major concept in Hegel's system—the dialectic, the absolute, the progression of spirit through history—maps directly onto Hermetic doctrine. Voegelin, working from a different angle, showed that this was not merely an intellectual curiosity but a civilizational threat: the deliberate replacement of transcendent reality with an immanentized becoming—the attempt to create heaven on earth through human will and political power. These scholars cracked open a door that most of the academy had spent two centuries bricking shut.

It was Stephen Coughlin and Rich Higgins of Unconstrained Analytics who took this academic insight and forged it into an operational intelligence framework. Their work, particularly *Re-Remembering the Mis-Remembered Left* and its Appendix B on "Hermeticism in Hegel," demonstrated that the modern Left is not merely influenced by esoteric thought but is, in its operating system, an esoteric religious movement. Coughlin identified Plato's *Republic* as an operational oligarchy formula. He nailed the *Timaeus* as the metaphysical origin of the esoteric system. He strongly hinted at the *Symposium* as an in-group control mechanism. He identified the New Age link to the esoteric tradition. And he hinted at the nature of modern intelligence agencies being infected by this same spirit. Coughlin's contribution to this field cannot be overstated, and I owe him a substantial debt, even where we disagree about the effect of Aristotelian metaphysics and categories as imported by Thomas Aquinas.

I also owe a debt to James Lindsay, who, through his podcasts and writings at New Discourses, made the dense world of Leftist academia easily accessible. I could listen to his work during long commutes to legislative duties in Concord, and his analysis of Critical Theory, Queer Theory, and the practical structures of Woke ideology sharpened my understanding considerably and made vast amounts of Leftist academic works available to me that I would never have had time to read in print. I wish to be clear, however, that while James did great work in describing the problems, once he turned to positive solutions I believe he erred considerably – particularly in expending much hard-won credibility and ethical capital in building up the term "woke right" only to then throw it away by wielding the term against anyone and everyone not of a secular liberal persuasion (to include his anathematizing this author as "anti-American"). I still recall the early days of arguing online with James that Communism was, in fact, a religious system. I distinctly remember in his work, long after his accepting the religious premise of Leftism as true, that he admitted plainly that he could identify the problems and transmit that analysis to the masses (he is legitimately a powerhouse in scholarship), but that he had little in the way to offer of strategy to move forward. He stated that he hoped somebody listening would be able to formulate a strategy to fight back based on his work. I was already doing exactly that, and I've been putting it into practice ever since. Lindsay's diagnostic work remains invaluable. Utilize his accessible readings of difficult literature. His prescriptions, however, being rooted in many of the same philosophical sandboxes as the problems he identifies, and in his preference for a happy misdiagnosis of our current circumstances over the reality of the beast we face, are flawed.

I owe a greater debt than these to the reader—to extend the work of these men and cement it on the firm foundations of traditional Americanism. What this book offers beyond their framework is, I believe, both deeper and truer, according to a presuppositional basis grounded in the American Protestant tradition—the tradition of the Puritans and Presbyterians who built and fought for this country. I am also, to my knowledge, the only analyst writing from the perspective of a practitioner: a sitting state legislator who has watched these dialectical operations play out in real time on the floor of the New Hampshire House of Representatives and who has fought them with the tools described in this book. The theory has been tested in the field. I have put the strategy into direct contact with reality and received feedback.

Beyond these extensions, the analysis in these pages offers several insights I have not found elsewhere: the theory of mind—the way esoteric belief necessarily distorts how its adherents perceive and model the minds of others—inherent to the tensions of esoteric beliefs; the connective tissue that renders these almost insane sounding things both normative and mechanistic; and, importantly, the identification that the philosophies of Plato and Aristotle are not merely in opposition but form a set of paired errors—as per C.S. Lewis, paired errors sent out each attracting a different sort—that pit their respective adherents perpetually and inexorably on a path to decline forming, together, their own in-system dialectic of sorts. The oscillation between Platonic Hermeticism and Aristotelian empiricism is not a story of one hero and one villain but of two Greek systems, each flawed in its own way, each exploitable by the esoteric tradition, and each incapable, on its own terms, of providing the firm foundation required to resist the dialectical destruction we face. That firm foundation exists, and it is neither Greek. It is the tradition that built the West, and it will be the subject of a thorough future work.

The lineage itself, as I trace it, runs thus: from the alchemy of Kemet through the Pythagorean mystery cult to Socrates and Plato's Academy, from the Academy to the gnostic and Hermetic sects that attempted syncretism with early Christianity, from these into Kabbalistic mysticism, through the Renaissance rediscovery and translation of the *Corpus Hermeticum*—the collected texts attributed to the legendary Hermes Trismegistus, purporting to contain the original divine wisdom of the Egyptian priesthood, translated from Greek into Latin by Marsilio Ficino in 1463–71 under Medici patronage—that electrified the European elite, to the Rosicrucians, a German secret society claiming direct descent from ancient Egyptian wisdom, the Knights Templar, and the Masonic lodges that would incubate the Enlightenment and the French Revolution. From the lodges to Hegel, who systematized the whole esoteric project into a single philosophical architecture. From Hegel to Marx, who stripped out the spiritual language and dressed it in the costume of economics. From Marx through the Bolsheviks, the Frankfurt School, and the New Left to the postmodernists, the Critical Theorists, and finally to Crenshaw's intersectionality—the latest denomination in the mystery religions of Babylon.

And running parallel, a softer tributary: from Blavatsky's Theosophy through Alice Bailey, Blavatsky's ideological successor who systematized the esoteric program for institutional penetration, through the New Thought movement and its offspring in Christian Science and New Age spirituality, into the foundations and institutes that would embed social-emotional learning into American public education—the Fetzer Institute, a spirituality-focused foundation that bankrolled the creation of CASEL, and the cultural machine of Oprah and Chopra. Two rivers, one source. Both emptying into the same sea.

The Four Levels of Progressivism

What follows is dense but essential—it is the anatomy of the religion you have been living inside without knowing it, broken into four layers that operate simultaneously. Esoteric Progressivism, with a direct line to ancient Hermeticism and Platonism, constitutes a religious faith—eschatological, coercive, and structured around gnostic elements demanding intolerance despite operating within "liberal" and "tolerant" frameworks. This faith operates simultaneously at the levels of presupposition, faith, ethics, and strategy, with specific linkages to Platonic and Hermetic ideas in each domain.

At the *presuppositional level*, esoteric Progressivism presupposes a teleological view of history as an inevitable unfoldment toward perfection, mirroring the Hermetic principle of the universe as an alchemical process (*solve et coagula*)—"dissolve and reconstitute"—and Platonic emanation from the realm of Forms, where the material world is a shadowed ascent toward ideal truth, guided by those with "ears to hear" and "eyes to see."

At the *faith level*, the eschatological conviction in a man-made Eden available after all oppressive hierarchy is deconstructed reflects Hermetic rebirth into divine unity (the adept completing the great work) and Platonic return to the ideal state under philosopher-king rule, where gnosis-bearers realize the promised harmony disrupted in the fallen world, and all hierarchy naturally dissolves into perfect unity.

At the *ethical level*, justification for deception, manipulation, murder, and atrocity derives from the Platonic noble lie (permissible falsehoods to maintain social order among the ungifted) and Hermetic pendulum and creation mythology, where dissolution of existing structures is morally required for higher coagulation and rebirth as the elect gather the divine shards and transcend distinctions toward at-one-ment.

At the *strategic level*, the vanguard's role in driving history forward, with openness among initiates, echoes Platonic guardianship (philosopher-kings educating and directing society covertly when needed) and Hermetic transmission of knowledge among adepts, proclaiming doctrine evangelically while concealing operative details from the profane.

The Timeline in Brief

The lineage, compressed: In antiquity, gnosticism and Hermeticism existed beside, and repeatedly attempted to syncretize with, Judaism and Christianity. Plato advanced early forms of these ideas. In 1807, Hegel amalgamated several streams of esoterica into a single theosophy in his *Phenomenology of Spirit*, spreading them through cult followerships called Young Hegelians. Marx, a zealous Young Hegelian, dressed the system in materialist economics and published *The Communist Manifesto* in 1848. The Young Hegelian associations in America gave rise to Progressivism. The Bolshevik revolution of 1917 produced Vanguard Marxism. The

Frankfurt School, founded in Frankfurt am Main in 1923 and relocated to Columbia University in 1934 as Nazi power consolidated, abandoned the worker as change agent, shifted to race and sex, and birthed Cultural Marxism. Gayle Rubin's "Thinking Sex" (1984) solidified insurgent Gender Marxism—the application of the Marxist dialectic to biological sex and sexuality. Kimberlé Crenshaw's *Critical Race Theory* (1995)—in which she referred to those in attendance at the founding conference as "a group of Marxists"—gave rise to Woke Marxism through the incorporation of intersectionality as a simple paradigm allow a common operational interface among the many tribes.

Each denomination carries the same Hermetic kernel in a different costume. The full denominational history, with the detailed map of each branching and the commentary that makes sense of it, is the subject of a later chapter. What matters here is the unbroken thread.

The Hermetic Kernel

Nothing seems to make sense—or, at least it would not to somebody teleported to our present from a mere two decades past. They would not understand the question, "what is a woman?" They would not understand very many things, because the distinctions—those things differentiating between particulars—have been blurred or obliterated.

What if I were to tell you this was not done as a random accident of history – not an emergent property of *idiocracy* – but a purposed, zealous, and religious drive towards pure abstraction and undifferentiated oneness of all things? This is the religious rite of Hermeticism—the religion of alchemy—which says that god does not know himself to be god, because he has no opposite to contrast himself against, so he created this mundane world and imbued mankind with *mind* (*nous*) such that man can, through this process of recognizing and then eliminating distinctions, bring god to knowledge of himself. At the end of this religious prophecy of eschatology—a belief about the final destiny of mankind—humanity will be reabsorbed into god (the *absolute*), and all will be utopian. The trick is to understand that this material world is merely an illusion to be transcended.

The Wizard, the Spellbound, and the Based

In modern texts it can sometimes take a near-herculean effort to tease out true meaning by pulling thread after thread until a web of associations can be discerned that exposes esoteric intent. Plato, though not entirely forthright, and writing in the form of "dialogue" (the same word in Greek as "dialectic"), often spoke plainly enough that a person of average intelligence with no background in such matters could, in fact, discern the evil on display in his works. In order to obfuscate such obvious and hideous evil, the Academy, then and now, undertakes a spell-casting routine of extreme obfuscation in order to convince the "educated" and "respectable" people that Plato meant something else—anything else, really—than what he plainly said.

They will argue that his works were highly allegorical, metaphorical, that the *Republic* was "an epic work on justice and civil government." They will suggest that Plato was actually looking inward and writing on "a properly ordered mind," and had no intention of applying his seminal work on the "ideal state" to actual, literal government. They will argue that his extensive formula for eugenics, murder, and spiritual evolution does not even exist—"what book did you even read?" they will query.

This is the fundamental paradigm for our times between the three categories of persons engaged in this war: the *wizards* with their grimoires—their books of spells—who go about casting spells and constructing socially enforced barriers to truth, those under the spell and trapped within the wizard's circle—the *spellbound*—and those consciously alert to the existence of both, ever seeking to be *"based"* in reality and reason (*Logos*). We will return to this model and develop it in detail throughout the remainder of this book.

You have now seen the unbroken thread—from the alchemy of Kemet through the mystery schools and secret societies, through Hegel and Marx and the Frankfurt School, through Blavatsky and the New Thought movement, all the way into intersectionality and the social-emotional learning programs operating in your child's school. The lineage is real. It is documented. It is not a conspiracy theory—it is a conspiracy, conducted in the open, hidden behind the sophistries of an academy that has spent millennia perfecting the art of obfuscation amid a mountain of literature you will not read.

But every thread leads back to a single figure. Every lineage converges on one source. We have named him repeatedly. Now it is time to open his books and read them as the adepts read them—not as allegory, not as quaint philosophy, but as what they operationally are: a regime change mechanism masquerading as religion masquerading as science. We turn now to Plato.

Chapter 8

PLATO

The formula for what you see all over your television set – and, if you live in a big blue city, out your window – was laid down over two millennia ago. Some may call it "the fourth turning," a cyclical theory of American history popular in some conservative circles, others "mass-formation psychosis" or "demoralization." However, it has a proper name from antiquity, and that name is "initiation."

Welcome to the United States of Plato's *Republic* as understood by those who know how to read information out of events, instead of *into* them.

We have quite thoroughly linked the revolution of today's West to the peculiar ideas of Plato. We have reviewed and summarized the *Republic* as a blueprint for our times, and we have made the case that "democracy" exists as little more than a mirage to keep you thirsting—a mirage of moisture amidst a desert of corruption, as the oligarch class manipulates the masses and pits them against one another in perpetuity. This is the underlying formula of all Platonic philosophy, and the game-theoretical reality of what occurs when the elites adopt its strategy.

Let us open the texts and see for ourselves.

A caveat is necessary before we proceed. I have no interest in arguing in perpetuity about the finer points of Platonic scholarship or anyone's pet theory of what Plato "really meant." Whether the interpretation presented herein is the "correct" one in some academic sense is, ultimately, beside the point – guessing at the key to the heart of a Greek dead for millennia is not the ultimate aim. What matters—what matters enormously—is that the interpretation of Plato presented in these pages is an interpretation that was, demonstrably, acted upon by groups of people throughout the millennia to great and terrible effect, just as described. The victims are real. The bodies are real. The revolutions are real. The institutional capture is real. The incentives are real. Whether Plato himself intended every consequence that followed from his writings or whether his ideas were appropriated and weaponized by those who came after is a question I leave to your own discretion, though I certainly have my opinion. I am concerned, foremost, with the operational reality that has formed our present circumstances.

TIMAEUS AND THE LIVING UNIVERSE

The *Timaeus* provides the cosmological operating system for the entire Platonic project. In it, Plato describes a universe that is not merely a collection of objects in space but a single living organism—endowed with soul, intelligence, and purpose. This concept of the "living universe" is the metaphysical origin of all esoteric thought that followed. It is the reason collectivism is not merely a political preference for these people but a cosmological imperative.

Plato writes: "The creator, reflecting on the things which are by nature visible, found that no unintelligent creature taken as a whole was fairer than the intelligent taken as a whole; and that intelligence could not be present in anything which was devoid of soul. For which reason, when he was framing the universe, he put intelligence in soul, and soul in body, that he might be the creator of a work which was by nature fairest and best. Wherefore, using the language of probability, we may say that the world became a living creature truly endowed with soul and intelligence by the providence of God."

And further: "It would be an unworthy thing to liken it to any nature which exists as a part only; for nothing can be beautiful which is like any imperfect thing; but let us suppose the world to be the very image of that whole of which all other animals both individually and in their tribes are portions. For the original of the universe contains in itself all intelligible beings, just as this world comprehends us and all other visible creatures."

And: "In order then that the world might be solitary, like the perfect animal, the creator made not two worlds or an infinite number of them; but there is and ever will be one only-begotten and created heaven."

Read carefully, the world is a single living creature. All beings are *portions* of it. There is only one. This is not a metaphor or some wordplay. This is the cosmological founding that, when coupled with the ethical imperatives, everything else "Left" flows from: if all beings are portions of a single cosmic animal, then individuality is an illusion, (discriminating) distinctions are harmful, and the purpose of existence is reunification into the whole. This is why collectivism is a religious imperative for these people—it is the cosmic destiny of the universe to become one again by, ultimately, the realization that *we are gods*. It is summarized much more succinctly in modern esoteric literature, "All is One" and "All is Mind."

THE CREATION MYTH

In the *Symposium*, Plato provides the creation myth for this strange system. Through the character of Aristophanes, the comic playwright appearing as a guest at the drunken and debauched "dinner party," he tells us that the sexes were originally three: men, women, and the union of the two. These beings cartwheeled around—having four hands, four feet, and two faces. Terrible was their strength and swiftness, and they were preparing to scale heaven and attack the gods.

Zeus, faced with this threat, devised a solution: "Let us cut them in two; then they will only have half their strength, and we shall have twice as many sacrifices." He split them, the primal unified androgyne, and these halves went about looking for one another, ready to embrace until they died of hunger in one another's arms.

The division is said to have produced in mankind three types of erotic desire: those from the original man-woman are "lascivious and adulterous." Those from the original woman form female attachments. Those who are a section of the male follow after the male. The pair are inseparable, "yet they cannot tell what they want of one another. But if Hephaestus were to come to them with his instruments and propose that they should be melted into one and remain one here and hereafter, they would acknowledge that this was the very expression of their want."

"For love is the desire of the whole, and the pursuit of the whole is called love."

This is not mere trash romance in ancient type. This is the Hermetic creation story—or, more precisely, it is the origin of the to-be Hermetic creation story that would not be fully spiritualized for half a millennia more. The primal androgyne—the unified being split by the gods—is the same figure found in Hermetic texts as the divine hermaphrodite, the original unity before differentiation. The "desire of the whole" is the same drive toward undifferentiation and reabsorption into the Absolute that we traced in the previous chapter. The pursuit of the whole (wholism/holism) is the beating heart of the esoteric project: the elimination of distinctions, the destruction of categories, the reunification of all things into one.

It should require no great leap to see the modern transgender movement as a direct application of this myth—the assertion that biological sex is a false distinction imposed upon a superior unity, that the categories of male and female are prisons from which the enlightened must be liberated, that the "true self" exists beyond and prior to the body, and that the severed "soul" might then be in mismatch with the outward vessel. This is not remotely a modern invention. It is Plato's creation myth—itself a syncretism of Egyptian and Greek traditions—operationalized through the great new alchemy of modern medicine. One must also recognize the gnostic influence clearly here: the flesh as a prison for those "mismatched" according to their desires. The body is not a gift to be stewarded but a cage from which the enlightened soul must be liberated—and if the body does not conform to the desire, it is the body that must be cut, drugged, and remade by pharmakeia. This is gnostic anthropology—the doctrine of what man truly is—applied via scalpel and pill.

The Political Blueprint

In the *Republic*, Plato lays down the political program. Traditional stories about the gods are to be censored, signaling a revolution in cultural mythos enforced by the sword (this was a significant part of the official rationale for the execution of Socrates: denying the mythology of Homer, heresy against the gods, and worship of false Egyptian gods). God should be presented to the guardians as good, and as a cause only of good, as unchanging, and as refraining from deception—even though the guardians themselves are taught a "willingness to tell lies when necessary." The guardians are to confine themselves to the austerity in their lifestyle. Restrictions are imposed on music, diet, and physical education. Socrates designs a "patriotic myth to be believed by subsequent generations" as a new founding mythology in which faith is to be placed, to be upheld by the philosophers under the *noble lie* – a lie not made "noble" in intentions, as in an ethically justifiable lie, but by *noble* by virtue that the people lying are *nobles*. In other words, whatever lie escaping the lips of the philosopher is good by virtue of the station occupied, which makes that office divine in a manner of speaking – man making himself as the Most High.

In Book 5, Socrates proposes that women and children should be held in common among the guardians. Female members of the guardian class should perform the same tasks as male guardians in an early nod to egalitarianism, radical equality, and blank-slate prototypical presuppositions. There should be no separate families. Sexual and eugenic regulations are required—selective breeding to maximize the production of "gold" quality persons, with children to be raised communally with no knowledge of who their true parents are. (The concept of "evolution" far preexisted Darwin, and in the Greek paradigm it was the soul that is subject to evolution through reincarnation, activism, and "enlightenment," until a state of perfection is reached ending the cycles of reincarnation). These arrangements are designed to achieve a unity among the guardians that can then extend to all citizens under their sword.

Even the introduction to the Cambridge edition of the *Republic* cannot fully suppress what is plain: "Look rather towards its restriction of political power to a tiny elite, consider their status as moral paragons and saviours, their centralised control of the moral and cultural as well as economic life of the society, their eugenic techniques, their resort to censorship and to outright deception in order to preserve order and promote good behaviour, and you may think you are reading a prescient charter for fascism."[4]

They said it. Not me. Though I would argue the term "fascism" is itself a misdirection based on the same faulty "no such thing as Left-wing authoritarianism" trope the academy has been pushing for a century. The *Republic* is really the direct ancestor of Socialism generally—the communal property, the abolition of the family, the eugenic breeding programs, the censorship regime, the philosopher-king vanguard. Fascism, insofar as it is a distinct phenomenon at all, is a creation of disenchanted Communists who retained the methods while discarding the distinctly Communist internationalism. Plato's blueprint is Communist to its marrow. And yet this book is still taught in every university in the Western world as a "work on justice."

THE CONTROL MECHANISM

What we have the absolute displeasure of discussing now is the "how." That is, how do they maintain their conspiracies without frequently losing the allegiance and devotion of conspirators? After all, anyone with any time looking at the issue of crime knows that, overwhelmingly, convictions of criminals occur based on "flipping" a conspirator to point the finger at others. Why does this not routinely happen among elites who partake in the sort of conspiracies against America, the West, and society?

Well, it just so happens that Plato has a book for that, too.

To understand the workings of the innermost cogs of this machine—the "inner circle"—we look to Plato's *Symposium* once more. *Symposium*, billed rather uninterestingly as a series of drunken speeches to Eros, the Greek god of lusts, hides in plain sight, barely between the lines, the mechanisms for control of such conspirators.

The truth is, the *Symposium* is a series of monologues that elevate the practice of pederasty to religion. Like Plato's other works, this book is an account of conversations among oligarchs while engaged in their debauched and drunken self-aggrandizement. And these were oligarchs in every meaningful sense: of the seven men at Agathon's table, three—Alcibiades, Phaedrus, and Eryximachus—would be indicted in the religious and political scandals of 415 BC, just one year after the dramatic date of the dinner party. Alcibiades himself would go on to instigate the oligarchic coup of 411 BC. Socrates's wider circle included Critias, who became the leader of the Thirty Tyrants, and Charmides—Plato's own uncle—who served under them. Even Xenophon, a sympathizer, was forced to concede: "Among the associates of Socrates were Critias and Alcibiades; and none wrought so many evils to the state" (*Memorabilia* 1.2.12).

Described within these pages is the institution of the *paidagōgos*—a household slave appointed by fathers, as Pausanias tells us at 183c, "to prevent them from conversing with their lovers." This was a protection deployed by aristocratic fathers against other aristocrats—an intra-elite measure revealing that even within the oligarchic class, the practice was understood as a threat from which one's own children required guarding. Pausanias himself distinguishes between what he calls "Heavenly" love—directed at older youths of intelligence and good family—and "Common" love, which he damns as indiscriminate and base, directed at "women and boys" alike "with the least possible intelligence" (181b). The institution of pederasty, as described in the *Symposium* and corroborated across every Greek source we possess, was strictly an aristocratic affair—a rite of passage within the ruling class, not a predilection of the commons. That the appetites cultivated by such a rite resulted in ever greater depravity is a reasonable inference from fallen human nature.

This was not simply a "cultural difference," as many of the modern Academy might argue. Even within the aristocratic class, the practice was hedged with anxiety and regulation – spoken of in a manner that gives the impression that the nastiest of business is always just below the surface, and unsaid. Aeschines, in his prosecution *Against Timarchus* (sections 9–12), recounts the Solonian laws governing the protection of boys—restricting school hours to daylight, barring unauthorized adults from entering rooms where boys were present on penalty of death, and providing public oversight of "slave-attendants of school-boys." The lawgiver prescribed that "if any Athenian shall outrage a free-born child," the offender, if convicted, "shall be delivered to the constables and be put to death the same day" (*Against Timarchus* 16). These are not the laws of a society at peace with the elite practice of pederasty. When Aeschines prosecuted Timarchus before a jury of ordinary citizens on charges of sexual degradation, he won—demonstrating that arguments about the sexual exploitation of citizen males were persuasive to the common people. Aristophanes, performing before audiences of some fifteen thousand, consistently mocked pederasty and presented non-participation as a mark of excellent moral virtue. In the *Wasps*, he boasts of never having been "found in the exercise-ground corrupting the boys." It was not the common people who had a taste for, or sympathies for those who did have a taste for, pederasty. That was an appetite reserved to the oligarch class, and particularly the revolutionaries among them, and the common people knew enough about it to be disgusted. And lest anyone think this mere speculation about what the commoners would do if confronted with the full extent of these practices, recall that a jury of five hundred ordinary Athenians tried Socrates on the charge of "corrupting the youth"—and they killed him for it.

In Plato's Charmides (155d), Socrates—having been told by a companion that if he could see the boy naked 'you would think he had no face, so great is the beauty of his form'—catches a glimpse beneath the youth's cloak and confesses that he 'caught fire' and 'could no longer contain himself.' The Greek is more vulgar than the Victorian translators let on: ephlegomēn, rendered politely as 'caught fire,' is the standard Greek term for burning with sexual arousal, and ouket' en emautou ēn—physical heat associated with increased blood flow. 'I was no longer within myself'—describes a man on the verge of orgasm at the sight of a child's naked body. This is the great philosopher of the West, the man the Academy has spent two and a half millennia sanitizing.

Also described in some detail was the extent of the appetites of individual oligarchs within this inner circle. Socrates's erotic attraction to boys is not confined to the *Symposium*—it is attested across virtually every ancient source we possess. In the *Protagoras* (309a), a companion teases him: "Where have you been now, Socrates? Ah, but of course you have been in chase of Alcibiades and his youthful beauty!" In the *Meno* (76c), Socrates confesses "my weakness for handsome people." In the *Gorgias* (481d), he declares himself "the lover of Alcibiades, the son of Cleinias, and of philosophy." Xenophon records him saying plainly: "I cannot name a time when I was not in love with some one" (*Symposium* 8.2). Even Xenophon's defense amounts to an admission: Socrates warned that a beautiful boy is "more dangerous than the scorpion" and urged his companions, "as soon as you see a pretty face, to take to your heels and fly" (*Memorabilia* 1.3.13). Bear in mind that Plato wrote the *Symposium* after his mentor had been convicted and executed for corrupting the youth. What follows in this dialogue is the defense attorney's manipulations of history, not the prosecution's telling—and the prosecution won. Other oligarchs appeared less lustfully inclined towards children but apparently partook nonetheless. Alcibiades himself describes being drawn into Socrates's orbit as a youth, offering sexual gratification "by which I could learn everything he knew" (*Symposium* 217a), only to have the dynamic reversed—the older man creating the conditions in which the younger pursues him, providing the predator with plausible deniability. Alcibiades warns the company directly: "Do not be deceived by this man; learn from my experience" (222a). He reveals that this was a serial pattern: Socrates had done the same to "Charmides the son of Glaucon, and Euthydemus the son of Diocles, and many others"—"beginning as their lover he has ended by making them pay their addresses to him" (222b).

One does not have to read between the lines much here to see that if the commoners were liable to kill an oligarch who was exposed for his ways with children (which they explicitly did do with Socrates, eventually), and that all the oligarchs partook in such in spite of what their natural inclinations may have been, that there was something more to this pederasty than a mere individual crime of evil passions. There was a conspiracy here: pederasty as ritual, as elite bonding, and as blackmail material, to secure a position among the inner circle. It was an evil bargain struck to secure power, wealth, and a place in "high society." The ancient evidence supports this reading directly. In Crete, the ritual *harpagmos*—the abduction of a noble boy by an adult male of the aristocratic class—functioned as an explicit initiation rite, after which the boy received a military cloak, an ox, and a drinking cup, and took the title *parastates*: comrade in battle. In Sparta, after the age of twelve, every boy of the citizen class was expected to receive an adult warrior as his lover, creating immediate accountability between senior and junior members of the military elite where the elder would be punished for the transgressions of the younger. In Thebes, these bonds were militarized into the Sacred Band—150 pederastic couples who routed Spartans at Tegyra and Leuctra before being annihilated at

Chaeronea. Pausanias himself, in the *Symposium* (182c), provides the political theory: in tyrannies, he says, pederasty is suppressed because tyrants fear the solidarity bonds it creates among citizens. (Of course, the "tyrants" here are seen not as those oppressive of the masses, but of the oligarchs). The implication is plain: pederastic bonds are dangerous to outside rulers precisely because they forge unbreakable loyalty within the ruling class – within the secret societies.

The degree to which such practices were undertaken by various groups, sects, and societies throughout history is difficult to pinpoint, as it is only occasionally that such practices come to light, either through the written word, as in the *Symposium*, or in scandal documented in history.

However, we can know conclusively that these practices were transmitted through the ages by these varied organizations.

Perhaps the best place to start this proof is to look to the nearly modern and extremely influential "father of the New Left," Herbert Marcuse. Marcuse wrote of the "road to higher culture" leading "through the true love of boys"—alluding directly to the *Symposium*, the work from which his *Eros and Civilization* gets its name.[5] The passage appears at p. 211 of the 1966 Beacon Press paperback; attempts to verify it against widely circulated digital editions have encountered passages that appear incomplete relative to the physical text, which is itself worth noting. This entire passage is an esoteric justification of pederasty wherein Marcuse suggests that the fulfillment of pedophilic sexual gratification leads to the inculcation of "higher" forms of desires and gratification. In other words, the gratification of desires available to the oligarch class will lead to the development of the desire for pederasty, which in turn will lead to further debauched desires in an upwards spiral towards the realm of forms (because it could not possibly be a downwards spiral toward Hell).

Marcuse was not merely some German Communist come to America to spread this mind virus within academia. During the time of World War Two, Marcuse would find himself recruited by the United States Army as an early member of the Office of Strategic Services, or OSS. The OSS represented the first major formalization and implementation of professional unconventional warfare and intelligence services within the United States government. After the war the OSS was scrapped for a time before being reorganized and instituted under a new name: the Central Intelligence Agency.

Consider what Marcuse brought with him into the OSS. He had spent his career developing and refining the Frankfurt School's strategies for institutional capture—the counter-hegemonic methodology of entryism, narrative control, and the dialectical subversion of existing organizational cultures from within. These were not mere abstract theories and navel gazing nonsense. They were operational doctrines for the takeover of institutions. Marcuse did not leave these doctrines at the door when he put on a uniform. A man whose life's work was the theorization and practice of institutional capture was placed inside the most powerful and least accountable institution in the American government—one designed, by its very nature, to operate through compartmentalization, secrecy, and the cultivation of factions within target organizations. The OSS was reorganized after the war into the Central Intelligence Agency, and the men who built it carried with them whatever operational culture had taken root. These esoteric organizations excel foremost at one thing: institutional takeover. The fingerprints are visible in the record that followed and in the factional nature that characterized the CIA through its storied history.

We can also see the fingerprints of these organizations on various historic scandals, from the Kincora Boys' Home in Northern Ireland which operated during the period known as "the Troubles" as a sexual honeypot trap utilizing orphaned children to obtain blackmail materials by British intelligence, to the memory-holed recent scandal of Epstein in America: a known intelligence asset associated with the United States, Britain, and Israel, trafficker of children for sex to elites across the globe at his private tropical island, whose apparent murder must have involved numerous elites to see him succumb within a jail cell in New York.

THE COHERENT WHOLE

These Platonic works, together, produce not just some interesting academic work on the conceptual evolution of justice and comparative religion. These works fit together, just as was later accomplished by the Neoplatonists, as a comprehensive worldview to enable revolution, regime change, establishment of an oligarchic class of elites, control of the masses via information warfare and brute force, and the substitution of traditional religion with a system of nonsense that cracks epistemology and ontology irreparably in all directions.

The *Timaeus* provides the cosmological premise: the universe is a single living organism, all beings are portions of it, individuality is mere illusion to be repressed and transcended. Without this premise, nothing else in the system holds together. If reality is objective, if individuals are real and distinct, if creation is ordered by a transcendent God who made things as they are and called them good—then the entire Platonic project collapses. The *Timaeus* exists to prevent that collapse by establishing, at the deepest metaphysical level, that separation is the original sin and reunification is the purpose of existence.

The *Symposium* provides the creation myth, the emotional engine, and the personal gratification. The primal androgyne—split by the gods, forever seeking its other half—sacralizes the destruction of categories and makes the longing for undifferentiation feel like love itself. "Love is the desire of the whole." It is the mechanism by which the esoteric system recruits: it takes the deepest human longing for connection and belonging, and the fallen orientation towards an external locus of control, and redirects it toward the dissolution of the self into the collective. And for the inner circle, the *Symposium* provides the bonding mechanism of shared transgression—pederasty and debauchery as initiation rite, blackmail as glue, mutual complicity as the unbreakable chain that holds the conspiracy together across centuries.

The *Republic* provides the political program and permission structure for extreme violence: how to organize a society according to these premises. Censorship to control what the masses may think. Noble lies to shape what they believe. Eugenic breeding to control what they are, and in what numbers. Communal children to destroy the family as a competing locus of loyalty. Philosopher-kings to rule without accountability. And the entire structure defended by an information warfare regime so total that even questioning the system is rendered unthinkable as the cave-dwellers watching shadow puppets demonstrated.

Together, these three texts form a complete system: a cosmology that demands collectivism, a creation myth that sacralizes the destruction of categories, and a political program that implements both through deception and force. This was not meant to be read in this manner by the public. It was meant to be read ion this manner by initiates. The *Republic* is not a book about justice. It is a manual for oligarchs. The *Symposium* is not a book about love. It is a manual for conspirators. The *Timaeus* is not an obscure and weird novelty. It is a book about cosmology that roots the whole project.

Recall the tripartite model introduced in the previous chapter: the *wizards*, the *spellbound*, and the *based*. You are now looking at the original architecture of all three categories. Plato's philosopher-kings are the prototype of the wizard class: those who know the system, who wield the noble lie, who possess the grimoire and cast the spells. The masses living under the censorship regime and the patriotic myth are the original spellbound—captured within a pseudoreality constructed for them by their betters, never permitted to see the machinery. And the task before you, the reader, is to become and remain *based*—rooted in reality and reason. The purpose of this model is practical: it offers a quick categorization in complicated and confusing circumstances that should cause you to adjust how to engage, and whether to engage at all. Your goal is to move those in the spellbound category into the based category, while reducing or eliminating the effectiveness of the wizards, and retaining the based on-side without being splintered off into wild-eyed theories – a very real risk after being disconnected from the sources of information that deceived them. This stands in stark contrast to the "consciousness" and "woke" language of the Left, because it does not represent a gnosis-gaining exercise but an exercise in reconnecting concepts to the real world—accomplished along lines of remoralization and, generally, by disconnecting people from mainstream sources of information that have been captured toward oligarchic ends.

Assurance

For the rest of you, do not be overwhelmed or dispirited by all of this. Tomorrow will be tomorrow just as yesterday was yesterday. What must change, however, is how you discern, to whom you give the benefit of the doubt, and you should be beginning to understand that political warfare is not merely at the intersection of information warfare and kinetics—it is also at the intersection of spiritual warfare.

You have now seen the architect and his blueprints. Three texts, one system: a cosmology of enforced unity, a creation myth of sacred dissolution, and a political manual for oligarchic control. What remains is to understand the weapon he forged from them—the dialectic. It is the mechanism by which these ideas are transmitted, enforced, and weaponized against populations. From Hermetic polarity to Hegelian sublation, from spells to grimoires, from the principle of polarity to the weaponized problem-reaction-solution of modern political warfare—the dialectic is the edge by which their sword cuts. It is a religious rite aimed directly at the destruction of knowledge itself, and it is the subject of our next chapter.

Chapter 9

THE DIALECTIC

You have a grasp on the who, the what, and the why. Now we stare directly into the abyss of *how*. This is the linguistic and intellectual equivalent of the neutron bomb—a disaster that lingers on a timescale barely human: the dialectic.

The dialectic can be difficult to understand and even more difficult to properly describe. This is not because it is an especially deep concept, but because it is the central theme of a religion that has undergone many, many changes over the millennia. As such, the dialectic is best understood—like so much of the esoteric—by first understanding the origins, fleshing out the spiritual aspect of the concept, and then demonstrating how it applies in the modern world.

HERMETIC ORIGINS

The dialectic emerged from the application of Hermetic theology into practice. It is overwhelmingly linked to the Hermetic principle of polarity—that all things contain their opposite, and that these opposites are identical in nature but different in degree, such that the distinctions between them are merely illusory and can be transcended—but it also encompasses the other principles of Hermeticism.

Mentalism—that all is mind, the universe is mental, and that ideas are more real than reality itself, meaning the dialectic operates purely in the mental sphere divorced from the objective world.

Correspondence—as above, so below; the notion that patterns repeat across all planes of existence, binding the material to the spiritual and the individual to the cosmic, such that what is done on one plane necessarily affects the others.

Vibration—that nothing rests, all is in motion, and that all matter is merely energy at varying rates of frequency, lending itself to the belief that consciousness itself can be shifted or manipulated through dialectical agitation.

Rhythm—that the pendulum swings in all things, that the measure of the swing to the left is the measure of the swing to the right, creating the conditions for the dialectical ratchet that always inches in one direction while resisting correction.

And cause and effect—the principle that every cause has its effect and every effect its cause, and that the swing of this pendulum can be directed strategically at unwitting identity groups to absorb the impact that should rightly be borne by the Communists themselves.

From mentalism to the pendulum of cause and effect, the dialectic draws on the full architecture of Hermetic theology. It flows from the Hermetic creation myth.

According to the creation mythology of Plato and the Hermeticists, God—known variously as undifferentiated act, absolute spirit, the All, Source, or the like—could not know itself to be God without an opposite to compare itself to. God, being perfect, could not recognize its own perfection without something imperfect as a contrast – "what is perfection, without the imperfect that makes it so?" So, God overflowed, superabundant, into *mundane* (imperfect) creation. In this process, everything that was created was imbued with a shard or spark of divine perfection, but encased within mundane existence. In this manner, it is said that the true nature of all things is one with God, and that mundane matter is merely an illusion. Then—all things being at one with God in their true nature—the difference between all things itself must be an illusion, part of the mundane existence, and something to be abolished.

A man is then no different than a woman, nor is a mineral different than an animal, nor is good different than evil. These are all merely illusory distinctions to be overcome.

The process of creation in this myth did not complete the process of bringing God into full knowledge of itself—*actualization*. Creation was merely the first half of the equation. The second half falls to mankind to complete. As the lowest (evolutionarily) of all created beings endowed with *nous*—mind—it is the duty of man to recollect these shards of the divine and, through the mental process of pure thought (dialectics), recognize that these distinctions between things are mere illusions, and to mentally overcome them by recognizing their sameness. This process of recognizing the likeness of all things, which is prophesied to end in the realization of an individual that they are, in fact, a god, is commonly known in the modern era as *enlightenment*.

This is the origin of the dialectic, and this description is in accordance with Plato's own assertion that dialectics are a purely mental exercise, wholly disconnected from the material world, and oriented towards the esoteric realm of forms (*spirit*, as modern practitioners would say). It is in this process of transcending distinctions that dialectics takes its shape. Because the material world is but mere illusion, the products of dialectics are considered to be more true than reality itself – unfalsifiable by any appeal to fact or observation.

THE CATASTROPHE OF ABSTRACTION

Take a simple example of how this works in practice. A trout swims up a cold river, eating flies and fighting the current. A flounder eats sea worms amid the crashing waves where the vast sea meets land. What does the trout have in common with the flounder? At a higher order of categorization, we recognize them both as fish. According to the theory of the dialectic within the Platonic Hermetic faith, our recognition of the trout and the flounder as both being fish—thereby transcending the distinctions between the two—brings our collective consciousness, which is linked to God, into a higher knowledge than merely to know them as particulars. In this manner, we mentally undertake the creation process in reverse – man no longer tasked with giving things a rightful, specific name, but destroying that paradigm altogether.

According to the Hermeticists, all of existence started as undifferentiated, coming into existence merely as a mental projection of god, and it is to this state of undifferentiation which we must mentally return if we are to recognize ourselves to be as gods and ascend to the higher planes of existence. There can be no man or woman, but first a return to the original *whole* state of the hermaphrodite. There can be no trout or flounder, but only fish. Later, there can be no fish and mammal, but merely animal, as we climb the mental ladder towards At-One-Ment.

You have already seen the Hermetic drive toward undifferentiation—the purposeful obliteration of distinctions. Now consider what this looks like applied in a practical example.

Consider an apple. When you consider an apple, you might think of the flavor, the color, the shape, and so on. However, when you consider first the color of an apple, you are eliminating nearly all apples that are not that particular apple in your mind's eye. These nested hierarchies of abstraction begin with the particular apple, move up to the variety—McIntosh, say—move up further to all red-colored apples, and further yet again to all types of apple, and then higher to fruits.

Now, assume you are the agricultural minister for a little dictator of a small nation, and you are tasked with centrally planning agriculture. You order that one million apple trees be planted forthwith in order to feed the poor people of your country. Your underlings go out and plant one million Red Delicious apple trees and return to you, all smiles. But instead of rewarding them, you ream them out and scream, "I said plant one million apple trees, not a million Red Delicious trees!" Your underlings then go out and uproot one million Red Delicious saplings and plant one million McIntosh apple trees, and again return to you all smiles.

Again, instead of rewarding them, you have your number two hung in public while screaming, "I said plant one million apple trees, not a million McIntosh trees!" At this point everyone is quite confused, but you keep screaming about socialist plant science, and you have already hung a man publicly, so everyone gets busy trying very hard to look like they are working without actually doing anything at all—because it appears that doing anything at all will result in their demise.

This is the reality of dialectics. It cannot ever produce anything useful, including knowledge. It can only produce confusion, and sow destruction.

If you want to undertake the process of planting even one apple tree you must choose, from among the very many varieties, one single variety to plant. Even then, among the very many seeds of that variety, you must choose one single seed that will become your tree. Taking any action in the real, objective world requires the greatest degree of distinction—right down to the level of the individual unit. You cannot undertake a category of things as an action, because a category is purely an abstraction.

You cannot perform an abstraction in the real world—you can only perform a particular that excludes the possibility of all other particulars. When one commits himself to the elimination of distinctions and blurring of boundaries, he begins making himself incapable of any sort of discernment between particulars as to which is better, or which is terrible, or evil even. This is the methodology by which Communism—and Fascism and Nazism—destroys entire societies. It destroys the sense-making capacity of the population writ large such that they attempt to override reality with abstraction and social construction.

Reality cannot be overridden. There is no *absolute* spirit, and there is no perfecting anything through the elimination of distinctions. Distinctions are necessary at all times for discernment, and discernment is necessary at all times to simply avoid the terrible death that nature would happily inflict upon you with its veto over your stupid abstractions.

You can also see within this concept the mechanism for perpetual revolution. There is no end to the process of transcending distinction until all distinctions have been transcended. Distinctions cannot truly be transcended in practice at all, because they are purely abstract at higher orders of category. Therefore, there is no end to this process of trial and error and trial and error and trial and error, *ad infinitum*. It is, in practice, a perpetual motion machine of misery.

HOLISTIC PHENOMENOLOGY

If the catastrophe of abstraction is what the dialectic *does*, phenomenology and holism are the philosophical frameworks that *justify* doing it.

Phenomenology, as used in the modernist sense, is the ultimate philosophical practice of looking inward in an effort to understand and describe the nature of the realm of ideas. As such, phenomenology is a purely subjective practice and, like dialectics, not tied to any objective reality. Further, a central premise of the field is the supposed ability to dispense with one's own presuppositions and beliefs and simply take in raw experiences for unbiased analysis. Of course, this is a sheer impossibility. The entire structure of both knowledge and identity is predicated on presuppositions, and while they can be altered, they cannot be eliminated.

Phenomenology in the esoteric sense of Hegel's *Phenomenology of Spirit* (1807) was a bit more than just this. It is specifically dialectical and also, therefore, historicist in method. In other words, it is the subjective interpretation of one's own existence and thoughts that *pretends* to dispense with presuppositions and metaphysics—while advancing the presuppositions of Hermeticism and describing the process of History driving with purpose, as in a spirit of History, towards the endpoint in which mankind becomes God. In this manner, phenomenology is the ultimate exercise in philosophic navel-gazing.

This endpoint of man as God, per Hermetic theology, occurs as a result of transcending distinctions between all things until absolute undifferentiation is achieved. It is in this process and belief system that the word *actualization* originates—meaning to literally come into conscious knowledge of one's own state of consciousness, with the attendant presupposition that *the universe is mental*, and therefore that a knowledge of one's own consciousness comes with supernatural abilities. Remember: because this belief system holds that all is mind, to achieve actualization and come into a conscious awareness of one's own consciousness is the same as to be as God – cocreators. Specific terms within this cult religion used to describe this state of actualization include *enlightenment, ascension,* and *Christ consciousness,* and states approaching this perfect consciousness on the evolutionary path of enlightenment are commonly known as *critical consciousness.*

These are also the ideas that undergirded the establishment of the field of psychology. Translated directly, *psyche* means "soul," and the field arose entirely out of the Hermetic syncretic faith and continues to smuggle with it those beliefs and presuppositions. These ideas are also at the center of the New Age religion, the New Thought cult as promoted by Oprah Winfrey, Christian Science, Theosophy, social-emotional learning, the United Nations, and others.

HOLISM IN PRACTICE

Holism is a very closely related field of philosophy that emphasizes how all things are interconnected. You may be familiar with sayings that begin with "a butterfly flapped its wings," suggesting that the tiniest variation can lead to dramatic outcomes—such as a butterfly causing a hurricane. Like the Platonic use of phenomenology, this concept of holism flows from Hermetic theology, which suggests that all is one. This is the academic dress of what we earlier termed *wholism*—the esoteric project of eliminating distinctions.

This field of philosophy suggests that you cannot understand the particular without understanding the universal—which is simply another way of saying that you cannot really understand anything at all, since a perfect, absolute knowledge of all things is not achievable.

Let us ground this in something practical. Anyone familiar with industry and handiwork will likely have, at some point, utilized a battery-powered hand tool—perhaps a drill or saw running on an 18-volt lithium battery. The application of holism to this might suggest that we need to understand the workings of the internal brushless DC motor, the chemistry of the lithium storing the energy, and so on. Now, surely the engineers at these corporations need this knowledge to design and build these products. However, to build a shed at home, all I really need to know is how to pull the trigger and where to cut.

This easily demonstrates the failure of holism in practice. When we function doing anything at all in the objective world, we do so without a holistic knowledge of things. We must operate this way simply because we do not share in the mind of God. We lack a perfect knowledge of all things. Yet we manage to survive and even thrive at times.

Heuristics—How We Actually Function

How do we accomplish this without a perfect knowledge? We do not have unlimited mental processing capacity. Our capacity is limited, and this limit is often expressed in terms of bandwidth. In any given task or thought, we must limit our incorporation of data and variables to stay within our available bandwidth. We do not want to randomly include or exclude variables—that would be a recipe for disaster as we dismiss important things while incorporating inane things.

The process we use for deciding what variables are sufficiently important to include among our limited calculations is called *heuristics*. By this process, and through improvements to the specifics of the heuristics we use, we can operate, function, survive, thrive, and avoid pain and suffering with a limited knowledge of the world. For instance, we do not need to incorporate the butterfly flapping its wings because that energy will rapidly dissipate as a tiny amount of heat—and it simply is not meaningful compared to weather patterns, sun cycles, ocean surface temperatures, and so on.

Heuristics inform your everyday life right down to that category of thought commonly known as "subconscious." When women get that disgust or fear around a man, when a man picks up on a small set of cues from a guy on the street that tells him that a predator is on the hunt, they are not pulling that information out of the ether. They are relying on information they gather through sense perception that amounts to far, far less than a holistic knowledge. The guy kept patting his waistband, looked around to see if anyone was observing him, and was eyeing people up and down when they walk past. This was enough to strongly suggest, even if you couldn't verbalize it, that he was looking for an easy target and he is armed. That's more than enough information to make a simple decision: cross the street.

Here you can see the relationship between holism and Hermetic phenomenology, as both incorporate the principles of "all is one" and "all is mind," and both strive for an unobtainable perfect knowledge and sharing in the mind of God through ascension. Holism goes so far as to suggest that all information short of holistic information is worthless—which can only be justified when you make the argument that objective reality itself is an illusion, as is the suffering produced by the Hermetic ideology.

No Limiting Principle

So why then do these obviously flawed models of thought persist to this day, to the extent of becoming the predominant governing and legal philosophies in the West?

Returning to Plato's *Republic*: recall that the esoteric, initiate understanding of Plato as passed down through the Academy was that of a manual for the corrupt accumulation of power and wealth by a select few—an oligarch class. In this way, the application of phenomenology and holistic philosophy removes any limiting principles from government regulation.

As a thought experiment, consider a gentleman who, upon becoming inebriated by wine at a party, goes on to choke on a grape and dies. With a traditionalist view, based in Biblical presuppositions and metaphysics, we would assign the highest reasonable degree of agency and responsibility to this gentleman and suggest that this tragic occurrence was of nobody else's fault but his own. After all, he chose to drink the wine and become inebriated. He went on to choose to eat the grapes while inebriated and likely while being preoccupied socially. It is unfortunate and should serve as an example of what not to do—and perhaps drive people to undertake on their own the attainment of skills to resolve such an emergency in the future.

However, if we apply holism and phenomenology to this scenario, we suddenly find that the host of the party is ethically and legally implicated for providing the food and beverage, for failing to ensure that partygoers were versed in the Heimlich maneuver, for allowing the guest to over-serve himself, and so on. More: we can also implicate the other partygoers for distracting the gentleman socially. We can implicate the manufacturers of the glass he drank from and the bowl he ate from, and doubly so for the grower of the grapes that produced both the wine and the physical obstruction of his airway. Perhaps he who grew the grapes, being doubly responsible, should be tried for murder.

You see, in this manner, quite literally anyone can be implicated for anything at all, and the opportunity for regulation is infinite. With infinite regulation comes infinite opportunity for pay-to-play, kickbacks, regulatory capture, and monopoly through public-private partnerships—and unlimited arbitrary power is accrued by corrupt officials. This also enables a rapid switching between assigning limited or no agency, and assigning maximal or reasonable agency, to victims and villains.

If this sounds familiar, it is because it is, first, the precise method for the creation of a critical theory as defined by the cultural Marxist Frankfurt School scholars, and it is also the principle that our governments, and especially our judiciaries, have been and are being transitioned to. There is no difference between the critical legal theory of 1980s Harvard Law and a holistic approach to judicial matters. In fact, the entirety of the fields of social science, as developed and deployed by Marxists, is premised on the concepts of holism and phenomenology. This is a significant contributor to the replication crisis in these fields of "science," as they are not in fact science as we would consider it at all, but merely extensions of the dialectical seminaries akin to modern mystery schools.

You ought to also see in this the mechanisms that enable anarcho-tyranny – where government simultaneously is overbearing on the decent while seeming nonexistent when dealing with the criminal – as the variable assignment of agency enables anyone accused of a crime to be seen themselves as the victim in some higher, cosmic sense, and thereby freed while the conviction falls on the brokenness of the world that produces such criminals – a world that must now be overthrown to correct this.

Now that you understand the history and structure, it is time to show you how, exactly, it has been deployed to bring us to where we are today.

Chapter 10

HISTORICAL THEORISTS

With a theological and philosophical framework of the dialectic now firmly underfoot, we can delve deeper into the concept and bring it to life as we explore the ways it has molded modern culture, government, and religion. What follows is the history of how three men—the fathers of post-modernity—took this theological principle and hammered it into a weapon.

Imagine a child playing with one of those little shape-sorter games. The little one picks up the star-shaped block and attempts to place it in the square hole. It does not fit. The child then tries the circular hole. Much closer, but not quite. Then, finally, the child places the star in the star-shaped hole. Success—but we are not done there.

Say the child smuggles this little star block out of the home and takes it on a field trip. Where might it fit in the real world? As the child's parents fuel the vehicle at the petrol station, the child sneaks a try at shoving the block in the fuel tank. No luck. Looking up, the child sees the rear window is open and tosses the block through it. It fit through the window, though it was not exactly a tight fit. Then the little one gets back in the car and finds that the cup holder is a snug, firm fit for the star block. After a gas tank and an open window, this cup holder feels just right—and provides a sense of success to the child.

The block represents the dialectic. Though not a game, the theological and philosophical process of dialectics places an onus on the initiate to attempt to fit this block into quite literally everything, everywhere. In application, there will be places that the dialectical block fits with varying degrees of fitment. When applied, the dialectic will produce real-world effects—these occur as a consequence of enacting the resultant dialectical ideas in the world. Bad ideas tend to produce bad effects. But as anyone who plays the markets will understand, there is money to be made in bad occurrences, if only for the know-how and ability to predict the occurrence. The ability to inflict bad things at will can, if utilized in an intelligently evil manner, be utilized to accumulate wealth and power.

This is the beginning of *gnosis*—that belief that one has had something of a direct revelation from the mind of God—and it assures the initiate that he must be on the right track – that he surely now understands the world better than you or I. After all, he fit his star block in a cupholder. . .

ROUSSEAU

Jean-Jacques Rousseau (1712–1778) rejected his Calvinist upbringing and became associated with French lodge Freemasonry—a connection evident in the Masonic influence on his thought, though the precise nature and timing of his affiliation remains debated among scholars. He went on to formulate his dialectical, conflicted concept of the noble savage. With roots in early Greek thought, this romantic, vast oversimplification of culture suggested that the savage—those cultures and tribes without modern technology, dependent more directly upon and subject to nature—are inherently good, morally superior, and represent a better way of existing.

This concept directly tied the evil of man to the corrupting influence of culture and society. Man is inherently good, noble, and virtuous—but modern society, not being in accordance with nature, corrupts him such that he becomes evil. This evil then becomes the mechanism by which social inequality is perpetuated, as the industrialist becomes wealthy through the hierarchical domination of those in his employ.

Here we have the value judgment that a perfect, total equality between persons is desirable and good—a principle of esoteric Freemasonry. Further, that to be a privileged elite removes one from his natural good state and inculcates an evil in him, and that this evil is perpetuated on society to further inequality, cyclically and perpetually, in a manner trapping man "in chains." This sets up the dialectical, conflicted relationship between the idea of the noble savage against the corrupted, civilized man—objects for an attempted synthesis: to bring the noble savage to the modern city, to live virtuously in modernity (though, in reality, for Rousseau, like Marx after him, he mostly just loathed working and wanted to justify perpetual layaboutism and navel gazing).

The genesis of these ideas is extremely interesting for those who appreciate irony. Rousseau never did much travelling and never met these noble savages, as he called them. He relied on the writings coming back to Europe by those entrepreneurial explorers who did meet them—and who had their own reasons for concocting and perpetuating this myth of the innocence of the natives they encountered, and for omitting such native practices as human sacrifice and cannibalism.

Rousseau was a central figure in the Romantic Enlightenment movement, criticizing the intellectual consistency and centrality of logic in some Enlightenment thinkers, and in the Reformation traditions. He emphasized an emotional approach to understanding and life that is not necessarily tempered by reason—a pathos without logos.

Rousseau also put the esoteric interpretation of Plato into action in his defining of a *general will*—the suggestion that the majoritarian opinion of the mob, democracy, was of the spirit and constituted the perfect idea for that time in History. This became a central theme of Progressivism: that democracy would move History forward towards a utopian end. Of course, Rousseau would have been familiar with Plato's formula for the manipulation of that mob through the control of information—and undoubtedly believed himself qualified to effect it. *Vox Populi, Vox Dei* was never really meant to empower the people, but those who pulled the puppet strings.

The influences and esotericism of Rousseau shine through in his declaration that "man is born free, but everywhere he is in chains"—suggesting that the natural state of mankind is a good and perfect state, but man is imprisoned by the demiurgic (referencing a demon who imprisoned man's spirit in a fleshly body in gnostic mythology) forces in this life, forces which he mostly chalked up to society and the state. His path forward: mankind must adopt the social contract, surrendering his rights to society, and in so doing find freedom and happiness among the collective and the democratic will.

Rousseau's ideas, deeply inspired by the esoteric traditions, would go on in turn to deeply influence the same traditions—especially those of the esoteric Lodges, which went on the influence the American revolution before becoming fully empowered in the French Revolution.

HEGEL

Georg Wilhelm Friedrich Hegel (1770–1831) was likewise raised in the ostensibly Protestant tradition. He was raised in Württemberg, a region whose dominant Pietist tradition—through figures like Oetinger and Bengel—was deeply influenced by German mysticism, Boehmean theosophy, and Kabbalism, as documented by Glenn Magee in *Hegel and the Hermetic Tradition*.[6] Hegel turned firmly towards Platonism. As a throwback to the concept of Platonic forms, Hegel adopted a speculative idealist philosophy and crafted his dialectic of abstract, negative, concrete.

What does that mean? Far from the modern view of *speculative* as being a guess of sorts, the true meaning of *speculum* is mirror. This was meant to suggest that you must hold an abstract idea up to the mirror of one's mind until the negative idea—sometimes viewed as its opposite—appears, putting the original abstract idea in conflict. Then the ideas are considered until a higher-order idea that resolves the conflict arises in the concrete. It is a form of navel gazing until you experience some thought accompanied by such a feeling that implies the achievement of gnosis – it's little wonder why drugs have always played so heavily into esoteric spirituality and philosophy.

The true meaning of *idealism*—again, far from most current perceptions—is that ideas are more real than reality or the material world, and ultimately can directly shape the material world. This is a direct rewriting of Platonic forms and the principle of mentalism of Hermeticism.

Following on the philosophy of Descartes—*I think, therefore I am*—Hegel viewed consciousness as the principal aspect of things. *All is mind; the universe is mental.* His dialectic was built around the belief that a person can adopt different consciousness, positionally, and that these consciousness come into conflict dialectically, and that they must be worked out through his dialectical process of History.

Hegel brought this idea into maturity in his version of the master-slave dialectic—a direct lineage from the noble savage. He postulated that the nature of human relations between consciousness can all be categorized according to the master-slave dynamic, with all persons adopting one or the other depending on circumstance. In this theory, the master forgets something important about existence that causes him to become dependent on the recognition of his authority, thereby finding his identity in the subjugation of the slave. The slave, however, through his labor and service, becomes self-aware and develops a consciousness that exceeds that of the master—his sense of self seen as more authentic, arising from his own self-actualization in labor and not dependent on the affirmation of the other (*in labor* should be noted, here, as fundamental to the esoteric traditions of thought thereafter, including the infamous "labor will set you free" signage that hung outside German concentration camps).

Hegel postulated that it is this struggle or conflict between the two consciousness, according to his dialectic, that brings about resolutions—becoming more perfect with each cycle of the dialectic, driving History forward towards the Hermetic eschaton—the prophesied end of History. The dialectical process of History is often visualized symbolically as a coiled spring, or some other similar-looking thing—such as a snake climbing a pole.

Hegel became something of a rock star in his day, with adherents globally calling themselves Young Hegelians or Old Hegelians, spreading his ideas to every corner of life through these cults.

MARX

Karl Marx (1818–1883), a zealous Young Hegelian in college, initiated into the mysteries via various memberships of orders and societies common to Germany and to England, took Hegel and recrafted his ideas to hide the metaphysical, religious nature of the system—wrapping it in something vaguely materialistic and economic. Hence the proper name given to Communism by Marx: dialectical materialism.

Like those before him, Marx adopted this idea of different consciousness in conflict, and he too saw man everywhere in chains—according to the

Gnostic disposition of the material world as a prison for the spirit. The materialist shape he hammered this doctrine into took its cues from the gnostic Hermetic creation myth—that demiurgic demon that imprisoned man in a physical body—but in the stead of the demon is "capital."

For Marx, *capital* does not have the meaning the uninitiated prescribe to it today. Capital does not simply mean money. Capital is quite literally a magical property which, possessed by some, instills within them a false consciousness of an evil, corrupting sort—one that causes them to subjugate as master over the laborer. This magical property, through instilling this consciousness, perpetuates itself cyclically throughout History as a flat circle, preventing the advancement or evolution of mankind.

On the other hand, the laborer develops the slave consciousness, providing that authentic knowledge of self. Marx postulated that it must be the laborers—the proletariat—with their special knowledge, that moves History forward towards the eschaton, and to undo all of creation toward a return to absolute spirit.

"All that exists deserves to perish." Quoting Mephistopheles of *Faust* was his favorite refrain, as was his reinterpretation of that sentiment through "ruthless criticism of all that exists." Recall: Hermeticists believe that the duty of mankind is to undo creation, undertaking the process of creation in reverse, until all returns to the unified All.

So the laborers must be empowered over society and government. How? Through revolution. *Workers of the world, unite.*

Your schooling might have skipped over the simple fact that economic theories do not tend to be teleological toward an end in which man returns to Eden (or absorption into Absolute Spirit). Engels drafted the Communist Manifesto's predecessor in June 1847 as a question-and-answer catechism titled the *Draft of a Communist Confession of Faith*—until he and Marx thought better of it and hid the overwhelming religious nature of the system as economics.

Marxism has always been a religious sect of the faith of Platonic Hermeticism, as was Hegelianism before it, as are the ideologies that synthesized Hegel and Marx—Fabianism, Progressivism, and Wokeism.

THE CONFLICT ENGINE

Here you have the most critical components of the evolution of dialectics that has brought us into our modern circumstances. While none of the preceding philosophers called it such explicitly, this concept was later coined as *conflict theory*—and it is the predominant worldview of sociology, which adopts the metaphysics, theology, and eschatology of Hermeticism as understood through these initiates. The dialectical conflict between various consciousness identities, with those various slave identities coined *critical consciousness* and the master identity termed *false consciousness*. Note the inversion: it is the traditional, reality-based worldview that is labeled "false," while the revolutionary worldview claims for itself the mantle of "critical" awareness.

According to these theories, it is only this conflict between identities that can bring us to utopia. According to this logic, it makes sense to actively increase conflict on purpose—as a matter of religious duty—to speed up the process of History toward the eschaton, towards a man-made Eden. *Accelerate the contradictions, comrade*, as Lenin would say.

We will learn in a later chapter how the American state was transitioned from one of transcendence to one of Hermetic immanence—the state of Hegel. *The state is the divine idea as it exists on Earth*—under the presidency of an avowed Young Hegelian, Woodrow Wilson. But, first, let us delve into a real-world example from my legislative experience on how dialectics are used to control the people you elect.

Chapter 11

DIALECTICS DEEP DIVE

The dialectic does not have to be complicated. It can be simply thought of as third-way-ism—the practice of taking two competing ideas and "synthesizing" them into a new concept that accounts for both. Somebody wants to cook dinner at home, another wants to eat dinner out, and the negotiated synthesis might be getting takeout to eat in. This process is readily weaponized, however, as it has been by the Left for centuries, into a mechanism whereby Leftist ideas are synthesized with rightist ideas in a way that always favors the gradual progression of Leftism.

This is accomplished by handicapping the rightist ideas through "scientizing" them—various linguistic tricks that place the rightist idea, properly considered in the realms of theology or philosophy, into the realm of "science" or "experts," who can then speak to the rightist ideas as "false" (making an objective claim with no basis in objectivity). Alternatively, rightist ideas are placed outside the Overton Window and thus made unacceptable socially. These practices favor the Leftist ideas during the negotiated process of synthesis such that it effectively builds out a *dialectical ratchet*—so named for the tool that moves by ever-so-small increments in one direction while resisting movement in the other.

Further necessary to the understanding of this incremental process is that the "science" we typically consider to be science is not the same "science" that they mean when they engage in the process of political warfare. This was outlined in the political theology of Hegel in the division of "science" into two categories—one rudimentary and process-driven, the other metaphysical and prophecy-driven. Very much of what the modern

Left refers to as "science" is actually of the latter variety, and more properly called Scientism.

By capturing the broader sciences and infecting them with Scientism, the Left has managed to remake institutions and repurpose them as reification agents of Leftist dogma. The Left can, through the dialectical process described above, point to the institutions it has captured and the "science" it has infected with Scientism to label rightist ideas and policy as "objectively false" or "scientifically harmful"—while in reality referring to a religious ideology, not actual science. They get away with this because they have ideologically captured the institutions that would, in a functional system, serve as a check on their false claims to expertise.

Do not take my word for any of this. Clinical psychologist Jeremy Shapiro published a piece in Psychology Today in December 2020—"Dialectical Political Messaging: A Strategy for Democrats?"—laying out the strategy for implementing this process, citing dialectical behavioral therapy as the model, detailing how they intended to negate rightist ideas and policy through this dialectical process. The author of the piece gives away the game at the end: "In principle, Republicans could use this strategy too, but the main problem currently besetting that party is the rejection of factual and scientific information." In other words, the Republicans do not get to use this strategy because their ideas are not correct according to the institutions that the Left controls.

Shapiro is one small instance of a very large pattern. The Left reliably adopts what empirically works. Deng Xiaoping said it plainest—it does not matter whether the cat is black or white, so long as it catches mice—and moved the Chinese economy into substantial privatization in frontal contradiction of Maoist orthodoxy, because the methods produced the material results the regime needed. The same pragmatism governs the twentieth- and twenty-first-century Western social-science apparatus: empirically validated techniques of persuasion, conditioning, mass psychology, and behavioral modification—drawn from behaviorism, cognitive science, marketing research, and intelligence tradecraft—were adopted without any concern for whether they cohered with stated humanistic or egalitarian values. CASEL and SEL did not arrive in American schools because their designers had become empiricists. They arrived because the empirical work on childhood ethical formation had matured to the point that it could be weaponized at scale. The vanguard holds its nose and picks up the hammer that drives the nail.

I ask you then to consider, with this new knowledge, what the actual purpose might be of a training event for lawmakers from both the Left and the Right—learning to utilize the dialectical process to "work together," to find "common ground," and to "reduce polarization." Would it be helpful to know that this training event was run by a psychologist? Do not assume the worst of those involved in bringing in this training, however. It is entirely likely they did not, and do not, know the true intentions of it.

I know this because I was there. And having since conducted a forensic examination of the organization behind that training, I can now tell you the full story.

The Trust: A Necessary Prologue

Before we turn to the organization itself, a historical parallel is necessary—one that should be taught in every school and is not, because its implications are too dangerous to the people who run them.

In the early 1920s, the Soviet secret police—the GPU, predecessor to the KGB—established a fake anti-Bolshevik resistance organization called the Monarchist Organization of Central Russia, known internally as Operation Trust. The organization presented itself as an underground network of loyalists working to restore the old order from within the Soviet system. It recruited genuine White Russian émigrés, anti-Communist officers, and foreign intelligence operatives into its ranks. It held meetings. It planned operations. It gathered resources. It looked, in every respect, like the real thing.

It was not the real thing. It was a GPU front, designed from inception to identify, attract, control, and ultimately neutralize the genuine anti-Communist resistance. By drawing real resisters into a managed structure, the Soviets accomplished several objectives simultaneously: they identified who the real opposition was, they channeled oppositional energy into activities that posed no actual threat to the regime, they gathered intelligence on foreign support networks, and they demoralized the broader resistance by ensuring that every effort undertaken through the Trust's auspices failed at the critical moment. The Trust operated for years before its true nature was exposed. By the time it was, the damage was done—the authentic resistance had been gutted from within.

The principle is timeless: if you cannot destroy your enemy's resistance directly, build a version of it that you control, and let your enemy's best people walk into it voluntarily. The operation need not be a perfect conspiracy. It need not involve every participant as a knowing agent. It need only be designed—at the top, by those who understand its structure—to produce the desired outcome. The sincere participants are not obstacles to the operation. They are its most valuable assets, because their sincerity is what makes the operation credible.

Keep this pattern in mind. We are about to see it again.

Braver Angels in the New Hampshire House

In late 2022, shortly after being elected to the New Hampshire House for the first time, I received an invitation from House leadership to attend what was billed as a continuing education event: *Managing Difficult Conversations with Colleagues and Constituents*. The training was scheduled for December 15th, 2022, in Representatives Hall—the House chamber itself—and was put on by an organization called Braver Angels, described in the official House Record as "a nonprofit working to bridge the partisan divide." The session was to run approximately two hours and was open to all Representatives-Elect. Members would be paid mileage for attendance. It was followed immediately by the Annual Legislative Christmas party at the Upham Walker House—refreshments and fellowship to seal the experience with warmth and goodwill.

I attended—not because I was taken in by the billing, but because I was deeply suspicious that it would be exactly what it turned out to be: a political warfare operation. A "bipartisanship training" event, run by an outside organization, conducted behind closed doors in the House chamber, led by a psychologist, and aimed at freshly elected legislators who had not yet established their bearings? Everything about it triggered the instincts I had developed over years of studying these methods. I went to see it with my own eyes and confirm what I suspected.

I was not disappointed.

The session was led by a Washington, D.C.-based representative of the Braver Angels organization—a psychologist, as was stated openly—and was conducted according to the methods of dialectical behavioral therapy. This, too, was stated plainly. To my knowledge, the session was never broadcast publicly or live-streamed. It was an intimate affair, conducted inside the House chamber, with newly elected legislators as its subjects. I understood what I was watching in real time.

The format proceeded in stages, each building on the last.

First, the exercises were relational. Legislators from opposing parties were paired together and guided through structured intimacy-building exercises—getting to know one another on a personal level, sharing experiences, establishing rapport. There is nothing sinister about getting to know your colleagues. But this was not the point of the exercise. The relational stage was the preparation of the ground for what followed.

Second came the negotiation exercises. Here the method revealed itself. Participants were required to adopt the frame of mind and policy positions of the opposing party—to inhabit the other side's perspective, to explore that frame from within, to understand it not merely intellectually but *empathetically*, in the captured sense of that word we examined earlier. Having thus inhabited the other side's frame, the participant was then guided to moderate his own position toward it—to find the middle, the synthesis, the third-way resolution.

This is the dialectical ratchet in live application, administered by a trained psychologist to elected officials in the seat of government.

Consider what this process actually does when you account for the presuppositional depth asymmetry we have been developing throughout this book. The ethics of the Left tend to be shallow, operational, and relativistic—socially constructed, situationally negotiable, and anchored not in transcendent principle but in the social context of the moment. The Right—at its best, at least, and certainly at the level of its deepest commitments—tends to stand on transcendent ethics, deep principles, and opposition to social constructivism. These are not symmetrical starting positions. The conservative participant is being asked to step off of bedrock and wade into quicksand. The progressive participant is being asked to move from one patch of quicksand to another. The conservative *loses something real*—contact with his principles. The progressive loses nothing, because his position was never anchored to anything deeper than social negotiation in the first place.

The exercise was designed to break conservative participants away from their deep ethical commitments and draw them into the realm of social constructivism, where social context and interpersonal relationships trump principles, where feelings outweigh foundations, and where the Left can and does serially dominate. The Left *lives* in relativistic social constructivism. It is their native territory. Asking a conservative to meet them there is not finding common ground—it is an away game on an opponent's field with the opponent's rules and the opponent's referees.

This is how the dialectical ratchet operates in a legislative environment. Each "bipartisan" exercise, each "bridge-building" session, each "depolarization" workshop functions as one click of the ratchet. The conservative is moved incrementally leftward. The progressive holds position or advances. The net motion is always in one direction. And the whole operation is dressed in the language of goodwill—*common ground, bridging the divide, managing difficult conversations*—so that anyone who objects to the process can be dismissed as partisan, unreasonable, or unwilling to work with others.

THE ORGANIZATION BEHIND THE OPERATION

Having experienced the method firsthand, I set about examining the organization that delivered it. What I found was not reassuring.

Braver Angels—the largest grassroots "depolarization" organization in America—was founded in December 2016 in South Lebanon, Ohio, weeks after Donald Trump's election. Its founder and president is David Blankenhorn, a self-described liberal Democrat educated at Harvard and the University of Warwick, where he studied in the social history program established by Marxist historian E.P. Thompson. By Blankenhorn's own admission, he carried Saul Alinsky's *Rules for Radicals* "in our back pocket" during his years as a community organizer, and considered Alinsky "our ultimate teacher." He also visited the Highlander Folk School in Tennessee—the legendary training ground for civil rights and labor organizers, and a well-documented node of Communist organizational infrastructure in the American South.[7]

An Alinsky-trained community organizer educated in a Marxist historian's program. This is the man who built the bridge that conservatives are invited to walk across.

To his credit—or to his cover—Blankenhorn spent years building credibility on the Right. He founded the Institute for American Values in 1987, a think tank focused on marriage and fatherhood. His 1995 book *Fatherless America* made him a prominent voice in the social conservative movement. His 2007 book *The Future of Marriage* argued that marriage is fundamentally oriented toward uniting biological, social, and legal parenthood. He aligned himself with the conservative position on same-sex marriage—one of the central cultural flashpoints of the era.

This is the Trust pattern. You do not build a controlled opposition by announcing your intentions. You build credibility with the target population first. You invest years. You say the right things, defend the right causes, build the right relationships. You become trusted. And then, at the moment of maximum leverage, you turn.

Blankenhorn's turn came during *Perry v. Schwarzenegger*, the federal trial challenging California's Proposition 8. He served as the defense's principal expert witness—one of only two witnesses the Prop 8 proponents dared to present. His testimony was catastrophic for his own side: he conceded under oath that same-sex marriage would "likely improve the well-being of gay and lesbian households and their children" and identified twenty-two benefits of same-sex marriage from his own book, disagreeing with only five. He told the court: "We would be more American on the day we permitted same-sex marriage than we were the day before." The judge ruled his testimony unreliable and entitled to essentially no weight.

Two years later, Blankenhorn published a *New York Times* op-ed titled "How My View on Gay Marriage Changed." The capitulation was complete. His former colleague Maggie Gallagher, who had left the Institute for American Values years earlier over precisely this trajectory, wrote a response that now reads as prophecy: "The truth about something as important as marriage cannot be the price we pay to live with each other... Giving up marriage is too high a price to pay. And it is not the last good we will be asked to surrender."

She was right. It was not the last good. Blankenhorn's next project would ask conservatives to surrender something far more consequential than a single policy position. He would ask them to surrender the very method by which they hold any position at all—their grounding in transcendent ethics.

Two readings of Blankenhorn's biography are possible. The charitable reading is that he is a sincere man who changed his mind, found that his social relationships with progressives were more important to him than his prior convictions, and channeled that experience into an organization designed to help others do the same. The analytical reading—the one informed by the Trust pattern, by Alinsky's own methodology, and by the observable outcomes of the organization he built—is that Blankenhorn operated for decades within conservative institutions, built trust and credibility, and deployed that credibility at the critical moment to undermine the cause he had championed, before pivoting to build an organization whose structural function is to replicate that same trajectory in others.

STRUCTURAL ASYMMETRY

The co-founding team tells the same story. Bill Doherty, the University of Minnesota family therapy professor who designed the workshop methodology, had previously organized a group called "Citizen Therapists Against Trumpism"—not against polarization generally, not against political extremism broadly, but against *Trumpism* specifically. This is the man who designed the "neutral" therapeutic process. The third co-founder, David Lapp—raised Amish, now Catholic, who writes for *The Federalist* and *American Conservative*—provides the requisite conservative credential, the essential window dressing that allows the organization to claim bipartisan bona fides. Every Trust needs its sincere participants.

Braver Angels itself discloses a sixty-forty funding split between left-of-center and right-of-center foundations. The organization grew from half a million dollars in revenue in 2017 to over five and a half million by 2024. The founder draws a salary of nearly a quarter-million dollars. The Carnegie Corporation funds it under its "Democracy" program. The William and Flora Hewlett Foundation provided seed funding through its Madison Initiative. The organization operates within a broader ecosystem of roughly four hundred "depolarization" organizations tracked by the Civic Health Project at Columbia University. One of the most prominent sister organizations in this ecosystem—Living Room Conversations—was co-founded by Joan Blades, who also co-founded MoveOn.org, one of the most aggressive progressive political organizations in America.

The right-leaning funding isn't truly "Right" at all, but socially liberal, Chamber-of-Commerce libertarianism. It is not. The neoconservative movement was funded by right-leaning money for decades while operating as a dialectical pole to the neoliberal establishment. Koch-funded organizations have a long history of funding libertarian and "reform conservative" initiatives that channel conservative energy away from populist and traditionalist priorities. Templeton funds inquiry and dialogue as institutional values—which is precisely the frame that makes the dialectical operation possible. Money follows mission, and these missions are compatible with the structural asymmetry Braver Angels produces.

The personnel confirm the pattern. The organization makes conspicuous efforts at balance—hiring a Republican CEO, maintaining a Focus on the Family director on its board, employing a former Republican congressional candidate as its national ambassador. But examine the type of conservatism represented. The Republican ambassador ran in California against Maxine Waters and associates with the American Project at Pepperdine and the Progress Network at New America Foundation—reform conservatism, heterodox conservatism, the kind of conservatism that the progressive establishment finds tolerable precisely because it has already been detached from the transcendent ethical commitments that make conservatism a threat. There is no one from Heritage Action on this board. No one from the Freedom Caucus. No one who represents the populist, the traditionalist Right, or Evangelical Christians that actually challenges the institutional progressive order. The conservatism on display at Braver

Angels is the kind that has already undergone the very process the organization administers – Jeff Flake conservatism.

And most revealing of all: Braver Angels' own internal data shows that across its events, Democrats consistently outnumber Republicans. The organization's own Red Caucus page describes itself as "a minority within Braver Angels" that wants "our voices to be heard." A 2024 investigation found that in conservative areas, the workshops' most documented effect was empowering liberal participants "to come out of the closet"—an outcome benefiting progressive expression, not conservative retention. As one liberal participant candidly observed: conservatives suspect that "what you're really going to do is get them in a room and then explain to them how they're wrong." That suspicion, it turns out, is analytically precise—the explanation just operates through therapeutic technique rather than overt argument.

The academic evidence on effectiveness is equally damning. The most rigorous study found workshops produced a modest reduction in partisan hostility at one week, with effects decaying rapidly. A 2025 meta-analysis of the broader depolarization field concluded that such interventions produce only approximately five-point shifts on a hundred-and-one-point scale, that effects decay within two weeks, that repeated exposure does not produce cumulative benefits, and that "current approaches are unlikely to scale effectively to solve polarization at a societal level." In other words: the therapy does not even work on its own stated terms. It does not reduce polarization. What it does—the thing it actually accomplishes, as measured by observable outcomes rather than stated intentions—is produce a handful of Republican legislators in each state who have been psychologically conditioned to prioritize relational comfort over principled commitment.

THE PROOF IN NEW HAMPSHIRE

The proof is in the outcomes.

In the years since that December 2022 session, a bipartisan caucus emerged from the Braver Angels training—a group of legislators from both parties who continued to meet and operate under the Braver Angels framework. That caucus, which has since rebranded itself as *Granite*

Bridge, has serially disrupted Republican votes and undermined GOP policy commitments despite Republican majorities. The Republican members of the caucus have become unreliable voters for the party platform and the ethical commitments their constituents elected them to uphold. Meanwhile, the Democratic members of the caucus continue to vote largely as a unified bloc—as they always have. The ratchet clicks. The synthesis favors the Left. The Republican defectors provide the margin.

This is precisely the pattern we would predict from the theory. The dialectical process does not produce genuine compromise. It produces *managed defeat* for the side operating from deeper principles, because the act of "meeting in the middle" requires that side to abandon depth while the other side merely shifts laterally within its own shallow plane. The GOP members who underwent this training did not become more effective legislators. They became more pliable ones—more susceptible to social pressure, more willing to substitute relational comfort for principled commitment, more inclined to mistake agreeableness for virtue.

The purpose of a thing is what it does. What does Braver Angels do? It produces Republican legislators who vote against Republican priorities while Democratic legislators continue to vote as a bloc. That is what it does. That is its purpose.

What you must understand is this: when a psychologist, operating from the methods of dialectical behavioral therapy, places you in structured exercises designed to detach you from your principles and move you toward "synthesis" with positions that are fundamentally incompatible with those principles—and when the organization behind that psychologist was built by an Alinsky-trained operative who personally walked the exact path they are now guiding you down. So-called "bridge building) is a political warfare operation conducted on the floor of a state legislature, with your ethics as the target.

Chapter 12

DIALECTICAL POLITICAL WARFARE

DESTRUCTION OF KNOWLEDGE

The phenomenological foundation connects critical legal theory and its offspring—the "living document" framework, disparate impact doctrine, intersectional jurisprudence—directly to the esoteric metaphysical tradition traced throughout this book. These judicial philosophies are Hermetic-gnostic in their epistemology, not merely Leftist in their politics. The premise is that fixed textual meaning is an illusion—that the law, like all determinate things in the Platonic-Hermetic system, is a threshold to be transcended rather than a boundary to be respected. The judge reading "evolving standards" into constitutional text is operating from the same presupposition as the alchemist dissolving fixed categories on the road to undifferentiation: both claim that the initiated interpreter possesses access to a higher truth unavailable to plain reading, accessible only to those trained in the methods of the elect. The philosopher-king judge, whose gold-souled education and certifications qualifies him to tell the bronze and iron citizens what their own supreme law actually means—regardless of what it plainly says—is a direct institutional expression of the Platonic program. The judicial oligarchy is oligarchic in its character in a familiar way.

The dialectic is utilized as a weapon against language—or, more precisely, against the meaning of language. This is accomplished by developing a false concept with which to slowly replace a real concept. This can be done in days, weeks, or months, but in many cases it is a years-long or even generational undertaking.

Recall the progression from *illegal alien* to *undocumented migrant* that we walked through in detail earlier. Each linguistic move served a strategic purpose: weaponizing empathy, nullifying the law conceptually, and ultimately remaking the conception of human nature itself—away from that of a settled, nationalistic peoples towards a nomadic, unsettled nature that can be readily manipulated. *You will own nothing and be happy.*

The utility of language lies in its ability to reflect a reality that we are in contact with. Language acts as a sort of shortcut to knowledge—another person does not have to directly experience a phenomenon in order to achieve some degree of knowledge of it. The more accurately language reflects something that is real, the more utility that concept has, the more valuable the language becomes, and the less punitive the feedback received from reality as we act out the idea. However, the less language reflects something real and true, the more punitive the feedback onto ourselves will become – the stove is hot, after all.

Ours is a time of low-fidelity language, and we are feeling these punitive effects. You cannot escape reality.

Binary Control

The dialectic has been weaponized against meaning, interpretation, and understanding for a very, very long time. C.S. Lewis noted (in *Mere Christianity*): "The devil always sends errors into the world in pairs—pairs of opposites—and he always encourages us to spend a lot of time thinking which is the worse. You see why, of course. He relies on your extra dislike of the one error to draw you gradually into the opposite one." A nearly perfect description of dialectical destruction of meaning through yet another mechanism: the false binary.

In this manner, you are often presented with two options—one bad and the other worse—and you are made to feel as though you must choose one. The truth, however, is that decisions are rarely truly binary. There are nearly always alternatives. By keeping you within the binary, the dialectical operator is able to move you incrementally toward his goal. By presenting you with bad and worse, knowing you will choose that which is merely bad, he has gained a small victory toward his ends.

A high-level example of this concept in action is that of elections dominated by two political parties. In the general election, you are presented with a binary of two persons you must choose between. However, that is a false binary. You do not really have to vote for either if you do not want to. There are often third-party candidates, and if not, you can always write somebody in or refuse to vote altogether. But you may respond that it is, for practical purposes, binary, since one or the other is going to win. That is not entirely correct. It may wind up being true that one does win, and one likely will, but it is not necessarily the case. In a time of significant disapproval of both, it is only the belief that it is binary—that you must choose—that results in one of them winning.

This is a concept known as reification, and closely related to reflexivity. In these concepts, something becomes true simply because people believe it to be. An older way of looking at this would be to say that they are under a spell. A simple example: place a bet against a company in the market, then place a story in the media that damages the company, thereby making your prediction come true.

Being trapped in this method of thinking makes you extremely vulnerable to manipulation via dialectical operations. Take the example of a war between two nations. This war is comprised of not one but many battles. It is almost certainly true that at least some of these battles could be lost, yet the wider war still won. It can be difficult to predict which battle might be so critical that it cannot be lost lest the whole war also be lost—but such discerning capacity can be developed through study.

Maintaining the war analogy, failure to accept that a battle is lost when it is manifestly so is a bad habit. It means dedicating men and resources solely to destruction with no upside. If the option of tactical retreat is removed from the table, you will find yourself forever under the control of dialecticians—forever manipulable into choosing between bad and worse. And this will not stop with just a politician. This is the foremost mechanism of controlled opposition, whereby you find yourself represented by those who will betray you, and those who represent you find themselves more and more compromised.

The Baited Hook

Yet another dialectical method of mystification is the baited hook—where you are presented with a target that shares some characteristics of reality, or at least what you have been primed to believe, that is just too juicy not to bite on. The less interesting, more nuanced, and more complicated truth is matched up dialectically against an outrageous lie that you have been primed to latch onto. Often this lie will be dressed up complete with realistic soldiers from the other side ready to defend against it. But it is a trap.

Consider the following. Imagine being at a cocktail party on the top floor of a tall building. We find there a man that absolutely cannot be de-escalated. He is intent on fighting you. He is yelling in your face, shoving you down, slapping you. He wants to fight you. He wants you to fight him.

Now consider that you have come into knowledge that there is a bomb in the building, due to detonate in mere minutes. How wise would it be to engage this stranger in fisticuffs at this moment? It would be extraordinarily difficult to take what he is dishing out without responding forcefully in an attempt to defeat him. But if you get suckered in, you will be killed when the whole building comes down. Maybe he will be killed too when the building falls. Or maybe he has a parachute in that backpack he is conspicuously wearing to a cocktail party.

Consider that there are times when it is the job of one enemy to keep you entangled and distracted while another enemy maneuvers to destroy you or your whole camp.

The Kraken

Such was the case when attorney Sidney Powell promised to "release the Kraken" in the aftermath of the 2020 election. According to the theory, the election was being stolen via electronic warfare by foreign nations in combination with domestic traitors—a special operations force was supposedly undertaking a mission in Germany to seize the servers that would prove it all. It was a juicy treat indeed, but inside that treat was a hook. Powell went on to file Kraken lawsuits in four states—Georgia, Michigan, Wisconsin, and Arizona—and lost every single one. Every case was dismissed. The suits were filed too late, relied on affidavits riddled with factual errors so basic that a cursory internet search would have exposed them, and requested remedies so extreme that one federal judge called it "the most extraordinary relief ever sought" in an election case. In Michigan, the presiding judge sanctioned Powell and her co-counsel, ordered them to pay the defendants' legal fees, and referred the entire legal team for possible disbarment—concluding that the lawsuit was "a historic and profound abuse of the judicial process" that was "never about fraud." The sheer scale of procedural incompetence across all four suits almost demands an assignment of purposeful intent.

There were countless verifiable, clear, and articulable problems with the 2020 election that should have made it impossible to claim with a straight face that it was "free and fair"—private third-party money used to place ballot drop boxes overwhelmingly in areas of a certain political persuasion, mass mailing of ballots with wholly inadequate verification mechanisms to prevent fraud, the legalization and institutional funding of ballot harvesting, and so on.

But when the hook was set by the Kraken, the entire true history of the election and any hope for a serious legal challenge was lost in the dialectical mystifications and false narratives that in turn allowed the even more false narrative of "free and fair" to dominate. We were caught out on a limb, and we handed the enemy the shears. We were defeated by professional operators—some of whom were wearing our colors, flying our flag, and propped up by our leaders.

This is the nature of dialectics.

The Many Names of the Dialectic

Not being quitters, and being quick to brush off the dried blood, Hermeticists have theorized and practiced many, many different variants of dialectics over the millennia. Each new iteration is destined for ultimate failure, being based on a nonsense premise, but each iteration does tend to become both more viral—spreading among more and more minds—and more destructive in scope.

A partial list of the sorts of dialectics employed over the years includes: the Platonic dialectic of Plato, Socrates, Pythagoras, and the Academy; Rousseau's master-slave dialectic; the Hegelian idealist dialectic; the Kantian dialectic; Marx's materialist dialectic; the fascist nationalist dialectic; the incrementalist dialectic of the Fabians and Progressives; the neo-Marxist critical dialectic of the Frankfurt School; the woke dialectic of modern American academia; and the weaponized dialectic—stripped of religiosity and purely utilitarian—of problem-reaction-solution infamy.

The application of dialectics is not limited to the material realm. Dialectics are just as applicable, according to Hermetic theology, to the mental and spiritual processes as well. Returning to the Hermetic creation myth: it is said that the true, original, or perennial philosophy can be achieved through a synthesis of all extant philosophy, knowledge, religion, science, and spirituality, as each system contains a shard of the divine or a portion of the truth. This means that Hermeticism is syncretic—it incorporates, as a matter of principle, other ideas, faiths, and practices into itself over time. It prophesies that at the end of time, the *prisca theologia*—the ancient, original theology—will be attained through the dialectical synthesis of all ideas. This explains why this religion looks different in every new generation and is able to deceive people anew with the same old bag of tricks.

Hermetic syncretism deserves more attention than it typically receives, because it is the tradition's primary infiltration doctrine and explains why it is so difficult to identify and exclude. A purely alien system can be recognized and resisted as foreign. A system that arrives wearing the clothing of existing traditions—incorporating Christian language, Eastern concepts, indigenous practices, whatever the host culture offers—presents as enrichment rather than replacement. The Great Invocation sounds almost like prayer. The SEL "illuminator" sounds almost like virtue. The "science of right human relations" sounds almost like ethics. Close enough to pass casual inspection; different enough at the presuppositional level to do the work the system requires.

Surface-level pattern recognition is an insufficient defense, because the vocabulary is specifically designed to be unsuspicious. The protection is presuppositional: people grounded in what their tradition actually teaches at the metaphysical level can recognize when something familiar is operating from incompatible premises. Which is the argument—practical, not merely theological—for the robust doctrinal formation in family and Church that sphere sovereignty requires.

Christians have not been immune to syncretism—the historical record makes that plain. But there remains a true faith, transcendently and presuppositionally grounded, recoverable through the careful unraveling of accumulated error and a return to original sources. That work of recovery is a central task of the Counterspell Group mission beyond this volume.

Over the years, the confusing and confounding effects of the dialectic have also taken many names—incantations, spells, and grimoires, to the more recent mass formation psychosis and demoralization. Those practitioners of dialectics have gone by many names as well: from philosophers to wizards, from magicians to sorcerers, from initiates to theorists, from academics to scientists, from alchemists to professors.

It was the dialectic that was responsible for the one hundred million plus bodies generated by Communism and Fascism in the twentieth century. It was the dialectic that brought about both world wars. It was the dialectic that precipitated the fall of Athens. It will be our demise too, if we do not learn to resist.

The dialectic always smuggles with it the metaphysics and faith of Hermeticism and Plato. They cannot be separated. Dialectics cannot operate according to the presuppositions of Christianity. The process of debate or dialogue—where two ideas compete and there is a losing concept that was demonstrated to be incorrect—is fundamentally not dialectics, though initiates will often seek to confuse by claiming it is. They like to play hide the ball amongst other sophist tactics.

While the dialectic may seem quite obviously fallacious as outlined here, we will in due course come to see the pernicious ways in which dialectics have sown the chaos all around us—often in subtle and concealed ways. You are not ready to enter the arena yet. You are only just now learning how to identify the enemy. We will have you in fighting shape soon enough.

We have seen how the weapon has evolved with the times, syncretized with other traditions, and sowed chaos everywhere it matured. Now, we meet the near-modern religion that obfuscated the spiritual nature of it all and wrapped it in a wholly "materialist" costume—just in time for the industrial revolution and the population explosions that would set the stage for the most massive campaign of murder in all of human history.

Chapter 13

The Church of Marx

To begin to understand what these things are—Socialism, Communism, Capitalism—you must first understand that none of them represent mere "economic" systems. Rather, they represent something akin to a theory of everything—which is to say that they are totalizing systems. They are facets of a full-fledged religious system of faith, duty, dogma, and praxis.

Marx and his comrade Engels, both initiates of the mystery cults, adopted the basic operating system of Plato as modified through the ages by those such as Rousseau and Hegel who, together, explicitly framed the mechanism for the evolution of society as that of dialectical conflict between the master and the slave. It was theorized that the resolutions of this conflict through time would cause the mentality of all persons to shift towards a single, collective, cooperative unit. Each unique, but not distinct, individual within this system would evolve to what Marx called "social man" through the realization that he is not truly a distinct individual at all, but only an aspect of the All.

Six Stages of Marx's Historicism

According to this theory, Marx separated all of History into six distinct phases of evolutionary advancement of "Humanity." According to the Hermetic principles of the beginning that envisions its own end as one—as represented by the ouroboros, the serpent devouring its own tail, an ancient Hermetic and alchemical symbol representing the cyclical return of all things to their origin—and the coiled-spring symbol of the dialectic—the first phase of Humanity mirrors the prophesied last phase, and was coined "primitive Communism."

Stage One: Primitive Communism

In this mythology of primitive Communism, which never truly existed, Marx said the beginning of human social evolution was marked by a perfect equality between persons living amongst nature—precisely the "state of man in nature" in which Rousseau framed his theories, and far in contradiction to the more accurate portrayal of early human circumstances from Hobbes—the seventeenth-century English philosopher—that life in a state of nature is "solitary, poor, nasty, brutish, and short."

Stage Two: The Slave Society

From this fiction of primitive Communism, Marx prophesied that Humanity transitioned into phase two: the slave society. This is directly pulled from Rousseau and Hegel's master-slave dialectic. He postulated that as man learned to oppress man, he took others as slaves to benefit from their labor, and that this set the stage for the rest of human social evolution through the dialectical synthesis of the master and slave consciousness. In this manner, the domination of one man by another is akin to the original sin of the Marxist faith.

Stage Three: Feudalism

Marx drew another line of demarcation in History with his prophesied phase three: Feudalism. The rise of agriculture saw the serfs—the slave-conscious—forced to work the land for the lords—the master-conscious. This, per theory, was a mere evolution of the expression of "slavery" from the direct theft of a man himself to the theft of his labor as he was forced to work the fields for the master.

Stage Four: Capitalism

This brings us to the prophesied, and much confused, phase four of Marx's History: Capitalism. It is important to know that this term probably does not mean what you think it does. As a rather unfortunate historical error, many on the Right adopted the term as a synonym for free-market economics. It is not that at all. When you mean the freedom to buy and sell, to own property, to engage in commerce without the coercion of the state—say that. Say freedom of commerce, say economic liberty. Do not gift-wrap your own rights in the enemy's terminology.

"Capitalism," according to Marx, and as interpreted along the lines of the master-slave dialectic, means that capital is not merely money. Rather, capital is a magical, spiritual property that inflicts, in a deterministic manner, the master consciousness on he who holds it. This traps the master in a state of limited consciousness where his concern is simply the oppression of the slave in order to perpetuate capital, and the broader society bred by capital, in perpetuity. In other words, capital is a sort of spiritual virus that exists only to replicate itself infinitely onto society using the master as host. This virus traps mankind in a state of conflict, unable to evolve further until a radical tipping point is reached called the "crisis point."

Of course, this, to Marx, simply represented a further evolution and obfuscation of the concept of "slavery," once meaning the direct theft of a man, then the direct theft of a mans labor, to the now (more insidious) indirect theft of labor and, moreover, the slaves natural social condition of abundant leisure time. (Ultimately, this is the same argument we hear from teenagers tasked with chores who simply expect that the necessities of life ought to be handed to them. Marx simply did not want to hold down a job, and he largely succeeded in that in life as he inflicted misery on his own family).

Another name for this crisis point during stage four of History is "late-stage Capitalism." It is at this latter part of stage four that Marx prophesied the proletariat, or working class, would begin to become conscious of their slave status and revolt against the bourgeoisie, or landlord and capital class. Note, here, that the terms utilized in Marxism are in French, not German, as they were pulled directly from Rousseau and the French Revolution.

It is worth dwelling for a moment on this concept of the crisis point. As you have learned, the dialectic of Marx operates according to conflict theory. So here we have a cult religion with millions of zealots who believe that conflict leading to crisis is necessary to bring about the next stage of History. Sit with that for a moment as you ask yourself why all these things occurring in the West are being allowed to happen by governments. More than that—they are not merely allowing these things. They are engineering the "polycrisis."

Stage Five: Socialism

This crisis point of late-stage Capitalism is where the revolution comes in. This is the point at which those possessing slave consciousness are prophesied to violently rise up against the master, invert and abolish hierarchy by force, and enact the transition into stage five of Marx's fictional History: Socialism.

During stage five, Socialism, the means of production are seized by the proletariat. However, not directly, as the idiot plebs cannot be expected to look out for their own best interests. Instead, a vanguard of educated, golden philosopher-kings must rise up to represent the people in a "true democracy" (in which there is no voting, as these golden-souled elites will surely act in the best interest of the demos).

Let me repeat that in its entirety, (read it) a little slower: During stage five, Socialism, the means of production are seized by the proletariat. However, not directly, as the idiot plebs cannot be expected to look out for their own best interests. Instead, a vanguard of educated, golden philosopher-kings must rise up to represent the people in a true democracy.

At this point, if you have been keeping up, you will recognize a sharp distinction between the exoteric theology and the esoteric recipe being advanced here. You will know that the philosopher-kings are, in fact, an oligarch class. You will know that democracy is the mechanism oligarchs use to divide a population to maintain their own power and supremacy. You will know that these oligarchs will never yield their power and wealth to the plebs. You will understand that what Karl Marx wrote was, very simply, a version of Plato's Republic updated for his nineteenth-century German audience steeped in the pseudoscientific language of economics and sociology.

Apply the tripartite model from our earlier chapters. Marx and the vanguard class are the wizards—the initiates who understand the true nature of the system and wield it as a tool for power. The proletariat, the true believers, the marchers and chanters who genuinely think they are fighting for liberation, are the spellbound—manipulated through the esoteric religion into serving the interests of the very oligarchs they believe they are overthrowing. Your task, as it has been from the beginning of this book, is to become based—to see through the economic costume, through the religious theology, to the naked regime-change mechanism underneath, and to help others see it too.

In other words, the reality of Marx's plan is that it was always meant to end in stage five—Socialism—where people like him would seize power as a new oligarch class over the masses to effect Plato's tyrannical recipe. However, for those who are not members of the inner circle, and therefore aware of Marx's true plans, there is a stage six of History: Communism.

Stage Six: Communism

Within the prophesied stage six of History, Humanity has synthesized all contradictions, transcended all distinction, eliminated all hierarchy, and made all persons absolutely equal under the banner of *liberté, égalité, fraternité*—just as the French Revolution was supposed to have delivered.

It is not worth dwelling excessively on this Communism phase of History that, according to Communists, has "never been tried"—despite the parade of nations that flew the hammer and sickle: the Soviet Union, China, Cuba, Cambodia, North Korea, Vietnam, Laos, and others, each of which arrested at stage five, with a vanguard oligarchy presiding over mass privation and mass murder, and none of which ever transitioned to the promised stateless utopia. It has "never been tried" because it was never meant to be tried. This is the point. Stage six was always for suckers—because stage five, Socialism, is the true end of Marx's plan. Marx himself did not dwell on the details of stage six. I strongly suspect much of the inner-circle of the esoteric cults are not themselves true believers, but it really does not matter much either way. For ideas on what they might have thought, you can review our previous chapters on Hermetic theology and eschatology. But it simply does not matter, as this was simply a rip-off of Plato designed to seize and hold power for a select few who did not, at present, have it. This is the prototype for the modern "color revolution" model.

Again, Marx did not invent this. He inherited it wholesale from the Platonic blueprint and the transmitted initiate knowledge of the mystery schools. The *Republic*'s program for mythmaking—the patriotic founding story, the noble lie, the censorship of all narratives that do not serve the guardians' purposes—operates on the identical structural principle of Marxist eschatology. The philosopher-kings construct a myth of cosmic destiny that gives the ruled a transcendent justification for the present arrangement and promises a perfected endpoint that legitimizes whatever the guardians must do to reach it. In this case, that mythology is the magical, self-perpetuating property known as "capital" that keeps the workers permanently boxed out of power, and society unable to move forward evolutionarily towards the next stage of history. The bronze and iron souls believe it because they are meant to believe it, and they have long since been robbed of their birthright foundations for sense-making. The philosopher-kings know the myth is constructed because constructing it is their job. The system requires the gap between promise and delivery to remain permanent—the fulfilled promise terminates the power of those making it. The proletariat that actually reached the classless society would have no more need of the vanguard. Fortunate, then, that such a thing is impossible. The adept who actually achieved union with the Absolute would have no more need of the hierarchy of initiates. Stage six is the Platonic founding myth in an economic costume.

At some ultimate level of truth, Marxism simply represents a timeless regime-change mechanism wrapped in an esoteric religion wrapped in economic garb. Strip away the economic jargon and you find a religion. Strip away the religion and you find a recipe for seizing power. It is well worth suspecting that Marx, along with the lot of his kind, understood from the beginning that the real goal began and ended with regime change that places them in power—and that everything else was packaging.

Chapter 14

The Esoteric Church

The Denominational History of Esotericism

In antiquity, the cult religions of gnosticism and Hermeticism were competitors with early Judaism, and later early Christianity. They were documented in the Scriptures. Plato advanced these ideas. What follows is a compressed history of the denominational tree—the branching and splintering of this faith as it mutated through the centuries, each new sect carrying the same Hermetic kernel in a different costume.

1807: Hegel, the German philosopher, Hermetic alchemist, and gnostic, published his seminal work, *Phenomenology of Spirit*, which amalgamated these varied theologies—including Rousseau's proto-master-slave dialectic—into a single theosophy and spread these ideas far across Europe and to North America, largely through cult followerships known as Young Hegelians.

1836: Karl Marx enrolls at the University of Berlin, where he studies exclusively the humanities and the philosophy of Hegel, and joins a student group of Young Hegelians.

1841: Marx receives his doctorate from the University at Jena with a dissertation quoting, in part: "Philosophy makes no secret of it. Prometheus' admission—'In sooth all gods I hate'—is its own admission, its own motto against all gods." The quote is notable in that the theology of Marx centers man as his own god, imprisoned in an unfair jail: this world. Marx was also said to be quite fond of Mephistopheles, the character representing Satan in the Faust legend.

1848: Marx publishes *The Communist Manifesto*, applying the Hegelian dialectic and the theosophy of gnosticism and Hermeticism to the concept of a "dialectical materialism" and "Scientific Social-ism"—loosely organized around a pseudo-economic prophecy of History and a largely unstated, but clearly between-the-lines, utopian eschatology, immanentized through gaining consciousness and cult rituals of denounc-ing the oppressive conditions of existence to "humanize" the world.

Late 1800s: The Young Hegelian associations in America give rise to the political Progressive movement, drawing on Hegel's historicism and the prophesied rise of the absolute spirit upon the perfection of the State. It inspired such influential persons as W.E.B. Du Bois—the first Black American to earn a doctorate from Harvard, who would later become an avowed Communist—President Woodrow Wilson, and education re-former John Dewey. The contribution of all three to the Progressive era was premised on the transition of the nature of American government from one rooted in transcendent Christian ethics to one rooted in the immanence of Hegel's Absolute Spirit, with the government operating as the hand of god on earth and in History. The effect of this transition was the removal of restrained, limited government as an operating principle and its replacement with the absolute will of the state—be it democratic, vanguard, or dictatorial—as the ultimate governing principle. This can, or could at the time, be considered another denomination in the broader church—but it has largely been intermingled with the others to such an extent that it no longer constitutes a cohesive, separate body of theology from modern Marxism.

1917: The Bolshevik Communist revolution in Russia quickly shifts away from pure Marx—the dictatorship of the proletariat—and towards the Platonic practice that places a class of educated elites in charge of the transition to Socialism and Communism. This denomination in the Church of Marxism is best called Vanguard Marxism, and it is reasonably speculated to have been the true intentions of Marx from the beginning, as it perfectly encapsules the formula of Plato's Republic.

1933: Hitler's rise to power causes German Communist Max Horkheimer—who had assumed directorship of the Institute for Social Research (Institut für Sozialforschung) at Goethe University Frankfurt am Main in 1930, a decade after the Institute's founding there in February 1923—to flee Germany. The Institute's endowment is relocated abroad in 1933, and by 1934 the Institute has re-established itself as the International Institute of Social Research at Columbia University in New York. Much of the original German contingent of Communists would immigrate to join the relocated Frankfurt School, including Theodor Adorno and Herbert Marcuse. The work of these Communists would, from there on out, focus on solving the problem of Marx's failed prophecies for proletariat revolution—where the working class was supposed to have overthrown nations such as America and England to install Communism, not backwater Russia.

Marx had prophesied that the revolution would proceed across advanced capitalist western nations first, as they were said to be in late-stage Capitalism already. When this failed to materialize, Marx was shown to be a false prophet of the Hermetic faith. The result was ultimately the abandonment of the worker as a revolutionary change agent and a shifting of the theology towards social dimensions such as race and sex, and the development of Critical Theories that can be summed up as "the relentless criticism of all that exists" applied to all categories of demos and faction. This new denomination in the Church of Marxism would become known as neo-Marxism, or Cultural Marxism. These new Marxists often use the disparaging term "vulgar Marxists" to refer to the followers of the original Marxist theology.

Others took up the mantle of prophet and modified these theories over time, changing the magical property of capital to other items—privilege, power, whiteness, heteronormativity, cisgender, and so on. They accelerated the contradictions by broadening the category of slave consciousness to include all manner of oppression under the broad banner of intersectionality. Thus, cultural Marxism was born of Marx's failed prophecy, by yet another slate of would-be oligarchs attempting to seize power via the attitude of Faust's Mephistopheles—"all that exists deserves to perish," or "the ruthless criticism of all that exists." They would rule even if over ashes. They have a religious duty to inflict crisis upon us.

1984: Gender theorist Gayle Rubin publishes "Thinking Sex," demanding a reimagining of gender and sex using a Critical and postmodern frame, giving rise to a field of study known as Queer Theory—and to yet another branch in the modern Church of Marx, best called Gender Marxism, or, as best-selling author James Lindsay calls it, Queer Gnosticism.

1989: Critical Race Theory is formally named and organized as a movement at the July Workshop on Critical Race Theory in Madison, Wisconsin, co-organized by Kimberlé Crenshaw and Neil Gotanda with some thirty-five participants. Its intellectual progenitor is Derrick Bell of Harvard Law School, whose 1980 "interest-convergence" article and 1987 book *And We Are Not Saved* laid the groundwork across the preceding decade. The same year, in a separate but related contribution, Crenshaw introduces the concept of *intersectionality* in her article "Demarginalizing the Intersection of Race and Sex" in the *University of Chicago Legal Forum.* Though, truth be told, there was not seemingly much new about these contributions that cannot be found in the work of Moscow and the ComIntern half a century prior. Crenshaw, a professor of law at Columbia and UCLA, was an indirect student of Herbert Marcuse of the Frankfurt School, with Communist Angela Davis acting as the intermediary.

1995: Crenshaw and colleagues publish *Critical Race Theory: The Key Writings That Formed the Movement,* in which Crenshaw is quoted as referring to those in attendance at the 1989 founding workshop as "a group of Marxists." This publication details the application of the Cultural Marxist doctrine of Critical Theory to the field of law as it relates to race—insisting on an anti-scientific approach of univariate analysis via disparate impact, or the examination of a single variable in isolation from all others to determine discrimination sans proving intent, which violates the most basic principles of both statistical and legal reasoning by ignoring confounding variables, selection bias, and the corresponding insistence that correlation does, in fact, equal causation. The incorporation of intersectionality into CRT gave rise to a new branch in the tree of the Church of Marx that might unite them all under one banner: Woke Marxism.

This pretty well carries us to the present day. You can follow these persons and threads and connect the origins of gnosticism and Hermeticism all the way through to your purple-haired neighbor. Mind you, these denominations are far more leaky than denominations within Christianity. Perhaps due to the nature that they often deny it is religious at all, many modern zealots fall into multiple camps. The ones seemingly most hostile to each other are, however, the dialectical materialists and the modern Woke—they just do not get along. Original Marx purists will deny to their last breath that modern Wokes are "Marxist." It should fall on deaf ears – modern Wokes are in many ways more Marxists than the vulgar Marxists are.

Naming the Enemy

You cannot raise an army to fight a thing you cannot call by a common name.

That is the first major utility of naming Marxism as what it is: a religion. The precise name chosen to represent this broader religious movement—Marxism—is true and correct as a proximate point for the origins of the enemy we face. It is likewise useful that others in popular culture—Chris Rufo, Mark Levin, Tucker Carlson, and others—have settled on this same name, or the closely associated term Communism. This name already has momentum and mass behind it.

What follows from naming it is settling on what victory looks like, so that decentralized actors can move towards a common objective. The stripping of the Church of Marxism from government is the medium-term victory, coming just after the most immediate victory condition: live to fight another day. In identifying the win condition, we orient ourselves toward common purpose and effectively multiply our efficacy and capacity to act decentralized.

Further, the finding that Marxian metaphysics supplanted American metaphysics—thereby undermining the ideological and ethical foundations of the nation—serves as the story, the narrative, to rally support around in the reformation of our collective understanding of American history from the late nineteenth century onward, as we correct the history written by Marxists. It has the added benefit of being entirely true and correct.

THE CASE

I put this case into legislative form as a resolution in the New Hampshire House declaring Marxism a religion and complete faith system.[8] The case is straightforward, and it is damning. Recall that the Manifesto's predecessor was Engels's 1847 *Draft of a Communist Confession of Faith*, a Q-and-A catechism—the religious nature of the system was only thinly concealed when the form was later rewritten as the Manifesto. Marxism presents fundamental metaphysical claims about the nature of reality and the human experience, agency, consciousness, and ethics. It asserts that the oppressor-oppressed dialectic of conflict theory forms the basis for understanding the progression of History. It gives rise to duties of conscience—to be on the right side of History by assisting the spirit of History towards immanentizing the eschaton through perpetual revolution, "doing the work," and struggle sessions of purging reactionary beliefs. It forwards a doctrine of Scientism as an aspect of faith under which "science" is to be interpreted and operationalized along alchemically inspired Marxist theory towards revolutionary goals—existing not to describe the world as it is, but to change it. It wields alchemically inspired spells—the ruthless criticism of all that exists toward perpetual transmutation of reality, the *aufheben* or synthesis of apparent contradictions towards ever greater perfection.

Modern Marxism asserts doctrines of social constructivism, individual subjective realities, structural determinism, and collectivism. Traditional "vulgar" Marxism asserts material determinism. All of these significantly or totally preclude and deny the possibility of free will and individual agency necessary for a republic to function. This doctrine is in direct opposition and mutually exclusive to American founding ideology as per the Declaration of Independence and the Constitution.

A proper First Amendment protection of religious freedom would not allow Marxists to coerce their faith on others, and thereby render Marxism's foremost means of replication nullified. Similar to other religions that receive protection—for instance Islam—there are limits to the degree of religious tolerance afforded under the Constitutional system. Honor killings cannot be justified under Sharia law in America despite the reasonable argument that it is fundamental to a religion. Likewise, Marxism, properly placed in that same box, is rendered impotent in its capacity to injure via official institutions. The cementing of the bureaucracy of experts and the judicial oligarchy are extensions of an unlawful State-Church.

TEACHING ABOUT, NOT THROUGH

There is nothing wrong with teaching *about* Marxism in schools—it is quite sensible to learn about the enemy (Sun Tzu would approve). In fact, Marxists who have been the primary authors of history books for decades have made it a point to *not* teach about Marxism, for this very reason.

There is a very important distinction between teaching *about* something and teaching *that* something. It is good to know about everything we can discern (what), but it is dangerously impossible to know *that* everything *is*—because if everything is (treated equally), then nothing is (real). It is that approach that lays the groundwork for the adoption of cultural and ethical relativism.

Marxism is already taught (in the manner "that is") in schools under names from Critical Race Theory to Gender Theory, and from Social Emotional Learning to Diversity, Equity, and Inclusion—except students are not learning about Marxist theory and history from the lens of Americanism. They are not learning about the millions of ugly deaths directly attributable to this anti-human ideology. They certainly are not being taught the tenets of Critical Theory. Rather, they are being taught everything—from the humanities through physics—*through the lens* of Marxism, and thereby being indoctrinated into Marxist religious presuppositions, metaphysics, and consciousness in government schools and beyond.

This effort stakes a claim to an America that has been much forgotten in the milieu of postmodernity—that which our founders understood as necessary for a populace socially, ethically, and ideologically. The words on the paper matter nothing at all if the people cannot understand them the way they were meant to be understood – meaning imbued upon their initial recording – nor if they care not to uphold the principles behind them.

The theology is laid bare. The denominations are mapped. But there is yet another failed prophecy to account for—and it is this failure that changed the shape of everything that followed. Marx's "seize the means of production" did not produce the kinetic revolutions he prophesied in the advanced western nations. The Black Panthers and the Weathermen tried to force the issue on American soil and were crushed or discredited for their trouble. So, the strategists adapted. Lukács, Gramsci—Marxist strategists who recognized the failure—and later Marcuse understood that if the proletariat would not storm the barricades, the revolution would have to take a different road—not through the streets, but through the institutions. Seize the means of *cultural* production. Capture the schools, the courts, the seminaries, the newsrooms, and the bureaucracies from within, and the revolution proceeds without a single shot fired – the tortoise might just finish the race that the hare forfeit. This is the counter-hegemonic strategy—the Long March through the institutions—and it is the subject of our next chapter.

Chapter 15

The Long March

Political Warfare and Institutional Capture

It is not immediately obvious to most what, exactly, political warfare is. That is not helped by the fact that any two "experts" in the field are likely to give extremely divergent definitions. So, allow us to bring you a lesson on the what of political warfare using a baseball analogy. Political warfare is the control of minds, meaning, and knowledge that is upstream of actions—and, ideally, without it ever being recognized as hostile, let alone as warfare.

Say you are a shortstop and a decent batter—a .350 record at the plate. This works well for the analogy because, as the shortstop, there is action happening both in front of and behind you. Say you are on the Cardinals, and the opposition is the Blue Jays. This also fits the analogy well, since you are in a red jersey and the opposition is in a blue jersey.

At the very first at-bat, the opposition Blue Jay wearing number 33 accumulates two balls and two strikes, and on the fifth pitch hits a popup fly. You begin estimating the location the ball will fall and, moving in quickly, you call out "got it!" to make sure the second baseman and pitcher do not collide with you as you make the play. You catch it in the soft web of your glove and give a little underhand toss back to the pitcher just feet in front of you as the home-team audience claps for the umpire's shout of "out!" You feel good, having set the tone of the game with an easy catch. "Easy day," you think.

The rest of the first inning progresses uneventfully. The Blue Jays manage to get to first with a walk but leave the man stranded with the third out on strikes. Coming up to bat in the second you are the first up, and the Blue Jays drove in two runs during their at-bat. The first pitch goes by—a curveball just outside the zone—which causes all the more irritation when the ump yells "strike!" The second pitch, a fastball, connects sweetly with your bat just as you extend on the upswing and sends the ball sailing into the outfield. Just barely, it has the legs to make it over the fence at center field. Home run. You take your time rounding the bases to the celebration of the crowd.

This is how the game goes. You trade some runs back and forth. Your personal performance is pretty darned good—better than your average day. However, the top of the ninth comes to an end with the game tied: ten to ten. It is going to extra innings.

You are coming to bat fifth at the top of the tenth inning, down one point, with a man on first and second and two outs. Then the main lights to the stadium go dark. Moments later the backup lighting switches on. You can barely see the field, but the stands are slightly better lit. The alarm is sounding, but you see that only about half of the audience is getting up and moving to evacuate. You walk over to your dugout, calmly, and you find that about a third of your team and your entire coaching staff is gone already. None of your teammates seem to know where they went—they just disappeared in the darkness.

You walk back out onto the field and notice that, while about a third of the audience is gone after evacuating and a bit more still filing out the exits, at least half of the audience is still seated and not moving. Walking toward one of the motionless sections in the stands nearest by, you begin to get a sinking feeling. As you approach, not a single person moves—they are all just sitting there, frozen. Now within about twenty feet of the fans you realize that the entire section of the stadium is full of mannequins. Nobody here is real.

You rush back to your dugout only to find that the remaining team members are being ushered out by soldiers with guns trained on them. They spot you and yell at you to get in a single-file line with the rest of your team. You comply, and the lot of you are led through the private entrance and out of the stadium where you observe checkpoints established outside by more armed soldiers. They lead you around the back to an alley where they demand you kneel against a wall.

It is only now that you remember: "I am not even a baseball player."

In political warfare a primary objective is to make you believe that you are playing a game—as part of a team, complete with an audience cheering you, an opponent, rules of the game, and more that do not actually exist. They will keep up this fiction for as long as necessary—extra innings, even—to maneuver into position to defeat you.

This all worked out for the enemy because you allowed the operators to convince you that you were playing baseball and not, in fact, on the battlefield. You saw the blurry, full seats from a distance, and you took for granted that the cheering was coming from them—not piped in artificially. You did not consider yourself an expert, so you placed yourself under the authority of the coach to teach you how to play and to call the shots—and you never questioned those strange decisions that kept the game tied and heading to overtime. The other team showed up in their blue jerseys to play by the same rules you did, so you believed that the rules were fundamental somehow, and that the other team would, necessarily, be bound by them.

You never questioned whether the entire game was a creative fiction designed to keep you out of the real fight.

The coaches, the rules, and the opposing team are the wizards—the operators of the spell. Your still-present teammates are the spellbound, playing the game in earnest because they were never told otherwise. The moment you remember that you are not a baseball player is the moment you become based—eyes open, spell broken, and dangerous to those who cast it.

THE DITCH AND THE FORTRESS

The phrase "long march through the institutions" was coined by the German student radical Rudi Dutschke in 1967. Dutschke did not invent the strategy. He named it. The strategy, in detail, had been worked out in a prison cell in Turi di Bari three decades earlier by Antonio Gramsci, imprisoned by Mussolini and writing what would become the *Prison*

Notebooks. Gramsci's central problem was that the frontal assault model — the Bolshevik capture of a weak state from the outside, executed in October 1917 — had catastrophically failed to generalize. Every Western European Communist revolution that tried to follow it in the years after Russia had been crushed. The reason, Gramsci concluded, was that Western states were not the thing that needed to be captured. The real fortification lay elsewhere:

In Russia the State was everything, civil society itself was underdeveloped and weak; in the West, there was a more balanced relation between State and civil society, and when the State was tested a sturdy structure of civil society remained secure beneath. The State was only an "outer ditch," behind which there stood a "powerful system of fortresses and earthworks."[9]

The outer ditch was the state. The fortresses and earthworks were the churches, the schools, the universities, the unions, the charities, the professional associations, the media, the family — every institution that mediates between private life and political power. No assault on the outer ditch could succeed while the fortresses stood. Which meant that the revolutionary project in the West had to proceed in reverse order from the Russian sequence: capture the fortresses first, and the state would fall once the foundations eroded.

This is the blueprint the twentieth-century Left executed. This is what the rest of this chapter describes.

Aufheben Der Kultur

Cancel culture is not a misnomer. Cancel culture is not, and never was, about canceling *people*. Though people feel the immediate pain, it is, and always has been, about canceling *culture* itself.

The formulation *aufheben der Kultur*—the dialectical abolition of culture—comes most clearly from Herbert Marcuse's 1937 essay "The Affirmative Character of Culture," applying to culture an operation that György Lukács had already deployed in his 1920 essay "The Old Culture and the New Culture." Lukács may not have been a formal member of the Frankfurt Institute, but his 1923 *History and Class Consciousness* was the book on which the Frankfurt School built; earlier, in 1919, during the five murderous terror months of the Hungarian Soviet Republic's existence, Lukács had served as Deputy People's Commissar for Public Education under Béla Kun, with responsibility for cultural and educational policy. Now, if you were to look up the definition of the word *aufheben* as commonly used you would find that the meaning is to eliminate, or be rid of something. However, the way it was used by Lukács, and later by Marcuse, Freire, and others up to this date, references back to a very odd usage of the term by Hegel.[10]

As anyone familiar with Hegel's works may expect, this peculiar usage of the term is in the context of the dialectic. Hegel's process—read: *cult*—of the perfection of society was to be accomplished through the perfection of ideas, and ideas, in turn, were to be perfected by the process of dialectical synthesis: readily summarized today as problem, reaction, solution.

The term *aufheben*, as used dialectically, implies a synthesis that both eliminates the former object but preserves something of its spirit as combined with the reaction. In this manner, *aufheben der Kultur* is not merely to cancel culture, but to replace it via a process of problematization, wild-eyed overreaction, and third-way solution that serves to perpetually move the culture by increments towards the desired goal.

The dialectic is utter nonsense. It is nothing more than the thorough obfuscation of readily identifiable sociological processes by alchemical magic, gnosticism, and initiate language—those common words with special meanings to those in the know, like "Democracy," "Justice," or "Liberation"—into a faith system. However, the application of the dialectic does form a potent sociological weapon when paired with a sufficient activist network. The purposeful problematization of traditional culture—and breaking of systems that worked for centuries—in order to introduce a process of reaction, is a fairly predictable method of political warfare so long as one can accomplish the initial problematization, and controls sufficient institutions to legitimate the solution (by paralogy – the illegitimate *legitimizing* accomplished by wielding captured institutions).

The cleverness of the *aufheben* formulation was not so much in Hegel's dialectic but in the later Frankfurt theorists' refinement of the weapon through Gramsci's *counter-hegemony* and institutional capture. Marx's "seize the means of [economic] production" failed, but Lukács' "seize the means of cultural production" would not. This is institutional capture via entryism: the systematic introduction of trained Communists to establish institutional beachheads and institute neutral-seeming but exclusionary policies to grow Communist control within the organization. By the seeding of trained Communists into varied institutions the dialectical methods could be applied internally to each institution. Here, the dialectic acts as a ratchet consistently moving the organization in the direction of Communism via a never-ending series of negotiated third-ways, but while retaining much of the language (redefined along initiate lines) and aesthetic of the organization—wearing it as a *skin suit*. This has been done to government, education, the media, and the Church over the last century.

Normally it takes a significant percentage of a population to move the Overton Window, and it moves slowly. This is a key to a stable society. Moving the cultural norms too quickly leads to backlash by traditionalists that would typically see the process slowed as third-way solutions are adopted over generations, not over days-to-months. Cancel culture is simply this process on fast-forward through the astroturfing of societal sentiment into radical territory. Typically, such revolutionary furor would be met by the traditional institutions of society to disrupt the revolution and protect itself. These institutions offered no such resistance once they were conquered.

Young Cannon Fodder

A nation cannot stand in the presence of one or more generations broken, entirely, from the founding mythos, ethic, ideals, and traditions.

The mass indoctrination of American youth towards revolutionary ends is not, exactly, a new phenomenon—it has been the foremost front of American Marxists for nearly six decades. It is far older than that, however. Two thousand years ago, Plato wrote this formula for revolutionary social change in his Republic, documenting the need to break the transmission of cultural values, norms, and mythos between generations by removing children from parents to raise and educate communally—a process effectively achieved through government-run public education—and through censorship and tabooification of the *olds*.

This campaign has shifted repeatedly through the dialectical perpetual revolution, first targeting the Christian nature of American government, culture, and ethics, replacing it with a veritable void of "do as thou wilt," and now the enshrinement of the new ethic of classic Marxism wherein the state is god and its ruling oligarchs speak with that authority—hence the old paradigm of the noble lie.

The manner of carrying out this program at the individual level is not particularly complex. Simply shift incentives and education towards the embrace of the gnostic disposition, wherein life is unfair and a prison, and elevate as moral duty the overthrow of the system that created it towards the liberation of all of mankind. Since the only manner in which all men are created equal is in dignity, there is no lack of attack vectors for this ideology: anything which makes any person less – in reality or appearance – than any other will do.

Not very bright? Tell them it is the intellectual class that is to blame. Not very attractive? Clearly, the oppressor is the celebrity industry for pushing what everyone wants to see. Rather poor in wealth? It must be the bourgeois landlord-corporate-million-billionaire class making you poor. Desire some kind of perverted shagging? You could do that all day every day if not for the pesky church-ladies and evil patriarchy. The dialectical method even has the capacity to get the public queer and the feminist girl-boss to fight for the liberation of the poor, oppressed Jihadist—such is the scope of its intellectual and ethical destructive potential.

It was the work of the Frankfurt School and its German Marxist scholars that wrote the modern strategy, with Marcuse penning the shift from the kinetic revolutionary activity of the Black Panthers and Weathermen to the classroom revolution of Paulo Freire that took place largely in the 1960s and 1970s. Of course, according to the clever principles of Gramsci, they did not merely seek to get themselves into the classrooms to indoctrinate children twenty or thirty at a time. They targeted the colleges of education and the institutions of accreditation, leveraging from their established beachhead in psychology and social science, in order to indoctrinate every single new teacher produced in America. This conquest was already largely completed by the year 2000, with the subsequent decades representing the period of natural transition as the new-school, new-Left neo-Marxists were elevated and the old guard retired. At this point you would be hard-pressed to find a single teacher in any school in America that has not been subjected to this indoctrination—and who is not indoctrinating, in turn, their students according to these *critical* methods (despite their lack of subjective knowledge of this fact).

This was also the basic methodology of Chairman Mao of the Chinese Communist Party as he undertook his second revolution and cemented his power. They utilized the "black" and "red" categories to divide among oppressor and oppressed, thereby shifting incentives to identify among the several red categories for the acquisition of real privilege. They vilified the olds, and banned them from the culture according to Plato's playbook.

The youth, with their underdeveloped minds, hypercharged emotionalism, flowing hormones, and cocksurety, make for an excellent revolutionary class to replace the stabilized proletariat. What a wonderfully devilish plan to take those dependents already tending towards rebellion against parental authority, and whom are coerced as a captive audience in government schools far more hours than they spend with their family, only to take their side against their parents in demanding their liberation from parental authority. Simply introduce this under the spell of "children's rights" as a dialectical negation of real and historic parental rights. What is more, it is not difficult to adjust education to make them even more emotionally charged—towards the paradigm of Rousseau—less intellectually developed, and more conceited, and this is precisely what they have done. These revolutionary classes in Marxism are only ever utilized as splinter movements to soften up the opposition. They are never allowed to achieve real power—Mao himself murdered much of his own Red Guard in work camps once their task was complete. This gives form to the truth that Marxism, for all its claims to "materialism" and "economics" which conceal a deep spiritual religiosity, itself further conceals a fine-tuned, long-established mechanism for regime change—the ultimate end of the mysteries.

Mao's contribution to the arsenal was the doctrine of mass lines—the development and simultaneous deployment of multiple narratives, each tailored to a different audience, all engineered to push disparate groups in the same revolutionary direction at the same time. Under mass-line doctrine, a labor grievance, a racial grievance, a feminist grievance, and a student grievance need not be coordinated at the organizational level; they need only be shaped by the same operational logic so that when the moment arrives, seemingly spontaneous uprisings erupt on every front at once. This is how a small vanguard manufactures the appearance of an organic mass movement—and it is among the most potent active measures in the political warfare playbook. Active measures encompass the full spectrum of subversion: disinformation, demoralization, the co-opting of persons and organizations, and the compromising and turning of enemy agents. Every tactic described in this chapter—counter-hegemony, entry-ism, educational capture, the manufacturing of pseudoreality—falls under this umbrella.

Social Emotional Learning

The whole program is downright insidious. The manner in which the most sickly-sweet, public-relations, human-resources language is weaponized to conceal the deadly and damnable content of the message—the linguistic-warfare equivalent of handing a child a grenade and instructing him to run over to the soldiers. It is little wonder why so many teachers have adopted the mannerisms of bad children's television presenters while waving the flag of Hamas and cackling about the demise of their enemies.

Though it really should not be a terrible surprise. At the risk of losing my audience by invoking Harry Potter, and since people seem to relate to the story as a totalizing social paradigm for their lives, the brainwashers and tyrannical indoctrinators of history have seldom looked and talked like Voldemort—reality has always mirrored Dolores Umbridge. From Orwell's *1984*: "It was always the women, and above all the young ones, who were the most bigoted adherents of the Party, the swallowers of slogans, the amateur spies and nosers-out of unorthodoxy."

The first thing we must remember is that all language, and indeed all ideas, stand on a basis of presuppositions. The language used, whether explicitly or implicitly, assumes certain things to be true about the world we live in, the manner in which humans relate to one another, and so on. More academically, language always assumes and stands upon certain types of epistemology, anthropology, and ethics. It is therefore very much possible to extract these presuppositions by analyzing the language used, and that information can then be compared to known historic systems of thought and related systems of government.

I captured a significant number of lesson plans from the SEL provider ChooseLove—a program deeply embedded in not just New Hampshire public schools, but also in the state bureaucracy, department of corrections, and police training—to analyze. From these we can identify the presuppositions and expose how they are diametrically opposed to all that America was founded to be. It is a wholly foreign creedal system.

The lesson plan prescribes a moral archetype of goodness, coerces children to sign pledges to abandon any ethics their parents have tried to pass on in favor of socially-engineered, Leftist-socialist, blank-slatist, highly esoterically spiritual ideals, and inculcates a totalizing ethical framework that is, quite likely, oppositional to the family's own. Our constitutions, Supreme Court precedents, and various legislation all serve to guarantee that the realm of ethical development remains the sole domain of the parent. Such Social-Emotional indoctrinators are actively, and with the most up-to-date scientific methods, overriding that guarantee. This is no different than having a child pledge to Allah and Mohammed, and it is in our public schools every single day. SEL is evil. The full depth of how this was accomplished—and how the American school was transformed from an institution of learning into a factory for ideological formation—demands its own examination at a later point.

Chapter 16

SIMPLE RULES

PRESUPPOSITIONS WE MUST STAND ON

First, we must start from the assumption that a real, objective world exists. We must presuppose it. We physically interact with this world and experience it through our senses and our bodies. Our very existence is dependent on our interaction with this world in a way that commands our attention towards our continued survival: eating food, breathing air, drinking water, and seeking shelter.

Our tradition in America is that of elevating truth as an objective good. Truth is an end unto itself, and no wonder: failing to conform to the truth manifests as interactions with the world that do not lend towards our continued survival. But elevating truth as an end to seek out does not mean we will not err in attempting to understand and describe the world. Often we err because of a fault in our senses, our minds, our logic, or our underlying assumptions about things.

Sometimes an error gets forwarded and becomes popular, even dominant within a culture despite being false. Often this happens because certain human social conventions will not allow for the testing of an idea as taboo. Or perhaps the idea itself occupies a position of first principles, or a position of religious faith taken as truth without being subject to reason. Some even believe that if the society as a whole simply reimagines reality, the pseudoreal, non-existent world they imagine can become real. They imagine we might create a new world, like Peter Pan, simply by believing something and acting like it.

When such a false idea becomes popular or dominant within a society, the idea as acted out by the population gives the impression to the onlooker that the error itself is true by virtue of popularity, and the error might then take up a position of tradition within culture. This elevation of fiction as fact, the way that a population upholds this idea through tradition, the social enforcement of the Overton Window, and acting it out in the world creates the abstract concept of pseudoreality—a fictional world that exists only in the minds of those inhabiting it, and which acts as the lens through which they view all things.

Paramorality

In the United States we still, to some degree, adhere to a morality based in Christianity, though over time this system has, and is being, transitioned more and more towards the immanent, god-state model and social construction. We still, under most circumstances, hold true to concepts such as "thou shalt not murder." Such a command means we may not take a life as a civilian unless it is done with justifiable cause, such as self-defense.

If I am out minding my own business and somebody were to attempt to thrust a knife into my chest, I would then be justified in drawing a firearm and shooting to end the threat, and probably the life, of the assailant. This is an example of morality as applied to reality. However, morality is also applied within pseudoreality. The morality itself may be roughly the same sort of morality held by you or me, but because it is being applied to pseudoreality one reaches very different moral conclusions.

For example, if in the pseudoreality the idea that "hate speech is violence" is elevated as truth, then one within the pseudoreality might reason that the very simple observation that trans men are, in fact, women—is cause enough to take my life. It is important to note here that people are not typically LARPing—play-acting—the pseudoreality and paramorality. They believe these things, truly and fully, and very many would desire, and perhaps a few might attempt, to take my life for such an utterance.

Paramorality, then, is simply the application of a moral system to a pseudoreality that results in seemingly incoherent moral assertions in the real world but is actually internally consistent in the false reality. These lessons will find their importance as we move forward.

Controlled Opposition and the Uniparty

The phenomenon of controlled opposition is a complicated subject and requires the consideration of mixed motivations. Those who are controlled opposition are the people who claim to be, or should ostensibly be, on the side of traditionalists, but for one reason or another act in ways against the traditionalists that effect their defeat.

Often these people seem to simply be vulnerable to paramoral assertions, perhaps as a function of trait agreeableness, such that they essentially become emotionally hostage to the pseudoreality. They, when met by a woman in an elevator screaming that they must vote against a well-qualified judge against whom spurious accusations have been made, because America itself is, in the pseudoreality, a "rape culture," fold like a cheap suit.

The effect of controlled opposition is the demoralization and splitting of the traditionalist base, as those controlled attack their own side from paramorality and demand that their side live up to its own principles—Saul Alinsky's fourth rule—in the face of an enemy that has no such compunction.

To salvage an increasingly desperate situation these forces of controlled opposition must be recognized, isolated, and gone to war with—politically—to wrest from them any grip on the levers of power. The controlled opposition must be defeated before any political warfare efforts against the Woke can achieve full effect.

The "uniparty" is a term describing the combination of the opposition, the controlled opposition, and those purely detached political actors who seek only personal power and wealth, cooperating generally to forward policies against traditionalists. As the term suggests, the uniparty is such the dominant force in American politics that it can be difficult to identify any meaningful opposition in some circles. Often the GOP members of the uniparty are said to follow a "managed decline" strategy for America.

The false binary and the controlled opposition are most clearly visible in their electoral expression—and understanding them requires thinking about elections as iterated games, not single rounds. The standard rational calculation—vote for the less bad option, every cycle, without exception—removes all cost from the apparatus of primary manipulation. If the base consolidates behind the nominee regardless of how the primary was engineered, then engineering the primary is costless and will continue indefinitely. The bad-worse binary perpetuates itself precisely because single-round rationality eliminates every incentive for the apparatus to stop producing it.

The iterated game inverts this. A demonstrated willingness to accept a bad outcome in direct response to a corrupted primary raises the cost of that corruption to the apparatus—potentially making honest primaries more attractive than manipulated ones in subsequent rounds. That is the rational recognition that disempowering those capable of engineering primaries may carry greater long-term strategic value than any single election outcome. The question shifts from "which option causes less damage now" to "which action best disrupts the mechanism producing bad-worse binaries in every future cycle." Anyone capable of engineering a primary is capable of producing this binary indefinitely. Treating elections as iterated games with memory is the specific shift that makes that capability costly – particularly when combined with a bottom-up strategy of our own counter-hegemony against local, county, and state GOP apparatus toward their eventual takeover by forces operating to win.

The Long March is not a conspiracy theory. It is the operational reality of six decades of patient, methodical, institutional conquest. Every school board captured, every accreditation body seeded, every newsroom turned, every seminary hollowed out and rebuilt as a factory for the new faith—none of this was accidental. None of it was organic. It was the execution of a strategy written by men who understood that the West would not fall to a frontal assault, but could be eaten alive from within, so long as the host never recognized the parasite for what it was. The question that remains is not whether the institutions have been captured—they have, overwhelmingly. The question is what the true political spectrum looks like in the aftermath, who the real combatants are, and how we distinguish friend from foe in a landscape engineered to make that discernment maximally difficult. That is the subject we turn to next. But before we can distinguish friend from foe, we must understand how the factory that produces them operates—and that factory is the school.

Chapter 17

The Ethical Factory

Public Education as Esoteric Formation

Before we examine what was imported, we must establish what cannot exist: neutral education.

Every pedagogical decision—what to teach, what to exclude, how to reward, how to discipline, what to celebrate, what to ignore—transmits ethical commitments and presuppositions whether or not anyone acknowledges them. The question is never whether education will form ethics but *whose* ethics it will form. You can minimize the transmission of explicit ethical content—you can attempt to focus narrowly on mathematics and reading and practical skills—but even that minimization reflects an ethical commitment: the commitment to individual competence, to practical utility, to the value of the autonomous person who can think and act independently, and to the value of reserving to the parent the ethical formation of the child. That is not neutral. It is a specific ethical vision rooted in specific metaphysical commitments about the nature of man, of education, and of civil government.

This is the same error we identified in the myth of "neutrality" in the public square. In the political context, the myth that governance can be religiously neutral masks the fact that Marxian metaphysics have replaced Christian ones. In the educational context, the myth that schools can be ethically neutral masks the fact that Hegelian-Progressive metaphysics replaced transcendent ones. The "neutral" school is no more neutral than the "neutral" public square. Both are occupied territory flying the flag of colonizers in the German tradition.

The American tradition that was displaced did not claim neutrality. The Protestant tradition of sphere sovereignty—the principle that family, Church, and civil government each hold distinct, limited authority—explicitly acknowledged that education transmits ethical commitments, and it placed the authority over those commitments in the hands of parents and, where authorized by parents, the Church. It was the parent who selected which school, and under which denomination or civil organization, the child was educated. The civil government's role was constrained to its own sphere. Education—particularly ethical education—fell under the authority of family and Church, not the state. This was not accidental. It reflected the Reformation conviction that there are multiple spheres of governance—family, Church, and civil magistrate—each with limited authority under a transcendent source of authority higher than any of them. The civil government has no more business forming your child's ethics than the Church has executing criminals or the family has demanding a tithe.

This tradition produced results. The Puritan educational model in New England generated one of the most literate, intellectually rigorous, and self-governing populations in world history. It did so precisely because it operated under covenantal authority with transcendent ethical commitments—parents educating children in accordance with what they understood as their obligations before God, and with local community schools serving a practical role funded not by typical civil taxation, but by tithing.

What replaced it came from Prussia. And the irony should not be lost on any student of history that the displacement began in Massachusetts—the very seat of the Puritan tradition—when Horace Mann, then serving as Secretary of the Massachusetts Board of Education and the first state education official in America, returned from his tour of Prussian schools in 1843 and set about dismantling the educational inheritance of his own forebears. The city on a hill became the seminary of statism, and they called it progress.

THE PRUSSIAN IMPORT

The Prussian compulsory education system was not merely an administrative innovation towards German efficiency. It was a metaphysical project.

In the aftermath of Prussia's humiliation by Napoleon at the Battle of Jena in 1806—a battle Hegel himself witnessed, famously describing Napoleon as "the world-soul on horseback"—the Prussian state undertook a radical reconstruction of its institutions, with education at the center. Johann Gottlieb Fichte, the post-Kantian Idealist whose philosophy directly influenced Hegel, laid out the program in his *Addresses to the German Nation* (1807-08). Education, Fichte argued, must be removed from the family and placed under state control, because the family transmits particular interests rather than the universal interest of the *Volk*. The child's natural will must be overwritten and replaced with a will oriented toward the national-spiritual whole.

This is not education in any sense the American tradition would recognize. It is ethical formation by the state, premised on the metaphysical superiority of the state over the family as a moral institution.

Hegel systematized this premise. In his *Philosophy of Right*, the state (civil government) is described as "the actuality of the ethical idea" and "the march of God in the world." The state is not merely an administrative convenience seeking economies of scale, but the highest expression of ethical life—higher than the family, higher than civil society. The State, to Hegel, is approaching "the good" in the Platonic sense. Education under this framework is not a service the state provides to families. It is the state exercising its rightful authority as the supreme ethical institution to form citizens for its own purposes.

The Volkish dimension of this Prussian project adds the organic-spiritual component that connects it directly to the esoteric lineage we have traced in this book. The *Volk* is not merely a political community but a living spiritual organism—the collective soul of the nation progressing through History toward self-realization. In some manner it is comparable to Rousseau's idea of the perfect democratic will. Education is the mechanism by which individual consciousness is aligned to this collective spiritual destiny. If you have absorbed the earlier chapters, you will recognize this immediately: it is the Timaeus cosmology operationalized through a state bureaucracy. The world as one living creature, all beings as portions of the whole, the alchemical process of dissolving individual distinction into collective unity—translated from esoteric philosophy into compulsory schooling policy.

Mann imported this system—compulsory attendance, age-graded classrooms, standardized curricula, state-certified teachers, state-controlled ethical formation. Here two distinct but related arguments must be kept clear.

The first is a sphere-sovereignty argument that does not depend on which metaphysics happen to inhabit the importing state. The civil sphere lacks legitimate authority over the ethical formation of children—that authority belongs to the family and, where parents choose it, the Church. Any assumption of that authority by the civil government exceeds its delegated scope and creates a structural vulnerability: it places the most valuable power imaginable—the formation of the next generation—in an institution whose incentives are misaligned with its ostensible purpose. It is a massive perverse incentive. Power over the formation of children is too valuable not to be corrupted over time, and the sphere-sovereignty violation creates the conditions for that corruption regardless of the initial metaphysical content. A Christian nation making this error begins on better footing but tends toward the same destination. The sphere-sovereignty principle was not a quaint Reformation peculiarity. It is structurally essential down to the bones of incentives, games theory, and theology.

The second argument is more specific and more immediate. The Prussian model was not a neutral administrative mechanism that happened to exist in a bad metaphysical and spiritual environment. It was the direct institutional expression of that environment—the product of Volkisch nationalism, the rejection of Christianity, and the embrace of Hermetic-gnostic immanentist metaphysics as the organizing principle of the state. Fichte's *Addresses to the German Nation*, which laid out the program Mann would import, did not merely recommend state control of education as a convenience. It argued that the family transmits only selfish interests, while the state embodies the universal spiritual interest of the *Volk*—and that education must therefore be removed from the family and placed under state authority so that the child's natural will could be overwritten with a will oriented toward the national-spiritual whole. Fichte might as well have been paraphrasing Plato from *Republic*: sever the means of social transmission between parent and child, and educate coercively towards the new, unifying mythos.

This is the metaphysics Mann imported. The moment you accept that the state is the proper vehicle for ethical formation—that the government and its certified experts possess the authority to determine what the child ought to believe and value—you have accepted the Hegelian premise that the state is the higher ethical reality whether you articulate it that way or not. The architecture *is* the metaphysics made institutional. What Mann imported was not a neutral administrative structure onto which Americans could graft their own values. It was a machine built to produce a specific outcome: regime change and power consolidation under the new oligarchs. A citizen whose highest loyalty was to the collective rather than to family and God, and whose concept of what was true and good was certified by the expert class – philosopher kings – rather than revealed by Scripture or transmitted by parents was necessary to the project. This was the single largest step in the destruction of American education, and it was a foremost project of the Progressive Era.

Young Hegelians in Control

John Dewey is the critical bridge figure who translated the Prussian-Hegelian metaphysics into a comprehensive educational philosophy and built the institutional machinery to perpetuate it.

Dewey was, in his formative years, an avowed Young Hegelian. He studied under George Sylvester Morris at Johns Hopkins, a committed Hegelian, and his early work—including his 1884 essay "The New Psychology" and his 1887 *Psychology*—operated explicitly within Hegel's philosophical framework. His later "pragmatism" is typically presented as a break from Hegel, but the eschatological and spiritual structure never truly disappeared. Truth is not discovered but *made* through social practice. Categories are not fixed but evolving. The purpose of thought is not to describe reality but to transform it. This is alchemy repackaged for the industrial age.[11]

Dewey's educational philosophy, laid out most clearly in *Democracy and Education* (1916), made the implications operational. Education is not the transmission of a fixed body of knowledge but the continuous reconstruction of experience toward social aims. The child is not receiving a heritage—he is being formed as an instrument of social progress. The school is not a conservatory of culture but a laboratory of change. This is Hegel's concept of *Bildung*—formation as the process by which Spirit comes to know itself through successive stages—applied to the institutional setting of the American public school in crafting the next generation who would, in turn, go on to press the next turn of the dialectic.

The question that would have exposed the entire project—"social progress *toward what?*"—was never satisfactorily answered in terms that a non-Hegelian would accept. Dewey's answer, stripped of its pragmatist clothing, was always the same as Hegel's: toward the progressive realization of the ethical idea through the dialectical reconstruction of society. Toward the end of History. But this was never stated so plainly in the education journals.

Dewey's contribution was not merely his philosophical works. It was institutional. He was a founding member of the American Federation of Teachers in 1916. The National Education Association, founded in 1857, was transformed during the Progressive era from a loose professional association into the institutional vehicle for Progressive educational philosophy. This point must be understood clearly: the NEA and AFT were not founded as collective bargaining organizations. They were founded as Progressive education lobbying operations. Collective bargaining came decades later—the NEA did not seriously pursue it until the 1960s. Their founding purpose was to professionalize teaching along Progressive lines, and excising the parents and Church from the process.

Practical step one: control the pipeline for teacher education and certification, and every new teacher emerges pre-formed in the Progressive mold. The union then ensures those teachers cannot be removed or disciplined for implementing the philosophy. The certification system ensures no one outside the pipeline can enter the profession. It is a closed, self-perpetuating loop—the institutional capture described in the prior chapter applied to the single most consequential institution in society: the mechanism by which the next generation's ethics are formed.

This is Fabian strategy—named for the Roman general Fabius, who defeated Hannibal through patient delay rather than frontal assault, and adopted by the Fabian Society of British socialists as their explicit methodology—in its purest expression. The wolf in sheep's clothing. Patient, incremental, working through institutional capture rather than confrontation. Reshape society one generation of students at a time. And it worked.

Chapter 18

The New Red Guard

Progressively Revolutionary

The Dewey-to-Freire shift was not strictly a betrayal of the Progressive project by the radical Marxists. It was its dialectical fulfillment.

The dialectic has no brakes. Every synthesis becomes the new thesis to be negated. Dewey's gradualism was always going to be supplanted by something more radical, because the dialectical engine cannot stop. Fabianism produces the conditions for its own radicalization—once the institutions are captured and the gradualist program has moved the Overton Window far enough, the next generation of revolutionaries will always emerge to say "not far enough, not fast enough." The product of broken institutions will always be viewed as necessitating more rapid application of the dialectic to perpetually worse circumstances. The Progressive project, Fabian or otherwise, necessarily manufactures the *crisis point* that will be exploited by revolutionaries towards further regime change.

Paulo Freire's *Pedagogy of the Oppressed* (1968) is the third most cited book across all social science disciplines—with over 130,000 Google Scholar citations—the most cited work originating in the education discipline in the history of academic publishing, and one of the most frequently assigned texts in education-foundations courses at top American schools of education. The person training your child's teacher was trained by someone who was trained on this book. That fact alone demands that we understand what it contains.[12]

Freire was a Brazilian Marxist whose "critical pedagogy" reframed education as *conscientization*—the raising of the student's critical consciousness so they can perceive and challenge the oppressor-oppressed dynamics structuring their reality. The teacher is no longer an instructor transmitting knowledge that necessarily but subtly transmits ethical commitments, but a facilitator of revolutionary consciousness that makes the radical ethics an explicit requirement. The student is not learning *about* the world but learning to *transform* it. Traditional education—what Freire derisively called "banking education," the depositing of knowledge into the student—is rejected as inherently oppressive. "Problem-posing education" replaces it: the teacher poses problems drawn from the students' lived experience, and the students develop critical consciousness by analyzing those problems through the oppressor-oppressed lens. It is tragically easy to get children to adopt a negative worldview by pointing out to them all that they do not have and cannot do.

The liberation theology dimension is explicit in Freire. He drew heavily on Latin American liberation theology, which synthesized Marxist class analysis with Christian salvation language. Salvation is reimagined as political liberation – something of the same mistake the followers of Christ made at first in expecting Him to deliver an earthly liberation by overthrowing Rome. In Liberation Theology, Sin is reimagined as structural oppression. The Church's mission is reimagined as revolutionary praxis. This is the esoteric-to-revolutionary pipeline, and its influence on modern education is palpable—you can hear it in the language of "social justice" pedagogy, in the framing of education as "transformative," in the insistence that the classroom is a site of liberating children from oppressive constructs of parental and societal authority.

Freire did not need to build new institutions. He captured the ones Dewey had already built. The colleges of education, the union pipeline, the certification monopoly, the federal reporting apparatus—the machinery was already there. The program running on it changed. Where Dewey's Fabianism said "reshape society gradually through patient institutional work," Freire's Marxism said "produce revolutionaries who will topple society that something better might arise from the ashes." The shift from the 1960s onward, as radical Marxists infiltrated American colleges of education, was simply the reprogramming of Dewey's machine with Freire's software.

Conscientization, applied to children, is the *aufheben* (cancellation) of childhood. The child's inherited understanding—the thesis received from family, church, and culture—is problematized by the teacher. The antithesis—the critical consciousness of oppression—is introduced. And the synthesis is the revolutionary subject, alienated from his inheritance and oriented toward revolution – destined to be the Red Guard cannon fodder that will, eventually, be discarded by the new oligarchs who use them. Because the dialectic has no brakes, the consciousness produced is never sufficient for the zealots. It must always be raised further, always perceive more oppression, always demand more radical action. The student who completes Freire's program does not graduate into productive citizenship. He graduates into a vehicle of perpetual revolutionary sentiment towards the culture his ancestors built.

THE OCCULT TRIBUTARY

Running parallel to the Dewey-Freire political line—and eventually converging with it—is a softer but no less insidious tributary. We traced its outline in an earlier chapter: from Blavatsky's Theosophy through Alice Bailey, through the New Thought movement and its offspring, into the foundations and institutes that would embed social-emotional learning into American public education. It is time now to trace that line in forensic detail.

The chain of custody is documented at every node by the organizations' own publications and statements. They convict themselves. Much of the forensic work that follows was done by mathematician and Critical Theory expert James Lindsay and his organization New Discourses, whose detailed examination of these primary source materials is indispensable.

Helena Blavatsky founded the Theosophical Society in 1875. Theosophy is, to put it plainly, occultism—a synthesis of Hermeticism, gnosticism, Kabbalah, and Eastern mysticism dressed in pseudo-scientific language. Blavatsky's influence radiated in several directions simultaneously: Annie Besant, one of the architects of the Fabian socialist movement, was her devotee. Margaret Sanger, the founder of Planned Parenthood, was a devotee. Adolf Hitler's Aryan ideology and adoption of the swastika derived from Blavatsky's "root race" theories, a connection considered uncontroversial even by mainstream historians. And Alice Bailey, who would become known as "the mother of the New Age," was her student.

Bailey joined the Theosophical Society around 1917 and was expelled five years later for conducting her own spirit channelings in the same spirit as Plato's subjects appropriating the Eleusinian Mysteries. In 1922 she created a publishing company to distribute her occult writings. She named it the Lucifer Publishing Company. In 1924, she renamed it the Lucis Trust—a change of label, not of substance.[13]

Bailey's book *Education in the New Age*, written in the 1930s and published posthumously in 1954, reads like a twisted prophesy for what would emerge six decades later as social-emotional learning. Bailey wrote that "the educator of the future will need to be more of a trained psychologist than he is today" and that "besides imparting academic knowledge, he will realize that his major task is to evoke out of his class of students a real sense of responsibility." He would "relate it all to the science of right human relations." Every subject—history, geography, mathematics, science, philosophy—would be infused with this "science of right human relations" to produce "better citizens" for the New Age.[14]

Bailey laid out the educational objectives in terms that map with disturbing precision onto what would later become the CASEL framework. Self-consciousness as the first developmental stage—matching CASEL's "self-awareness." Self-consciousness leading to group consciousness—matching CASEL's progression through "self-management" and "relationship skills" to "social awareness." The teacher as psychologist facilitating spiritual development rather than instructor transmitting knowledge. Every subject infused with the science of right human relations—matching CASEL's "systemic SEL" model. Children studied and categorized to determine their place in the collective and their proper vocation according to experts—matching the data-mining personality profiling that accompanies modern SEL implementation.

Bailey also envisioned children sorted into what she called "root races"—a categorization drawn from Blavatsky in which workers (Lemurians), intellectuals (Atlanteans), and the spiritually advanced (Aryans) represent ascending levels of human spiritual evolution. The "new race" that education was to produce would emerge "primarily in those lands where the fifth, or Caucasian, races are to be found." These are the same root-race theories that informed Hitler's racial ideology, and they sit at the foundation of the educational philosophy that produced social-emotional learning.

Bailey's treatment of parenthood is no less disturbing. She argued that the "need of an increasing birth rate will be eventually regarded as erroneous" because there are not enough souls of sufficient spiritual quality to fill human bodies—the surplus births produce spiritually inferior humans responsible for the planet's economic and environmental distress. (note: per a typical Protestant Christian spiritual doctrine a man or woman does not *have* a soul, but rather they *are* a soul, and there is therefore no moment of "ensoulment" when soul is bound in flesh). She explicitly invoked eugenics, calling for "the science of eugenics and of sex hygiene" to ensure only properly planned incarnations of ensoulment occur – yet another throwback to Plato, and explicitly spiritual in nature. Margaret Sanger—Bailey's occult sister in the same Theosophical tradition—would operationalize this through Planned Parenthood. The integration of Planned Parenthood and comprehensive sexuality education into public schools is not a coincidence. It is merely a reunion of sorts.

Now: John Fetzer, a radio magnate who became one of the 400 richest men in America, the owner of the Detroit Tigers, a former Seventh-day Adventist who became a 33rd-degree Scottish Rite Freemason, a practitioner of channeling and séances, deeply immersed in Hermeticism and Rosicrucianism—and, as documented in the Fetzer Institute's own spiritual library archives, a devoted reader of Alice Bailey who owned all of her collected works, read them frequently, and closed every formal meeting of his inner circle by reciting Bailey's Great Invocation. He and his associate Jim Gordon conducted channeling sessions in which they communicated, they believed, with the Archangel Michael to receive guidance on the Institute's direction.

Fetzer poured hundreds of millions of dollars into the Fetzer Institute—a building he designed with triangular architecture to represent the triad of mind, body, and spirit. The Institute's stated mission, in its own words: to explore how "the secular and sacred elements of life" can be "better integrated" and how "the insights of science and the power of technological innovation" can "be utilized to explore the capacities of the mind and spirit." It exists, explicitly, to combine spirituality and science in public education. That spirituality is explicitly esoteric and occult.

In 1994, a group of educators, researchers, and child advocates met at the Fetzer Institute. They introduced the term "social and emotional learning" and launched the Collaborative for Academic, Social, and Emotional Learning—CASEL. This is not an inference or a conspiracy theory. It is stated in CASEL's own handbook, on the Fetzer Institute's own website, and in the academic literature on SEL's history.[15]

The Lucis Trust—formerly the Lucifer Publishing Company—is today headquartered at 866 United Nations Plaza, adjacent to the United Nations headquarters in New York City. It produces and distributes its own advocacy material aligned with UN educational and spiritual programs, and holds Roster Consultative Status with the UN Economic and Social Council (ECOSOC). It conducts annual meditation retreats in support of the World Economic Forum meetings in Davos. Alice Bailey's books, including *Education in the New Age*, are listed in the UNESCO document library. UNESCO promotes SEL globally as educational best practice.

The connection between the Lucis Trust and the United Nations is not merely administrative. Robert Muller, former Assistant Secretary-General of the United Nations, developed what he called the World Core Curriculum—the pedagogical framework UNESCO disseminated globally. The Robert Muller School in Arlington, Texas, which piloted this curriculum, stated in its own published manual that its foundational philosophy was drawn entirely from the teachings of Alice Bailey as published by Lucis Publishing Company. The school's founder maintained an ongoing relationship with Lucis Trust's World Goodwill program, presenting the curriculum at World Goodwill seminars alongside Muller himself. Muller was a devoted student of Alice Bailey and credited her explicitly as the inspiration for the World Core Curriculum. When American education adopted what was rebranded as the Common Core Curriculum, it adopted a pedagogical framework whose spiritual architecture traces directly through Muller to Bailey to Blavatsky. The lineage from occult publishing house to United Nations education policy to American classroom standards is not inference. It is organizational genealogy.[16]

Jeb Bush founded the Foundation for Excellence in Education (FEE, later ExcelinEd) in 2008 and launched Chiefs for Change, the network of state superintendents that would push Common Core adoption across state lines. In January 2015 the *Washington Post* reported that the Gates Foundation had channeled $5.2 million into FEE during the Common Core push.[17] The fourth Bush this book has had occasion to name, and we will have more to say about the family in a chapter to come. The party label is Republican. The pipeline is the same.

From Blavatsky to Bailey. From Bailey to Fetzer. From Fetzer to CASEL. From CASEL to UNESCO. From UNESCO to your child's classroom. Every link documented by the organizations themselves.

Unfortunately, even where explicit the occult spiritualization of American public schools has largely gone unnoticed by practitioners. Sitting on the House Education Committee in recent years I had the opportunity to question a school counselor about these things. She was testifying on the terrible effect that removing SEL would have in schools, and her testimony seemed at many points to be brushing up against explicit spirituality. I asked her where that line was, and whether SEL represented any sort of spirituality education in schools. She assured myself and the committee that SEL is in no way spiritual whatsoever, stating it is "just, like, getting Zen." The direct invocation of eastern religion was entirely lost on her.

SEL FORENSICS

With the lineage established, let us examine just a tiny fragment of what is actually being taught.

The ChooseLove Movement—deeply embedded in New Hampshire public schools, the bureaucracy, the department of corrections, and police training—provides a representative case study. The program establishes a moral binary for children between the "illuminator" and the "diminisher." The illuminator is defined by "kind words, kind hands, kind choices."

The diminisher is defined by complaining, seeking fairness in situations perceived as unfair, and questioning authority.

Any student of religion or philosophy should immediately identify the most pressing question about kindness: *who defines what is and is not "kind?"* The answer is never stated explicitly, but it does not need to be. The attributes assigned to the "bad guy"—complaining, seeking fairness, questioning authority—are the attributes of the informed and autonomous citizen. The attributes of the "good guy"—obedience, compliance, never noticing double standards—are the attributes of Plato's subject. The program is engineering the perfect statist drone and telling the child it is teaching kindness.

The moral paradigm presented is totalizing. It is not offered as one perspective among many. It displaces whatever ethical framework the child received from family and Church and replaces it with a socially engineered alternative that is, quite likely, oppositional to the parents' own commitments. Children are coerced to sign pledges to adopt these engineered ideals—pledges that function identically to pledges of religious allegiance. This is no different, in form or function, from requiring a child to pledge fealty to the prophet Mohammad. They are tasked explicitly will condemning those earning the "diminisher" label, which is apparently not violative of the kindness principle. This is happening in public schools every single day.

Our Constitutions, Supreme Court precedents, and legislation all serve to guarantee that the realm of ethical development remains the domain of the parent and, if they so choose, the Church. These programs violate that principle at the root. They are actively and with sophisticated methods inculcating a totalizing ethical framework in children designed to override the parents' own teachings.

I can attest to this as a practitioner. As a sitting member of the New Hampshire House Education Committee, I watched bills to eliminate SEL indoctrination killed by a Republican chairman who invited lobbyists from the teachers' unions and the Department of Education to "orient" the committee—and invited no representatives of private schools, charter schools, homeschoolers, or parents. I watched this same chairman negotiate directly with Democrats to kill Republican education bills without input from the Republicans whose bills were being killed. I watched him push "mental health" mandates and digital social credit scores into schools—yet another delivery mechanism for social-emotional "wellness" practices and "empathy" training designed to create social activists and erode parental rights. The captured pipeline protects itself – and, in this case, the background of the chairman trained as a teacher in the Social Studies fields makes it very difficult to undertake the necessary paradigm changes to genuinely institute conservative policy. That indoctrination in that position is a veritable bulwark against necessary paradigm change. The fact that I genuinely liked that particular chairman as a person – the kind of guy I would be happy to share a beer and stories with – makes it all the more difficult to correct these entrenched failure mechanisms.

The legislative counter-offensive must be as comprehensive as the problem. The Countering Hate And Revolutionary Leftist Indoctrination in Education Act—the CHARLIE Act—directly names and prohibits the pedagogical practices we have described in this chapter: Hegelian and Marxist dialectical analysis applied to social conflict, Freire's critical pedagogy emphasizing *conscientização*, intersectionality frameworks, critical race theory, and similar approaches that frame society through lenses of inherent oppression and liberation narratives of overthrowing systems and hierarchies. It establishes that employment in public education is a privilege funded by taxpayers, not a right, and that violations may result in disciplinary actions up to certification revocation. It preserves academic freedom for neutral, factual discussion while prohibiting indoctrination and Marxian praxis—drawing the line that must be drawn. It represents the considerable paradigm change necessary in the field.[18]

Companion legislation—the Science in Education Act—attacks the epistemological corruption at its root by defining "evidence-based" in law according to the actual scientific method: falsifiability, reproducibility, and resistance to falsification through repeatedly consistent results over multiple experiments. It explicitly provides that (largely captured) peer review alone has no weight in evaluating truth claims, and it requires all pedagogical methods in New Hampshire public schools to conform to this standard. This is the legislative answer to the Platonic Scientism we have traced from episteme through Hegel to the modern captured academy—a law that forces education back into contact with objective reality by requiring that its methods actually work as demonstrated by repeatable evidence, and as aligned with transparent goals, not by institutional manufactured consensus towards social justice.[19]

As of this moment neither pieces of legislation have yet been passed and become law – it will surely require more efforts in coming years to affect these needed changes.

The Gnostic Turn

The esoteric content of education has not remained static. It has shifted—and the shift is toward something more destructive.

As we have observed throughout this book, the Hermetic and gnostic dispositions are two expressions of the same ancient religious tradition, and they oscillate through history as one comes to dominate, then the other. The Hermetic disposition emphasizes the alchemical process of transformation—perfecting the existing order through dialectical synthesis, evolving consciousness upward through stages, the state as the vehicle of History's self-realization. The gnostic disposition emphasizes liberation from the existing order—all hierarchy is oppression, all distinction is imprisonment, and the existing world is a prison from which humanity must escape violently. The Hermetic mode builds structures before collapsing them. The gnostic mode just annihilates them.

But this framing risks a misreading I want to correct before we proceed. It would be a mistake to read the Hermetic phase as merely unfortunate and the gnostic phase as the real catastrophe—as if Dewey's gradualism was a tolerable, if misguided, enterprise that was later hijacked by something worse. The Hermetic dialectic is not a gentler version of the same disease. It is the disease's first and necessary stage. The dialectic, at its root, is the systematic destruction of knowledge—the methodical elimination of distinctions, the progressive detachment of thought from the reality it is supposed to describe. Every cycle of thesis, antithesis, and synthesis moves language and concept further from the actual thing in the world, until the connection between word and reality is so tenuous that discernment becomes practically impossible. A population trained in dialectical thinking is a population that has been epistemically disarmed—rendered incapable of the firm judgments that a functioning life, a functioning culture, and a functioning civilization require. This process generates the precise corruption and illegitimacy in hierarchy that Marxists claim is true of functional societies.

The social and political effects of that disarmament are not abstract. The dialectic breaks the systems by which ordinary people navigate reality: the stable meanings of words, the inherited structures of family and church, the accumulated wisdom embedded in law and custom, the confidence that categories reflect something real about the world. When they are systematically problematized, synthesized, and problematized again over generations, the result is masses of people who are genuinely disoriented—who feel, in earnest, that the world is arbitrary and incomprehensible and that the structures around them are not serving them. That feeling is the accurate registration of an actual injury. The dialectic did that to them. It broke the instruments they needed to navigate existence, and then left them in the ruins, disenchanted and vulnerable. This is the Hermetic phase.

It should surprise no one, then, that the gnostic revolt tends to emerge from precisely the populations most thoroughly processed by the Hermetic machine. The gnostic diagnosis—the world is a prison, all hierarchy is oppression, the existing order must be annihilated—is not an independent ideological development that arrives from outside that sometimes captures the Hermetic project. It is what the Hermetic project produces if allowed to proceed according to its own internal logic. A person whose capacity for discernment has been destroyed by the dialectic, whose inherited structures have been systematically dissolved, whose conscience is still producing moral weight that the remaining conceptual apparatus cannot process—that person does not experience the world as ordered and navigable. They experience it as a prison. The gnostic framework is then handed to them as the explanation for what they are already feeling. The frustration is real. The diagnosis is constructed by the new would-be oligarchs.

The Dewey era was Hermetic in emphasis: patient, gradualist, institutional, focused on transforming consciousness within existing structures toward the Progressive end of History. The SEL era has shifted toward the gnostic: total liberation from all hierarchy, dissolution of all categories, the explicit rejection of every inherited structure of meaning. The shift did not occur because the project was captured by something foreign to it. It occurred because the project matured—because the dialectic had done enough epistemic damage across enough generations that the gnostic response became the path of least resistance for the people it had produced and the pain they feel.

This shift was facilitated by the incorporation of Frantz Fanon—the Martinican-French psychiatrist and Algerian independence theorist—whose anticolonialism was transmitted through the framework of intersectionality into the SEL apparatus. Fanon's *The Wretched of the Earth* called for the total annihilation of the colonial order, not its reform. All inherited categories—political, epistemological, ethical—are colonial impositions to be destroyed. Intersectionality, as developed by the critical theory establishment, applied this anticolonial framework domestically: every axis of identity represents a potential axis of colonial oppression requiring decolonization. SEL embraces intersectionality, which embraces Fanon. When SEL adopts the "transformative" and "culturally affirming" frameworks now circulating at the Department of Education, it is operationalizing this intersectional-anticolonial analysis through the CASEL infrastructure. Self-awareness becomes awareness of your positionality within intersecting systems of oppression. Social awareness becomes critical consciousness of structural power. The prescription is explicitly violent and explosive.

And the Luciferian dimension—through Bailey, through Fetzer, through the Lucis Trust—makes the spiritual nature of this project clear. The Lucis Trust, formerly the Lucifer Publishing Company, is not hiding what "Lucifer" represents in this tradition: the light-bearer, the liberator, the one who frees humanity from the tyrannical Creator's rules, the one who will make himself (and, maybe, you too) like the Most High. The "illuminator" in your child's SEL curriculum is not a secular concept. It is Luciferian salvation language. The dissolution of all hierarchy, the liberation from all inherited structure, the refusal to accept any authority above the self—this is the gnostic project funded by billions of federal dollars, backed by huge NGOs, and installed in every classroom in America.

The Factory Floor

If the theory of mind we develop later in this book is correct—that the epidemic of psychological disorder among the Left is the product of a shallow, socially constructed ethical framework in sustained conflict with a functioning conscience—then the public school is the factory floor.

The school is where the shallow ethical framework is installed, before the child has the intellectual capacity to resist. The thought-stopping cliches are rehearsed as classroom exercises. The weaponized concept of "empathy"—which we examined in detail earlier as a demand to project the oppressor-oppressed framework rather than to feel genuine compassion—is taught as the supreme moral virtue. The child is primed in vulnerability to sophistry and feminine taboo-making mechanisms of ostracism. The child's inherited ethical formation from family and Church is systematically problematized and replaced. The child emerges pre-loaded with the paramoral operating system which will be maintained by media and human-resource departments throughout adulthood.

This is why the "mental health" crisis skews young. The system has become more efficient at producing the spellbound, and it is catching them earlier. The feedback loop—shallow ethics producing conscience-guilt producing cliche-dependence producing escalation producing disorder—does not begin in college or in the workplace. It begins in pre-kindergarten, with a ChooseLove pledge and an "illuminator" sticker. It incentivizes the adoption of personality disorders in doing activism and theater-kid antics. The factory has been running for over a century. It is only now, with the gnostic turn, that its products are failing catastrophically enough for the general population to notice.

The restoration of parental authority over ethical formation is not merely a policy preference. It is the necessary precondition for breaking the production line. So long as the state claims the Prussian-Hegelian prerogative to form your child's ethics, the content of that formation will be determined by whoever controls the captured institutions—and as we have now documented in forensic detail, the people who control those institutions are operating from presuppositions that trace in an unbroken line to explicit occultism. The sphere sovereignty that the American Protestant tradition recognized—that education belongs to parents and Church, not to the state—was a functional bulwark. And it was dismantled on purpose, by people who knew what they were doing, to make room for exactly what we see today. They had to problematize and demonize the Puritans early in this process.

The bulwark must be rebuilt. But rebuilding requires knowing who will stand with us and who will not—and that requires understanding what the true political landscape looks like after a century of this factory's operation. That is where we turn after a short foray into The Science, and that technique that keeps the boot on your neck.

Chapter 19

THE SCIENCE

Throughout this book I have named the enemy—Hermeticism, Hegelianism, Marxism, Progressivism, Wokeism—and I have insisted, without apology, that the underlying thing these names represent is *a religion*. A prophetic, teleological, metaphysical system with a creation myth, end-times, a (false) doctrine of sin ("oppression"), a priesthood (the credentialed expert class), and sacraments. Everything we have traced from Plato through the Kybalion, from Hegel through Marx through the Frankfurt School right into your child's SEL lesson plan, is *religion*—and not in a trivial "spiritual but not religious" sense.

Yet when you attempt to say this out loud in polite company, something strange happens. You are not met with a religious rebuttal standing firm on a foundation of faith. You are not met with open theology. You are met with the accusation that *you*—the one noticing the pattern—are the religious kook, the science denier, the anti-intellectual, the tinfoil-hat conspiracist, the rube who cannot distinguish faith from fact. You are told that your objection reflects mere *beliefs*, while their position reflects *knowledge*. Their claims are "evidence-based," "peer-reviewed," "settled science." Your claims are "religious," "ideological," "anti-science."

This is the single most important tactical weapon the Left possesses in the entire arsenal of political warfare, acting as both sword and shield to elevate their religion, and their priest class, above your religion, faith, and the ethics that proceed from it.

The purpose of deploying Scientism is twofold. First, it immunizes the Left's actual religious doctrines—Equity, gender identity, apocalyptic climate change, systemic racism, COVID orthodoxy, the therapeutic state—from the ordinary skepticism that any foreign religious doctrine would normally face in our culture. Second, and more importantly, it subordinates the religious, philosophical, and presuppositional claims of their opponents to a lower social station. You are not merely of the wrong opinion; you are *unscientific*. And to be unscientific in a society that has been taught to worship Scientism is to be below the threshold at which one is permitted to speak in public.

You must understand this. You are not losing the public argument because your arguments are bad. You are losing because you have been maneuvered onto a battlefield where your arguments have been pre-classified as inadmissible before you ever open your mouth. The referee is not neutral. The playing field is tilted ninety degrees to the vertical, so every ball simply lands in your net by virtue of gravity.

Two Meanings of One Word

To see through the spell you must first see that the word *science*, as it is deployed in the public square, is equivocal—it does two entirely different kinds of work at the same time, and the speaker relies on you to confuse the two.

The first meaning of *science* is the one most people learn in school: the scientific method. A tool. Observe something, form a hypothesis, design an experiment that could falsify the hypothesis, run the experiment, see whether the hypothesis survives, then submit your results for others to independently reproduce. The gold standard of truth claims under this definition is not peer review and not the opinion of experts—it is *reproducibility*. A finding that cannot be independently reproduced is not yet knowledge. This is science as a mere hammer for smashing the world into constituent parts. You do not "believe in" a hammer. You do not place "faith" in a hammer. You pick it up and you use it when you encounter a nail, then you put it down.

The second meaning of *science*—the one our present rulers almost always mean when they invoke the term—is the old Hermetic, Platonic, Hegelian sense: *Scientia*, a metaphysical system of knowledge aimed at transforming the world to conform to a prophesied end. This "science" is not primarily concerned with describing reality as it exists; it is concerned with *effecting change on reality* in accordance with the adherent's desires. It is the *alchemical Science.* It does not seek falsification—it seeks confirmation by any means necessary. It does not welcome competing hypotheses—it declares dissent to be heresy. This is *Scientism.*

The trick, the sleight of hand, the entire basis of the sophistry they deploy, is that a speaker can use the word *science* in the second sense while relying on you to hear it in the first sense. When Dr. Fauci said "I represent science,"[20] he was not representing the scientific method. He was representing an institutional apparatus producing Scientistic outcomes aligned with perverse incentives. But you heard *science*, and you thought of hammers and nails and falsifiability, and the mental shortcut was already complete before you noticed you had taken it.

The result is that Scientism gets to clothe itself in the moral and epistemic authority that was rightly earned, over centuries, by the actual scientific method—a method subordinate to reason and standing on the presuppositional basis of a created order. And the speaker who called you an anti-science science-denier was never, at any point, actually defending science. They were defending a religion.

THE REIFICATION OF DOGMA

Once the equivocation is in place, the machine operates with terrifying efficiency. The Left takes a religious doctrine that could not survive ten minutes of honest public debate—say, "men can become women by believing they are women"—runs it through a captured journal, captured university, captured medical association, or captured federal agency—the public-private NGO complex—and emerges with a "scientific consensus." That consensus is then pointed to as dispositive evidence that anyone questioning the doctrine is *unscientific.* The religious claim has been *reified*—made real—by institutional laundering and naked sophistry.

Let me be precise about what I mean by reification. The American Academy of Pediatrics does not vote in a laboratory. It votes in a conference room. When it issues a position paper endorsing the chemical and surgical sterilization of children who experience gender dysphoria,[21] it has not discovered something in the natural world; it has held a meeting and taken a position. That position reflects the ideological commitments of the people who were permitted, via decades of institutional capture, to be in the room. The position paper itself is then presented to the public, to pediatricians, to school counselors, to courts, to legislators—as *the science*.

This is not proper science. It is just wearing a science costume. As I have said elsewhere in this book: truth knows nothing of credentials.

How "Public Health" Was Manufactured

Before I walk the roster of laundered doctrines, I want to dwell on a single case that demonstrates the entire mechanism in one frame. It is so clean, so precise, and so close to home that once you see it you will never stop seeing it. The case is the phrase *public health*.

Return for a moment to the chapter on language and the three-part test for truing our words. *Health*, in its plain and original meaning, is an *individual* reality. A body is healthy or unhealthy. A person is sick or well. A specific mother holds a specific feverish child. Health is inseparable from the concrete human being who possesses a body, who makes choices about that body, who bears the consequences of those choices, and who, under any legitimate ethical system, retains the moral authority to seek or to refuse treatment. Health is located where the body is located: in a person, individually, with agency, with responsibility, with dignity.

Now introduce the phrase *public health*. *The public has no body*. The public cannot get sick. The public cannot die. The public has no liver, no lungs, no conscience, no truly collective mind. The public cannot consent to treatment, cannot decline treatment, cannot weigh the relative moral claims of its own continued life against other goods. The public is not the kind of thing that has health or the lack of it, because the public is not the kind of thing that has a body at all. The term, on its face, is a category error.

And yet the moment the term is accepted into common usage, a staggering reorientation has already occurred. *Health* has been redefined. It now refers to a statistical profile of a collective that has been reified as if it were a single living organism. The *body politic* has been granted, linguistically, a mortal body. That body can now be said to be sick, at risk, vulnerable, endangered. The individual's actual, physical body has been relegated to the status of *a cell within the collective organism*. And cells do not have rights against the organism. Cells do not get to refuse the organism's demands. Cells are to cooperate for the good of the whole, and if a cell gets too uppity against the whole, its fate is apoptosis or phagocytosis: destruction.

This is the Hermetic vision in pure form. Recall from earlier chapters that the entire underlying metaphysics of Scientism treats humanity as *the One*—a single organism working its way through History toward unification and divinization. *Public health* is not a policy term. It is a *theological* term. It imports the Platonic fantasy of the city as a single body, Rousseau's *general will* that overrides particular wills, Hegel's state as the concrete expression of Spirit, and Marx's *social man* for whom the individual is only a momentary expression of class. The phrase *public health* smuggles this entire cosmology into the conversation under the guise of a neutral, clinical category.

Watch now what follows, mechanically, once the term has been accepted.

First, a new priesthood appears. The collective organism cannot feel its own symptoms, cannot know its own condition, cannot speak for itself. It requires an interpreter. The *public health official*—credentialed, appointed, insulated from accountability—becomes the sole authorized diviner of what the body politic needs. Of course, this great and powerful structure, devoid of accountability, is a prime location of capture for perpetual revolution and ever-greater radicalization.

Your own doctor, who can actually examine your body, now ranks beneath the diviner who cannot. The mother, who can actually hold her child, now ranks beneath the bureaucrat who cannot. Because it is not her child's individual body that matters in the new framework; it is the collective body, and she has no special claim on that one. The priesthood does.

Second, individual moral agency is reclassified as obstruction. Your refusal to accept a novel pharmaceutical product is no longer *your decision about your body*; it is a *threat to public health*. Your decision to gather with your family for worship is no longer *your right to assemble*; it is a *super-spreader event*. Your decision to keep your business open is no longer *your livelihood*; it is a *non-essential activity endangering the community*. The framework itself now makes your exercise of traditional liberty into a form of aggression against the organism of which you are merely a cell. And aggression against the collective licenses a response.

Third, traditional ethics is inverted. Under the older framework, medicine was ordered to *do no harm* to the individual in front of you. Under the new framework, medicine is ordered to optimize the statistical profile of the collective—and if that means withholding monoclonal antibodies from a white man with pre-existing conditions so that the *public's* equity score can improve, that is precisely what the framework demands. I document elsewhere in this chapter how the Biden FDA's scorecard weighted non-white skin color several times more heavily than significant pre-existing conditions in rationing a scarce, life-saving drug.[22] That decision was not a corruption of public health. That decision was *public health operating exactly as designed*—aggregating over the collective, silencing individual moral claims, and enabling ideological capture and collective punishment via *equity*.

Fourth, and most importantly for the purposes of this chapter, competing worldviews are delegitimized as *anti-science*. The Christian who objects to a mandate on conscience grounds is no longer exercising religious liberty; she is *endangering public health*. The parent who objects to a school policy of child-bureaucrat secrecy on parental-rights grounds is not defending his family; he is *contradicting the science*, and that pseudo-threat to the child via non-affirmation might just breach the threshold of *abuse* requiring legal action. The small-business owner who objects to closure orders is not asserting economic liberty; he is *science-denying* and eligible for forcible closure if not pogroms and mob justice. The phrase *public health* has pre-positioned every objector as a moral and epistemic inferior before he has uttered a syllable.

Public health is a theological construct masquerading as a medical one. It is Scientism's archetypal trick. And once you have seen it in this one case, you will recognize the identical trick everywhere it is deployed: *gun violence, the public interest, climate action, social justice...* Each of these phrases performs the same trick: dissolve the individual, reify the collective, install the priesthood, delegitimize the dissenter.

This is how the Left's religious system maintains its dominance. It does not argue against your worldview. It redefines the shared vocabulary in terms that make your worldview *unsayable*. They laugh at you, and, in too many cases, you shut up.

From Equality to Equity

If *public health* demonstrates the trick on the medical side, the substitution of *equity* for *equality* demonstrates it on the legal-political side, and the move is so close to identical that the two cases ought to be studied together.

Equality, in the American constitutional tradition, is a procedural rule that applies to *persons*. The Fourteenth Amendment's Equal Protection Clause guarantees that the state will treat each individual under the same rules regardless of class. It is a constraint *on the state*, binding the state to procedural neutrality between citizens. It says nothing about outcomes. It guarantees no proportional distribution of any good across any demographic aggregate. It is, in this respect, the political analogue of "health" in the older sense: located in the individual, predicated on the individual, recognizing the individual as the fundamental unit of moral and legal concern.

Now introduce the word *equity*. Stop and ask, with the same care we applied to *public health*, what those two letters of difference are doing. *Equity* no longer applies to persons. It applies to demographic aggregates. The unit of analysis has been silently swapped—from the individual citizen to the racial, sexual, or class collective. The standard of judgment has been silently swapped—from procedural fairness to proportional outcome. And the role of the state has been silently swapped—from constrained to creator. To deliver *equity*, the state must measure each person, classify her by group, calculate the aggregate distribution, identify the deviation from proportionality, and reapportion across persons until the deviation closes.[23]

Run the diagnostic from the previous section. The *linguistic move* redefines an individual reality (procedural treatment of persons) as a collective metaphysical entity (proportional outcomes across groups). The *metaphysical import* is Marx's *social man*, for whom the individual is only a momentary expression of class—the same theological substrate that gave us *public health*, now applied to law instead of medicine. The *Republic* blueprint installs the priesthood: the DEI officer, the equity auditor, the disparate-impact attorney, the demographer at the federal agency. The *noble lie* is the proposition that *equity is what equality always meant*—which is plainly false, but must be affirmed in public as a condition of membership in respectable institutions. The *censorship mechanism* reclassifies the citizen who insists on procedural equality as *racist, anti-equity, upholding white supremacy*—pathologized. And the observable, empirical reality—that no two persons are identical, that group outcome differences have a thousand causes, that procedural neutrality is the only standard a free people can administer without tyranny—is dismissed as *naive, simplistic, refusing to see the structural picture*.

Mark what then becomes possible. Under *equality*, the state cannot ration monoclonal antibodies by race without reproducible science identifying a causative effect attached to morbidity and mortality; doing so violates Equal Protection on its face. Under *equity*, the state can do precisely that, and call it justice. Under *equality*, the school cannot admit students by racial quota; under *equity*, it can. Under *equality*, the corporation cannot legally segregate its training programs by skin color; under *equity*, an entire compliance industry now exists to do exactly that and bill for the service. Each of these reversals is presented to the public not as a change in the law—because the constitutional text has not changed—but as a *more enlightened understanding* of what the law always meant. That is the laundering. The religious doctrine (*equality of outcome across groups, administered by experts*) has been dressed in the costume of the older procedural rule and walked past the constitutional checkpoint without being stopped, because the guards at the checkpoint have themselves been replaced by the priesthood.

And as with public health, the moment you object—even from the ground of the original constitutional text itself—you are reclassified. You are not a citizen invoking Equal Protection. You are a science-denying, equity-rejecting, anti-justice obstacle to the body politic's healing.

Two phrases—*public health* and *equity*—doing the same work, on different fronts, with the same machinery, in the service of the same religion.

Once you see one, you must learn to see the other immediately. The next phrase you should test against this template is the next one to come.

CASE STUDIES IN LAUNDERED DOGMA

With the archetype in hand, walk through a roster of the specific doctrines this book has already touched on. You will recognize every single one. You have been bullied about every single one. You have perhaps silenced yourself about some of them. You should not continue to do so. And in every case, the same six-part architecture will be visible once you know where to look for it.

1. A *linguistic move* redefines an individual, observable reality as a collective or abstract metaphysical entity.

2. A *metaphysical import* smuggles in Hermetic, Platonic, or Hegelian presuppositions without ever naming them: the primacy of mind over body, the collective as a single organism, the progressive unfolding of Spirit through History.

3. A *Republic blueprint* installs a priesthood of credentialed interpreters who alone are authorized to say what the collective needs, directly mirroring Plato's guardian class.

4. A *noble lie*—Plato's own term for the unified fiction the rulers propagate among the ruled for the good of the city—is treated as operationally required even when those who propagate it know it to be false.

5. A *censorship mechanism*—what Marcuse called *repressive tolerance*—suppresses every competing worldview by reclassifying it not as *a rival opinion* but as a *pathology* endangering the collective organism, to be enforced by the state or merely by taboo.

6. The observable, empirical, falsifiable reality to which ordinary citizens have direct and unmediated access is dismissed as *naive* in favor of the priesthood's *holistic* interpretation, which is by

definition unassailable to anyone outside the priesthood.

Run any Scientistic claim through this grid. You will find all six moves operating in concert, every time.

GENDER IDEOLOGY

That a man can become a woman by declaring he is one, that children in distress about their bodies should have puberty blocked and functional sex organs surgically amputated, that referring to a pregnant human female as a "mother" is hate speech, that the word *woman* admits of no definition that does not "include" males—none of these are empirical findings. Sex is bimodal, heritable, and tied to gametes. We were made male and female. Medicine cannot convert a male into a female, or vice versa, and it never will, because that would be a violation of essential categories. These are observable facts to which every citizen has direct access through the most ancient and universal of human experiences.

Run the diagnostic. The linguistic move here is perhaps the most audacious in the entire roster: the word *gender* has been forcibly detached from biology and redefined as an *inner, self-declared identity*. The body—the only datum actually in the room—is reclassified as *assigned at birth*, a phrase that ingeniously implies the body is a mere bureaucratic label applied by a stranger, while the *true self* resides elsewhere—*the soul is androgynous*. This is not a new metaphysics. It is textbook *gnostic dualism* of the exact kind I have traced in earlier chapters from the Hermetic tradition: the mind is real, the body is illusion, salvation consists in the mind's liberation from the prison of flesh. What gender ideology imports, under the cover of medicine, is the *Timaeus* cosmology itself—a world in which the forms are more real than the bodies that instantiate them, and the role of the enlightened practitioner is to remake recalcitrant matter to conform to the mind (*All is Mind*, after all).

The *Republic* blueprint is also perfectly in view. A credentialed priesthood of gender clinicians, endocrinologists, "affirming" therapists, and well-funded NGOs is installed as the authorized interpreters of the child's *true gender*—a thing the parent is incompetent to perceive, even about her own child. The noble lie is brazen: *trans women are women*, a sentence every adult knows to be false the moment she encounters a bearded male in a dress, but which must be affirmed in public as a condition of membership in polite society—a lie no less harmful than Marcuse's own affirmation of pederastic rites to be a member of the club.[24] His repressive tolerance does the rest: the mother who notices is *a bigot*, the doctor who dissents is *unsafe*, the peer-reviewed journal that publishes a contrary finding is forced to retract, and the child who might otherwise have outgrown the confusion of puberty is surgically and chemically committed to a permanent intervention before she can consent to anything. The observable facts—bimodal sex, natural desistance, the absence of replicable evidence for improved mental-health outcomes from gender-affirming care[25]—are dismissed as *reductive, simplistic,* or *refusing to see the whole person.* As I put it in an earlier chapter, the scientific study undergirding this regime is *so thoroughly corrupted by ideology that it is harmful to our understanding and cannot be utilized*, because it is not *that kind of science.*

APOCALYPTIC CLIMATE CHANGE

I am careful here. The planet's climate changes. Humans affect the environment; we were made to. None of that is at issue. What *is* at issue is the specific, religiously structured claim that we are living in the last hour before an anthropogenic apocalypse, predicted by absurdist models that never replicate in reality, which can be averted only by the complete political and economic reorganization of Western civilization under the supervision of the same class of credentialed experts who want, for unrelated reasons, to reorganize Western civilization.

Run the diagnostic. The linguistic move: *the climate*—a statistical abstraction that does not represent *weather*—is grammatically treated as if it were *a single living system* with moods, thresholds, and a looming death. *Gaia*, once openly named in the New Age sources I discussed in earlier chapters, now hides under the costume of *the Earth system.* The metaphysical import is precisely the Hermetic *holism* I dissected at length in the dialectic chapter: *as above, so below, all is one*, no part can be understood except through the whole, and therefore no one without the holistic credential is permitted to pronounce on any particular observation. The butterfly's wing becomes the hurricane, and only the climatologist-priest is licensed to calculate which butterfly to sacrifice. Recall how I described this failure mode: holism in practice demands a perfect, absolute knowledge of the whole that no finite mind can ever possess—which is precisely why it is so useful as a political weapon. The person who wields holism can always defeat the person who wields empirical particulars, because empirical particulars by definition do not constitute *the whole*.

The *Republic* blueprint is installed through the IPCC, the UN, the national academies, and the NGO-journalistic complex, which together function as a guardian class with sole authority to declare what the Earth system needs—invariably, the dismantling of the productive capacity of Western civilization and the subjugation of the sovereign nation to transnational management.

The serial failure of the prophecy—the North Pole still has ice, Al Gore's deadlines are decades past,[26] the predictions update faster than a horoscope—does not discredit the priesthood, because this is not a falsifiable hypothesis. It is, as I argued in the dialectic chapter, *prophecy*, and prophecy does not answer to evidence. It answers to the imperative of the eschaton. The "science" was always downstream of the religious imperative.

Systemic Racism

The claim that American society is structurally racist by necessity, that this racism is invisible and immeasurable yet omnipresent and determinative, that no discrete reform can address it, and that only the demolition and reconstruction of the society by anti-racist practitioners can resolve it—this is not a sociological finding. It is a doctrine of original sin (sans redemption) applied to a demographic group, an unfalsifiable theological claim dressed up in the language of research.

Run the diagnostic. The linguistic move is the redefinition of *racism* away from its plain meaning—the prejudicial treatment of a person on the basis of race, observable, particular, actionable—into *a structural condition of the society* that inheres regardless of any individual's conduct or intention. Racism is relocated from the individual to the collective, and once relocated, it becomes invisible, omnipresent, and immune to disproof.

The metaphysical import is *dialectical* in the strictest sense: oppressor and oppressed are treated as essential, ontological categories that carry their moral weight by virtue of membership in the class rather than by any act of the person. This is Marx's engine retooled on the axis of race, and it inherits Marx's *phenomenological* method—the claim that the oppressed possesses a superior consciousness of reality by virtue of her oppression, and that therefore her *lived experience* trumps any quantitative disconfirmation. *Lived experience* is simply Hegelian phenomenology in American vernacular, and it functions exactly as Hegel's phenomenology functions: to elevate the interior report of the anointed above the external observations of the rest.

The *Republic* blueprint—DiAngelo, Kendi, the DEI officer, the "antiracist" practitioner[27]—is installed as the priesthood with exclusive power to diagnose the society's pathology and prescribe the cure. That the priesthood happens to make its living from the perpetuity of the diagnosis is treated as impertinent. The noble lie is the proposition that *America is systemically racist*, a claim whose function is not to describe the society but to delegitimize its foundations and license the reconstruction proposed by the priesthood. The censorship mechanism is by now entirely routine: disparate-impact jurisprudence treats measurable, observable outcome differences as dispositive of invisible racism regardless of cause, while any attempt to inquire into actual causes is denounced as racism in itself. This is the pattern I dissected in the dialectic chapter as *destruction of knowledge*—the systematic elimination of the distinctions needed to investigate a question, until only the ideologically permitted answer remains sayable.

THE THERAPEUTIC STATE

The explosion of "mental health" diagnoses, the industrialization of SSRIs, the rebranding of personality disorders first as *health*, then as *identities to be affirmed*, the capture of psychology and psychiatry by revolutionary ideologies that pathologize the healthy and affirm the disordered, the framing of every social conflict as a public-health problem requiring expert management—this entire apparatus is theological, not scientific.

Run the diagnostic. The linguistic move is the elevation of behavior and the human condition into a clinical-metaphysical reality with its own diagnostic codes, billing categories, and insurance-reimbursable interventions. Sadness becomes *depression*; a normal energetic child becomes *ADHD*; a teenage girl's confusion becomes *gender dysphoria*; a healthy resistance to the regime's overreach becomes *oppositional defiant disorder*. The natural consequences of a childhood free from discipline and saturated in media exposure become a *sickness*—and, of course, nobody is responsible for that.

The metaphysical import is explicit, though disguised: as I argued earlier in the book, psychology was *founded* on Hermetic premises. The field, translated literally, is the study of the *soul* (*psyche*), but not of the soul as understood in the Christian tradition. It arose directly out of the Hermetic syncretic faith I traced from Blavatsky through the New Thought movement, and it continues to smuggle the commitment to ancient Greek categories and presuppositions.

The *Republic* blueprint is the therapist—licensed, credentialed, bound by professional standards set by captured guilds—installed as the sole authorized interpreter of the patient's inner life. The parent loses standing to discipline. The pastor loses standing to teach and correct. The husband (or suitor) loses standing to *autonomy* and the necessity of striking a blow against *patriarchy*. Only the therapist can pronounce on what the *true self* is, what it needs, and what it must be liberated from. The noble lie is the comforting framework by which the patient's disorder is always located somewhere outside herself—in trauma, in society, in toxic relationships, in internalized oppression—never in her own unexamined moral choices, because the therapist, bound by the guild's commitments, is structurally incapable of attributing error to the *oppressed*. The censorship mechanism is the pathologization of dissent and the weaponization of threats of self-harm. This is why the epidemic of psychological disorder I treat later in the book skews so hard Left: the therapeutic state is the Left's own sacramental apparatus, and it produces the very disorder it exists, ostensibly, to cure.

THE THOUGHT-STOPPING CLICHÉ

Herbert Marcuse, whom I have treated elsewhere in this book, understood something about human psychology that the empiricist camp was slow to articulate. He understood that *reason loses nearly every battle for minds against emotion*, and that if a society can be trained to feel a particular emotional response—shame, disgust, anxiety—on cue, that response can be used to prevent the person from thinking a particular thought at all. The cliché is the delivery vehicle. The slogan that lands, the taunt that sticks, the phrase that produces a flinch. Once the flinch is installed, the argument is over before it begins, because the subject will silence himself rather than feel the flinch again.

Consider the inventory of thought-stopping clichés that Scientism deploys:

Trust the science. The oldest and most direct. It is a statement of faith disguised as a demand for rationality. Real science does not ask to be trusted—it asks to be tested.

Do your own research—from reputable sources. A masterpiece of rhetorical engineering. The citizen is invited to investigate, and then the list of investigable sources is restricted to those that already share the dominant conclusion. It is the illusion of freedom of inquiry with the substance of catechism.

The scientific consensus is settled. Science is never settled. A settled question is not science but dogma. And consensus, as Michael Crichton famously said,[28] is a political category, not an epistemic one.

Anti-science. Applied promiscuously to any person who raises any objection, the implication is that one is against science as such, against method, against *knowledge*. In practice it means one has contradicted a specific priestly pronouncement.

Science denier. The same move, with the moral freight of Holocaust denial smuggled in as an added penalty for anyone who notices the rhetorical violence.

Conspiracy theorist. Deployed when the objection is to observable coordination among elite actors. Since coordination among elite actors is the empirically documented default behavior of every human society that has ever existed, declaring that its observation is a *theory* rather than a *recognition* is itself a remarkable act of unreality.

That's been debunked. Said about anything the speaker does not wish to engage with, often with a link to a Snopes or Media Matters article that did not actually debunk it. The function of the phrase is not to communicate information but to close the conversation.

Experts agree. Which experts? Drawn from which institutions? Selected by what criteria? Reporting what fraction of the actual distribution of expert opinion? The clichéd appeal to experts functions as a force multiplier for institutional capture—every time it is deployed, the capture becomes more self-reinforcing.

It's not a debate. The candid admission. They will not argue with you. They will ostracize you instead.

Each of these clichés is a small social weapon. Used once, it is nothing. Used ten thousand times, across every venue of public discourse, it installs a flinch reflex in the population. The flinch then does the work of the argument. The citizen silences himself not because he has been persuaded that his objection is wrong but because he has learned that raising it will produce the flinch, and he would rather avoid the flinch than speak. This is Marcuse's genius, evil though it be.

The Necessary Boldness

I need to be blunt with you about the stakes here, because I have watched many good people collapse under the weight of this machinery and I do not want you to be one of them.

You are not less educated than they are. You are not less intelligent. You are not less informed. You are not standing on superstition while they stand on knowledge. What is happening when a credentialed stranger invokes *the science* at you is not a moment of legitimate epistemic authority meeting a layman. It is an act of *dialectical subordination* in which a religious ideology, laundered through captured institutions, is deployed to silence a competing set of presuppositional commitments on the grounds that yours have been reclassified as unacceptable and theirs have been reclassified as beyond question. The entire performance is a shell game, and the whole game depends on your willingness to accept the premise that one side is science and the other is merely opinion.

You must refuse the premise.

Your presuppositions—that the human being is made in the image of God, that men and women are distinct and complementary, that children deserve the protection of their parents, that reality is objective and observable, that truth exists and can be pursued, that the family is the irreducible unit of society, that liberty must be ordered to virtue, that a nation has a right to its borders and a people to a measure of self-definition—are not *less rational* than the presuppositions of your opponents. They are, in fact, *more rational*, because they begin from an honest acknowledgment of their presuppositional character. Your opponents' commitments—that the self is fluid, that hierarchy is oppression, that difference is inequity, that reality is socially constructed, that the body is a prison for a true inner self, that History is moving toward a predetermined utopia, that the state is the vehicle of that utopia—are *equally presuppositional*. They simply refuse to admit it. They pretend their presuppositions are findings. They are not. They never were.

Once you see this, it cannot work on you anymore. You have been inoculated. You will still be called a denier. You will still be called anti-science. You will still be told to trust the experts. But you will see the maneuver for what it is: a frightened priesthood reaching for its trusty weapon—and, oh, what a sight it is to behold when that sheath flexes empty, and their faces reflect their horror.

Do not let them tell you your beliefs are *mere belief* while theirs are *facts*. Do not let them tell you a word laundered through a captured university is more truth-bearing than a conclusion you reached by reason and experience. Do not let them frame you as the religious one when the entire thing they are doing is religion—and not merely religion, but a specific religion with a specific metaphysical history, which this book has laid bare over hundreds of pages, that serially destroys entire civilizations.

The correct response, when a commissar of Scientism tells you *trust the science*, is not to fumble for credentials of your own. The correct response is to name what is actually happening. *That is not science. That is your religion speaking through an institution your faith has captured. I do not share your faith. I am not obligated to defer to your priesthood. And I know the difference between science and prophecy.*

Say it out loud. Say it in public. Say it when it is costly to say it. You will be surprised how many people around you have been waiting, silently, for someone to go first. The technique only works while the citizenry remains convinced that the priesthood's credentials are real credentials reflective of genuine authority. Name the thing, and the spell begins to come apart.

Chapter 20

The Left-Right Paradigm

Esotericism vs. Christianity

"Originalism" is the doctrine of interpretation of language fixed in meaning as a snapshot in time—unchanging, always imbued with the precise intent of he who spoke it at the time he spoke it. You may recognize this terminology as applied to jurisprudence and interpretation of the Constitution, and you may further recognize that it is broadly considered a rightist approach to interpretation, as championed by none other than Clarence Thomas. Leftist approaches to the topic of interpretation tend towards the euphemistic "living" language—meaning that changes over time to be interpreted as most appropriate for the purposes of modernity—and was the preferred framework of the late Justice Ginsburg. This *living* interpreter framework is both fundamentally and definitionally revisionist. What else could one call the revision of meaning to suit one's needs? Revisionism is not merely a concept applicable to language and meaning, but also to history, where it is, as with language, generally the territory of Leftist approaches to understanding.

What, however, is this left-right paradigm? Even in its most appropriate, true, and applicable manifestation, the left-right paradigm is a severely flawed conceptual framework for pegging deep political and ideological movements along a two-dimensional graph. The flaw is simply that two dimensions cannot remotely grapple with the intricacies or nuances of ideology except at the absolute lowest of resolutions.

That said, we can attempt to achieve a more correct version of this left-right paradigm through the adoption of the originalist interpretive framework and the rejection of the revisionist framework. First, let us examine the left-right version of media fancy: that of the Communism-Fascism scale. On this scale the far left is represented by Communism—more precisely, by international Communism in the vein of dialectical materialism—whereas the far right is represented by Fascism. By choosing this scale to elevate, the media invites us to determine where between Communism and Fascism our particular political persuasions fall. Would Progressives be, perhaps, just left of center? Just how close to Fascism are Conservatives, anyhow? More importantly, where did this scale come from in the first place?

As with very nearly every catastrophic idea of the last two centuries, it turns out this graph can be traced to Germany—though at the time it was still known as the Weimar Republic. In the early days of the twentieth century the Fascist Brown-shirts of Weimar took to the streets in a wave of violence that would portend the rise of Hitler. We all learned this as schoolchildren, but what we may not have learned is who they were taking to the streets against, and why. Before the Brown-shirts there were the Red-shirts: a group of committed international Communists who took up the mantle of the Bolsheviks in attempting a revolution in the image of Lenin's and then Stalin's Soviet Union. These revolutionary Red-shirts caused the streets of the Weimar Republic to flow red with blood in political violence against all non-Communists—they were not picky in distinguishing between Fascists, liberals, and conservatives. As with the laws of physics, the laws of society tend to dictate that for every action an equal and opposite reaction, and in the days of the Communist Red-shirts this opposite reaction came from the Fascist Brown-shirts who met the Red-shirts in the streets in pitched battles to put an end to the Communist violence. For those wondering how the German people could have ever sided with the Fascist Nazis, look no further than those who were perceived as worse: the Communists who, unlike the early Fascists, were not discriminating in their violence.

How ever did this Weimar Republic paradigm—that snapshot in time of early-1900s Germany—get transposed onto American politics? The

Communists of the Frankfurt School. As the writing on the wall became clear that it was the Fascists who would claim victory in Weimar, many of the Communists who could do so fled the country. Some fled to America, and some specifically to New York, where they would establish the American version of their Institute for Social Research at Columbia University. One can understand how a bunch of dysfunctional, angry Communist Red-shirt sympathizers who had just suffered defeat to Fascists might have that dichotomy color their thoughts, and thereby transpose this paradigm onto American politics.

Fascism was considered rightist by the Communists because Fascists sought to retain nationalism within their conceptualization of Socialism, whereas the Communists believed that Socialism was a project for the entire world to undertake in unison. Here are some things that Fascism has in common with Communism: Socialism, collectivism, Statism, collective ownership, equity (forced equality of outcome), utopian occult religiosity. Here is the one thing on which Communists and Fascists fundamentally disagree: internationalism versus nationalism.

This left-right, Communist-Fascist paradigm was never meant for America, and it never made any sense here. The American political tradition is not that of the French Revolution, Rousseau, Kant, Hegel, or Marx. The American political tradition was that of the Protestant Reformation, Smith, Locke, and Paine—individualism over collectivism, the rejection of broad state power, let alone state worship, and the devolution of power to the lowest fundamental units: the individual and the family. The American political tradition was never to spar with Communists and Fascists over the retention of national-identity Socialism versus Globalist Socialism. It was to tell both to go to hell, and stay off our lawn.

The American political spectrum runs from ordered liberty to statist tyranny, with the (originalist) Constitution at one end and every form of state worship at the other. That is the only spectrum that has ever made sense on this soil, and the sooner we discard the imported Weimar model and reassert our own, the sooner the enemy loses the framework that keeps us trapped in a false binary between two flavors of European Socialism.

ABANDON CONSERVATISM

What is "conservatism?" It is a serious question these days. It would be impossible to pin down a useful definition simply by incorporating commonalities among those claiming the title conservative.

Broadly, conservatism is the disposition towards the maintenance of existing and historic characteristics of society: politics, ethics, relationships, traditions, customs, mannerisms, and so on. Simply, it is the respect for, and perpetuation of, culture.

If you are paying attention in recent times, there should be several-fold reasons already apparent that this term should now be abandoned. The present and recent state of our public politics and ethics, the dissolution of our traditions and customs, the adoption of perverse mannerisms and practices—these ought not be something anyone otherwise inclined towards the label conservative should rightly want to conserve. It would amount to conserving only the last turn of the dialectical revolution.

It goes much deeper than that. Language is good when it is correct, precise, and suits the purpose of transmitting an idea that is clear in order that we might share an understanding of something. As the concept of conservatism is broadly applicable to the idea of maintaining and perpetuating culture, I must ask you to consider carefully this question: if somebody tells you they are a conservative, and you cannot see their face, you cannot hear their voice to determine accent or inflection, and all you know about them is that they live in America—is it at all clear to you *what culture* they aim to conserve?

Herein lies the problem that points to the insidious nature of what has been done in the name of multiculturalism. The project has been so successful at splintering and balkanizing American culture, and dissolving that which held for generations, that even the language we use to describe our circumstances has become useless at best and dangerously manipulable at worst.

Aristotle mentioned that tyrants import foreign hordes to oppress their own countrymen, because these foreigners make no claim against the tyrant. A people unified in culture and beliefs are the most dangerous thing there is to a tyrant – or to thirty tyrants. Where there is unity, the foe is he who is external to that which is unified. Where there is unity, a tyrant is intolerable. We now have so many built-in fault lines, from many, many years of immigration and importation of ideology, that it is hard to see where a persistent unity might be found.

This is the lens through which all policies facilitating mass migration should be viewed. It is done now, as it has for thousands of years, as a destabilizing mechanism against the citizenry to facilitate the looting and pillaging of the oligarch class. This is the reason that in our late hour we ought to nearly entirely abandon the term conservatism. It is worse than meaningless—it is an opportunity to keep us disunified through confusion and manipulation. We need to build out movements around more precise and useful language than this. We are American traditionalists, originalists, counter-revolutionaries—not "conservatives" of a thing no longer worth conserving. The trope about conservatives conservatively conserving conservatism is too right.

REPUBLICANISM IS NOT LIBERAL

You have probably been conditioned to either love or hate "liberalism." You have probably not been told why, or what the word actually means. The truth is that "liberalism," like "democracy" before it, is not what you have been led to believe.

"Liberalism" entered the lexicon properly around the turn of the nineteenth century. Prior to this, to be "liberal" was, generally, meant as akin to being properly or adequately generous—a virtue. The transition was, it seems, in describing the nature of government in extending freedoms to the people: generosity by rulers in extending freedoms to the people was seen as "liberal." From its roots in the Latin *liberalis*, meaning generous or noble, the word shifted in the late eighteenth century to a popular political call for more self-rule and less monarchy.

Liberalism, then, is not an ideology or worldview. Liberalism is simply a demand for "more freedom." As such, liberalism may represent a reasonable corrective in repressive times and under repressive regimes, pushing toward some greater amount of freedom—more generosity from the rulers. But as a relative term without first principles, liberalism always demands more. It lacks brakes against excess. An ideology in motion tends to stay in motion, and liberalism is the ideology whose only direction of travel is away from whatever arrangement currently exists.

The result is the dialectical ratchet we have already seen applied to other domains, now applied to liberty itself. Each "more freedom" demand erodes a constraint without reversal. Progressive taxation robs the few to redistribute to the many. Sexual "liberation" means the abandonment of family bonds. Even the refusal to return the shopping cart to the stall represents a tiny revolution of "more freedom" for the one at the expense of the many. None of these reverse. The ratchet clicks forward, never back. What was once called license becomes liberty, what was once called liberty becomes duty, and what was once called duty becomes oppression to be liberated from in the next iteration.

Democracy's excesses tie directly to this engine. Democracy as the contest of allied factions battling for spoils—what we have already seen in ancient Athens' *demos* as localized identity groups per Aristotle, leading to tyranny—is enabled and sustained by liberalism's unending "more." The factional spoils system feeds on the redefinition of claims as rights, and the expansion of rights into claims against others. Inherent rights are lost in the fog as the category itself is colonized by liberalism's ratchet. Applied to America's constitutional republic, liberalism overturned order in favor of anarchy: industrial-scale abortion libertinism denies the very nature of inalienable rights; student loan "forgiveness" liberates the one as it chains the many.

While liberalism might be symbiotic with despotism—reducing repression at the margin—it parasitizes virtuous systems. It descends on America's covenant community demanding absolute autonomy, liberation from duties, and excessive "rights" that necessarily deprive others of their rights. Even "classical liberalism," as it claims a sort of time-capsule quality never demanding excess, and stuck in the Enlightenment period ideologically, confuses the Christian metaphysical foundations with claims as being its own—and in so doing it parasitizes the very foundations of its own demands for Goldilocks-liberty. Not too little, not too much. Classical liberalism does not magically come with its own presuppositional basis, and it cannot magically shed the internal logic of its own claimed title: *more freedom*. The moment the Christian substrate is weakened, the ratchet accelerates, and whatever "classical" equilibrium was being claimed dissolves into the only motion the framework actually permits.

This is where the supplanting of "republicanism" by "liberalism" in the American lexicon becomes so important to the story, and so utterly damning. In early America, "liberalism" supplanted the far better term "republicanism"—the Founders' term for tempered freedom and ordered liberty under law and virtue. Republicanism disrupted democracy's factional spoils by prohibiting excess through enumerated powers and enumerated rights. The founders knew that there would be calls for ever-greater freedoms, and they also knew that there was an amount of personal freedom that, if exceeded, would represent a reduction in goodness and Godliness, as the freedom of the one would transgress the many. They built against that excess. Liberalism, by contrast, is built for that excess—it is the structural inversion of republicanism's balance of the one and the many.

The proper term, then, for that which the "classical liberals" often claim they desire—a correct amount of freedom tempered by the reality of duties and obligations—is republicanism. In fact, republicanism is what most really think of when they think "classical liberalism." Classical liberalism's supposed emphasis on limited government, individual rights under law, and free markets was usurped from the Founders' republicanism. Locke's proposed natural rights—life, liberty, and property—influenced *republican* constitutions, not unbridled liberalism or democracy. Classical liberals often cite these, but the term "liberalism" obscures how republicanism's balanced accounting of "the one and the many" prevents the parasitic destruction of the host inherent in liberalism's relentless "more." A reader who identifies with classical liberalism, and who does so because they want ordered liberty rather than ratcheting excess, is really describing a republican. The word they have been handed does not fit what they believe. The word that does fit is the older one, the American one, the one the founders used before the ratchet replaced it.

Reject liberalism's relativism and its demands for "liberty" for some that crush the liberty of others. Reclaim "republicanism" as the preferred term for tempered freedoms and ordered liberty under law and virtue. This is not a matter of pedantry or semantic hair-splitting. It is a matter of restoring the vocabulary that describes the thing you actually want, so that you stop being conscripted—by your own word choice—into the machinery that will eventually dismantle it. Language first. Always language first.

Chapter 21

Identify Friend or Foe

We face many, many threats, but most can be categorized among two categories: the ten-meter target and the hundred-meter target. That ten-meter target is shooting at us from ten meters away, and the hundred-meter target is firing at us from a hundred meters. Who do you suppose is the most immediate threat? It is certainly the ten-meter threat that represents the tactical priority for our fire. The hundred-meter threat, though still a threat, must wait until we have dispatched the nearer enemy. In our political context, the ten-meter threat is the controlled opposition within our own ranks—the managed Right that bleeds off resistance energy. The hundred-meter threat is the Left itself.

In combat operations it is imperative that allies be distinguished readily from the enemy. The failure to account for this necessity on the battlefield results in both catastrophic friendly fire and errors that allow the enemy to infiltrate inside the wire. In kinetic combat this is accomplished through a variety of means, many of which are visual, such as the wearing of a colored arm band or a professional uniform, as well as auditory means, such as a challenge and password, and, more recently, by electronic means as well.

In political warfare, however, this process of identifying friend and foe becomes much more complicated. Where in kinetic combat of a traditional variety most soldiers are uniformed according to their allegiance, and spies are relatively rare, in political warfare the spy is the norm. The tactic was not Lenin's invention, but it was perfected by his propaganda chief, Willi Münzenberg, whose Comintern front-organization apparatus across the 1920s and 1930s pulled tens of thousands of Western liberals, intellectuals, and moderate socialists into service as unwitting auxiliaries of Soviet foreign policy. Münzenberg's own description of how the mechanism worked, given to a closed meeting of his own staff: "These people have the belief they are actually doing this themselves. This belief must be preserved at any price."[29]

This quote was not mere bluster. The Soviet Union, as with many historical esoteric groups, made a habit of utilizing the concept of dialectics—a method of identifying opposites to place into conflict—in order to predict the nature their opposition would take, in order to send out Communists as spies to infiltrate opposition organizations, and even to organize and form new opposition organizations. These opposition organizations under the control of Communist spies—while wearing the uniform of anti-Communist as a disguise—would feign opposition to the Communists while secretly fixing the strategies, tactics, and techniques of resistance below the threshold of victory.

Put simply, Communists habitually form their own "anti-Communist" resistance organizations in order to attract the real social elements of resistance under their own control, which they then redirect towards resistance efforts that are no real threat to the Communists. Think of it as a lightning rod. It is erected to take explosive, natural energy and direct it safely to ground.

With this knowledge we must take a moment to analyze why, under these conditions, the concept of Hanlon's Razor is a defeat mechanism. The very nature of how esotericists operate is by conspiracy. They hide the nature of their allegiances and seek total subversion. Hanlon's Razor says: "never attribute to malice what you can attribute to incompetence." Now, consider a resistance organization formed by Communists in order to attract and negate real resistance elements. Certainly, without an admission of the conspiracy, we would attribute the failure of all such groups to incompetence—and in doing so we would totally miss the very real malicious nature of what is occurring.

The first necessary step is the thorough abandonment of, and taboo-making around, Hanlon's Razor. The second is the adoption of a new heuristic: "the purpose of a thing is what it does."

What does that look like in practice? Simple: we start with the outcomes and the initial assumption that the outcome is what was intended, and work backwards from there. Can an ally lose a battle despite best efforts? Yes, of course. However, if all the ally ever does is lose battles, it would be truly foolish of us to call him an ally in the first place.

When the GOP loses battles serially while perpetually claiming to champion the causes we hold dear, and when they lose despite ostensibly having the numbers to not lose, you must begin with the assumption that they lost because they intended to lose—because they are a controlled opposition.

One major source of this compromise as it presently exists was the neoconservative movement. Modern conservatism was itself midwifed by men steeped in the very esoteric tradition this book traces, and the movement that followed operated purposely as a dialectical pole to the neoliberal movement (the Leftist establishment's corresponding managed consensus). So shot through by spies we could not recognize has the GOP been that it elected multiple neoconservative presidents in the Bushes, as the Left was electing the neoliberal Clintons, as it was agreeable to the elites to alternate between these Left and pseudo-Right figureheads in order to keep government growing, spending levels ever higher, the war machine perpetually busy, and the intelligence community sated with serial sacrifices of the rights of citizens—all according to Plato's recipe.

The Bush family is the case study. Prescott Bush: Skull and Bones 1917, a society that built its Egypto-Doric tomb in 1856 and took as its founding year 322—the year, 322 BCE, celebrating Athens fall to permanent elitist oligarchy. Partner at Brown Brothers Harriman. The Harriman family, through Mary Harriman, founded the Eugenics Record Office at Cold Spring Harbor in 1910. In August 1932 the Third International Congress of Eugenics convened at the American Museum of Natural History in New York, its proceedings dedicated to Mrs. E.H. Harriman. At that same congress, Ernst Rüdin was elected in absentia to the presidency of the International Federation of Eugenic Organizations. The following year Rüdin co-drafted the 1933 Nazi sterilization law. In January 1947 Prescott Bush took the position of treasurer of the Planned Parenthood Federation of America.

George H.W. Bush: Skull and Bones 1948; population control advocacy in Congress; DCI appointment in January 1976 under Ford, framed as repairing institutional morale that Church Committee inquiries into CIA assassinations, domestic surveillance, and MKULTRA had punctured. The George Bush Center for Intelligence is named after him. Thematic echoes of Alice Bailey's theosophical writings on the New Group of World Servers and their points of light (illuminators again, it seems).

George W. Bush: No Child Left Behind paired with Good Start, Grow Smart, framed as federal tracking of "social-emotional development" from birth to age six—upgraded infrastructure for the ethical factory.[30]

The esoteric family business of three generations, with Republican credentials.

If those who represent you are losing, they are losers. They do not get to self-identify as anything else. Treat them like it.

THE CAT CARNIVAL

The Right, in practical politics, looks like a carnival of cats.

We mostly agree on the surface: secure borders, parental rights, biological reality, economic sanity, rejection of woke indoctrination, and the urgent need to roll back the administrative state. We put on a good show. Yet every attempt at sustained coordination, and every reach towards an ultimate victory, collapses into infighting, purity spirals, or silent defection the moment the tactical overlap ends.

This is not simply a personnel problem. It is a metaphysical one.

The Right is "herding cats" because our coalition is built on a negative wartime vision—anti-Communism—rather than a positive, transcendent first principle. Libertarians, Burkean traditionalists, civic nationalists, constitutional originalists, and various stripes of Christians all converge on immediate threats but diverge radically on *why* those threats matter and *what* ultimate order we are defending. Pragmatic politics—the only kind rewarded under democratic incentives—treats that divergence as radioactive. Foundational ethics become taboo, as when they are referenced the result is a breakout skirmish between libertarian postmodern relativists, libertine liberationists, various stripes of Aristotelians and Thomists, abstract-allergic pragmatists, and radical dispensationalists. The result is fatal for final victory.

DIVERGENT FIRST PRINCIPLES

The libertarian starts from socially negotiated individual rights—often ethnically or genetically deterministic. The traditionalist starts from inherited custom and traditions of social order—a second-order "first" principle raising up process itself as the good. The liberal starts from a presupposed but nameless "Nature's God," smuggling in more Greek than Biblical metaphysics. The civic constitutionalist starts pragmatically from parchment and procedure—a third-order "first" principle. And the consistent Christian starts from a transcendent ethic, sphere sovereignty, and a standard for authority that precedes and constrains all human government—the only first principle among these that does not ultimately rest on man's own authority or discernment.

You can see from even a cursory study of parliamentary or legislative review how these various dispositions play out. The civic-first conservative clings to procedure and decorum as his people suffer a bitter and catastrophic defeat. The liberal places one foot on the pillar of individual rights and another on the pillar of pluralism and winds up doing a split that would make a Belgian martial-arts action hero blush. The modern traditionalist appreciates the fruits of the revolution up through gay marriage and internet pornography but finally stepped off the wagon upon the literal castration of children en masse.

You are familiar with these archetypes of failure.

These are not minor emphases. They are irreconcilable presuppositions about reality, authority, and the good. The overlap on policy is real but both temporary and incapable of striking a winning blow in the wider war—a wartime coalition against a common existential foe capable only of managing decline. Remove the immediate threat and the coalition dissolves, because there is no shared metaphysic to hold it.

The Left suffers no such fracture. Their unity flows from a coherent, if demonic, eschatology: History as alchemical process—*solve et coagula*—*dissolve and reconstitute*—man as self-creator, and the vanguard elite wielding noble lies in service of the man-made Eden. Their first principles are presuppositionally locked and synchronized across the breadth of Leftist theory in precisely a manner that benefits strategy and tactics – a sort of memetic gain-of-function applied to ethics. That is why they coordinate across decades and institutions while we fracture over Twitter threads. The esoteric nature of their strategy is why they can write it down for the world to see yet it is almost never properly recognized.

The Left will always attack at least one ideological layer deeper than we are prepared to defend. Our coalition is assembled at the policy level—agreement on what government should do or not do in a given circumstance. Below that, at the ethical foundations of those positions, the coalition finds divergence rather than bedrock. Deeper still, at the metaphysical level—*what is a person, what is the basis of rights, what does authority derive from*—the divergence becomes fracture. The theoretical libertarian and the Christian hold different answers. The civic constitutionalist and the traditionalist hold different answers. Under normal political conditions those differences are managed. Under presuppositional attack they become the fault lines the Left drives its wedge into rather than a foundation capable of bearing weight.

The corollary is equally neglected: attacking the Left's policy positions (and their hypocrisy) does not destabilize it, because the unified metaphysical foundation holds regardless of policy-level defeats. Conservative policy victories are consistently reversed because the cultural and institutional infrastructure the Left's presuppositional unity sustains continues operating against the conservative position throughout the period of victory—and when political winds shift, the position collapses because it was never defended at the level where the real war is fought. We win battles. They fight civilizational, generational wars.

The asymmetry cuts in both directions, and the second cut is the one most often missed. The Left attacks at the presuppositional level because our unity lies several layers higher in policy. Their own presuppositions, being socially constructed and socially affirmed, are resistant to the same kind of presuppositional attack from the Right. You cannot undermine a socially constructed foundation the same way you undermine a transcendent one—the transcendent foundation stands or falls on its correspondence with reality and by faith, which means it can be attacked by severing that correspondence through confusion and mystification (scientization of metaphysical claims) or the taboo-making of faith-based claims. The socially constructed foundation stands or falls on social affirmation or stigmatization, which means it can only be undermined by disrupting the affirmation infrastructure and taboo-making—the institutional, cultural, and media apparatus' that produces and maintains the consensus. This is why the Right's argumentative victories are sterile: defeating a Leftist argument on its merits does nothing to the social-affirmation machinery that sustains the Leftist's presuppositions. And this is why the counter-offensive must target the machinery, not the arguments—the institutions, the language, the social enforcement mechanisms—because the foundation we are attacking is not rational but social, and it must be attacked where it actually lives: social taboo-making.

THE ATOMIZATION MACHINE

Democratic politics—which the republic was deliberately *not*—rewards the lowest common denominator and forces faction-building among disparate groups. Any candidate, organization, or movement that insists on first principles is accused of "dividing the Right." Foundational ethics are declared divisive, theological, or not politically viable.

Without a transcendent anchor, people retreat into private piety, consumptive hobbies, or black-pilled isolation. No covenant communities form. We remain a collection of consumers with overlapping grievances, filling our free time with sportsball and unreality TV, not *a people*.

When the cost arrives—doxxing, job loss, legal persecution, or worse—the atomized individual calculates utility and defects. The Left's false immanent transcendence—History, Equity, the Revolution—routinely produces suicidal and homicidal commitment. Our pragmatic substitute produces little of even a personal capacity for missing a meal to secure a victory.

This is a structural disadvantage that produces further controlled opposition mechanics in politics, as anybody asserting a logical and correct chain of reason beginning from a foundation of faith and presuppositions necessarily runs into the power-centers and seats of the GOP that are filled by those who could only achieve their position in the hierarchy by pragmatic and utilitarian maneuvering and alliance building. These are the precise sorts of persons most likely to be hostile to transcendent claims and paradigm change.

Anti-Communism as Glue

The reality of any on-the-ground political effort to the right of Mao tends to be plagued by varied ideologies, apathies, good-perfect-enemy-ism, anarchic utopian dreams, zealous libertarian evangelism, and pathetic decorum-ism. As a result, it tends to be the moderates—representing a third-way-ism conducive to sabotage of rightist cultural goals—who drive agenda.

We must build out a coalition that can represent both the largest representative bloc on the Right and also be the most intolerant—of any ideas to the Left—group in the room, in order to begin to shift policy rightward beyond the threshold of defeat by the modern Left. This coalition must hold firm in order to defeat, first, the GOPe RINOs, and second, the Left. That order is significant, as the Left cannot be successfully engaged by the Right until their blockers, the RINOs, are defeated, as spies in your own camp will always upset the battle on the open field.

However, to coalition-build on the Right is to herd cats. Somebody could show up, suggest limiting the government to the exact dimensions authorized by the Constitution and not one iota more, and he would lose half the room for being too radically anti-government and another third for being a statist. There is, seemingly, no way to present a positive, uniting vision around which the Right might unite except in the vaguest, most nebulously superficial appeals to "freedom."

If we cannot reasonably advance a positive vision to unite rightists against those who want to defeat us, we must, as an immediate response to our conditions, advance a *negative vision* to unite rightists and make them want to win. A negative vision is akin to a negative right: it means to advance a vision *against* something in order to be free of it, rather than *for* something to have it. The thing that must unite us, and that we must defeat, is Communism—and it has already arrived in America. It is, in fact, already the foremost operating principle of the federal government, and more and more of state governments also.

Thus anti-Communism as a negative vision becomes the future and hope of the Right in our present fight, that which has a victory condition of *live to fight another day*, and of the coalition we must now build. This is the common strand that unites us for the very simple reason that if it does not, and we fail in our task, it will destroy us—each and every one of us. We must pursue this coalition along the paradigm of political warfare, as, through no choice of our own, we are not currently in peacetime. This is a wartime doctrine, though conservative does not nearly do it justice. We are no longer looking to conserve. It just cannot motivate us. We are here for a refounding, a remoralization, and a political counter-revolution. Of course, this ought to be accompanied by a return to the faith tradition that made America great in the first place – only such a foundation can secure lasting victory.

Be an anti-Communist.

Chapter 22

Christian Nationalism

Anti-Communism holds the wartime coalition together, but a negative vision is a bridge, not a destination. The transcendent ethic is the only firm foundation on which a lasting order can be built—anti-Communism merely unites the democratic factions (a necessary evil) long enough to get us there. There are many people who want you to fear the idea that America's founding metaphysics are Christian. They promote the dialectical political warfare operation known as "Christian Nationalism."

The term "Christian Nationalism" is generally undefined and utilized as a "floating signifier." This is a political warfare concept where a label with a nebulous definition is slandered and coded as evil—placed outside the Overton Window as taboo—in order to apply it to any variety of political opponents at opportune times to negate their political will. They have done the same thing with the word "racist," where they changed the understood, reasonable definition of color-based hatreds into something only definable, and therefore only operational, by and for Leftist "experts." The mechanism is identical: create a term sufficiently vague that it can be affixed to anyone who threatens the revolution, sufficiently terrifying that the accusation alone produces social death, and sufficiently undefined that no defense against it is possible because the goalposts are never fixed. This operation is being run by the Democratic Party and their media apparatchiks. It is joined by some combination of opportunistic Christian Rightists (wisely or not) seizing the moment to build support behind their particular ideas, and also by bad-actor controlled opposition players bolstering the Leftist operation from inside the Right. Make no mistake: the origin and purpose of the "Christian Nationalism" label is a Leftist operation, and the sheer volume of Left-aligned media coverage invoking the term in recent years tells you everything you need to know about where it comes from.

This is the same dialectical weapon we have traced throughout this book—the *aufheben* of language. "Christian Nationalism" is not a description of a coherent political movement. It is a spell—and we know what spells are. Those who propagate it are wizards. Those paralyzed by the accusation are spellbound. And those who see through it are based. It is designed to make the articulation of the positive vision we just discussed—a return to Constitutional principles grounded in the transcendent ethic on which America was actually founded—unspeakable. It is designed to ensure that the only permissible coalition glue on the Right remains the negative vision of anti-Communism, because the moment anyone attempts to articulate what we are *for* rather than merely what we are *against*, the floating signifier descends and the speaker is cast out.

These political warfare operators want you to believe that the future will be some sort of dystopia of forcible conversions, slave-wives in weird robes, wars of fire-and-maneuver between sects, and on and on towards tyranny. Nonsense.

Some have voluntarily adopted the term "Christian Nationalism." Among them are those who are simply both Christians and nationalists, some are Theonomists, Postmillennialists, and other flavors of theologically informed political activists, some are would-be oligarchs themselves hoping to ride a revival wave to power, and others have adopted the term as enemies of the Right in order to assist the Left in making the term toxic. There is not, at present, anything approaching consensus within Christian America to transform American government into a Christian theocracy of the hard-establishment, State-Church type, and most Christians (including this one) would fight tooth and claw against any effort at State-Church sectarian establishment. After all, that is what the Puritans were running away from. What the vast majority want is simply a return to Constitutional principles and public—read: government—respect for their religion, traditions, and ethics – and a government responsive to the things that Christians believe the government ought to do, such as wielding the sword against evil, and leaving parents to raise up their children. In other words, Christians generally just want government to stay in its lane.

THE MYTH OF NEUTRALITY

The deeper problem is the assumption of neutrality that the "Christian Nationalism" smear exploits. Those most susceptible to the smear—often the liberal contingent within the Right coalition—operate from a presupposition that the public square can and should be religiously neutral. This belief in neutrality causes them to have something akin to an allergic reaction to any assertion of Christian metaphysics in public life, sensitized by the political warfare operation, and because they fundamentally do not view Christianity as *neutral*. So, the ideas of faithful Christians, even though entirely unrelated to the caricature of theocratic tyranny in pop culture, must be vigorously opposed according to this ideology of secular neutrality.

But neutrality has never existed in America, and it cannot truly exist anywhere. It has been taken for granted that American metaphysics are a human universal when in truth they are absolutely not. The Trojans killed their disabled infants in a eugenics program by tossing them from cliffs. Romans fed people to lions for entertainment. Communists murdered tens of millions for being "enemies of the people," largely through purposeful starvation. All these things could be classified under the "free exercise of religion" when placed in their broader context, as they follow from religious convictions of those societies, but they are not to be practiced in America under penalty of law. There is no right to practice, within America, those foreign religious practices so antithetical and subversive to the American metaphysic that they present a threat to it.

America was never *neutral* in the application of its presuppositions and law. It is not neutral now that the foundational metaphysics of America have become Marxian. The current regime punishes its enemies. It always has. The question has never been whether metaphysical presuppositions will govern public life—they always do. The question is *which* presuppositions.

A nation grounded in Christian metaphysics can withstand nonbelievers who, nonetheless, carry on with compliance to the basic laws rooted in that metaphysic: though shall not murder; thou shall not steal. But a nation adrift on the sea of relativism that has achieved the critical mass necessary to delegitimize the whole of the law will never find any option but submission to the zeitgeist – the *world spirit*. There is no way forward without, once more, recognizing the Christian basis of the American founding, and there is no reason to fear tyranny in so doing rightly—but there is every reason to fear tyranny if we do not.

WHY FREEDOM REQUIRES THE TRANSCENDENT

It is only under the paradigm of the Christian metaphysic that freedom is even possible. This is the case because it is only this particular set of metaphysical presuppositions that affirmatively lays out the good, transcendent ethic on which America was founded while simultaneously placing many elements of authority *outside* of the authority of the civil government. This *is* liberty.

The American political tradition recognizes that there are multiple spheres of governance, with the civil government being only one—others include the family and the Church—each with a limited range of authority, yet all institutions falling under the sovereign authority of God. It is not the job of civil government to enforce divine authority outside of the narrow prescription of authority delegated to it. It wields the sword, it does not coerce theological doctrine. The very concept of limited government depends on there being an authority *above* government that constrains it. Remove the transcendent, and there is no principled limit to state power—only the contingent, shifting limits of social negotiation, which the dialecticians will always win to their own uses.

Freedom is not possible under any other paradigm because, as all prominent, right-thinking theologians and philosophers have noted from Nietzsche to Augustine, mankind requires a transcendent ethic. Why should anybody do anything you or I say if all we have to appeal to is our own authority? Who the hell am I to lay down my own ethic? There are, in the end, only three types of ethics: the individually formulated, the socially mediated, and the transcendent. The individually formulated rests on no authority but your own—which is to say, none at all, and is therefore an impossible operating basis for a society. Every person cannot possibly lay down their own ethic if you expect to have an ascendent culture. The socially mediated rests on consensus—which is to say, on whoever controls the consensus-making machinery. Only the transcendent rests on an authority that no man and no state can override, which is precisely the foundation that the American Constitution rests on. Why would anybody else follow such a thing as an individually asserted ethic? And if the ethic is merely socially constructed—we have already seen where that leads. It leads to the Leftist feedback loop, the paramoral framework, the pseudoreality, and, ultimately, the gulag.

The "Christian Nationalism" smear exists precisely to prevent you from thinking this through. It is a spell—and now you know how to break it. Recognize the floating signifier for what it is. Refuse the premise of neutrality. And articulate, without apology, that the transcendent ethic is not the threat to liberty but its only possible foundation. The Left depends on you not recognizing the zealous religiosity of their own claim to legitimacy and rule.

What remains now is the fight itself—the practical counter-offensive. How do you break a spell? How do you smash a pseudoreality? How do you make the truth a weapon so sharp that the lies cannot survive contact with it? That is where we go next.

Chapter 23

Smashing Pseudoreality

Breaking the Spells

Reality truly exists.

Now, if you have been keeping up you will know that this is actually an article of faith: a presupposition about a fundamental thing. But as it is the basis of all action, it is not in any way worth debating. Seriously, it just is not worth debating with people who suggests we are a simulation, because nobody who says that actually acts like it and they therefore do not care about truthfulness – even with themselves. So, we take it on faith and we move forward. But what logic follows from "reality truly exists"?

First, we take it that reality is objective if it really exists. It is independent of our minds. It is *not* subjective. It is what it is—nothing less and nothing more, regardless of our perception. Our attempts to describe reality are, however, necessarily either less or more, as they are imperfect. We are subject first to the paradigm of perspective: we are limited in our senses. We also suffer imperfect reason. We make mistakes. As a result, every attempt to describe reality will too suffer from these defects. It is not our lot to know, with perfect fidelity, this objective world. Not in this life anyway.

So then, if a perfect knowledge is out of our grasp, what then should we grasp at? The answer, rather obviously, is a *more* perfect knowledge and understanding of things.

Every attempt to describe reality will be flawed, but each variation will be uniquely flawed. These unique flaws will, necessarily, render of any two competing visions one that is more correct and one less correct—even if only in the slightest, nearly imperceptible manner.

Another way to view this is that because reality is objective there is *always* a correct answer—that which represents the objective world with perfect fidelity. As such, any two non-identical descriptions of reality, both being wrong by degree according to our own imperfections, must be wrong by a varying and different degree. One is always more right. Because they are different, they are *never* equal.

This same analysis can be applied to any first principles of faith beyond that of an objective reality. So long as the first principles themselves are identical, the logic that flows from them—forming specific answers from general rules—will render of any two views one more and one less correct. Again, because they are different, they are never, ever equal.

This logic, applied to a people holding a common first principle, necessarily leads to the conclusion that, because there is always a right answer—even if unobtainable in practice—and because two dissimilar wrong answers are never equally wrong, relativity has not a leg to stand on in arguing for equal treatment of ideas, worldviews, cultures, or descriptions of reality.

Of any two worldviews, rendered down to their particulars and compared accordingly, there is always one that is of greater fidelity to objective reality or to an objective good.

Apologies for the necessary foray into a confusing topic, but you need this foundation more than you yet understand. This argument is a relativity killer. Postmodernism has nowhere to hide but in a reversion to nihilism. Relativity cannot possibly be true once we accept the premise that objective reality exists and apply logic to it. This argument effectively crushes any appeals to cultural or moral relativism. You need this argument in your quiver.

Truth as a Sword

We are at the tail end, and final push, of a century-long political warfare effort and revolution against the American founding and Anglo-Saxon political tradition established in the land. It appears that the most potent psychological tool of the opposition is the exploitation of agreeableness. We do not want to think of ourselves as bad or evil and will make the choice to be discriminating with language to avoid cognitive dissonance.

This often comes in the form of white lies—apparently minor untruths told to spare the feelings of another. The opposition takes advantage of this by aggressively asserting emotional arguments based on a paramoral framework. This paramoral framework is a largely internally consistent construct that follows from the pseudoreal (false) conceptualization of the world the opposition holds as a worldview.

In other words, the Left does not live or operate in reality. They live in a false pseudoreality with concerns that tend not to be totally aligned with reality—Covid risk, climate change doomsaying, transgender ideology—and are fundamentally religious in nature. This pseudoreality produces moral conclusions that, because it is applied in pseudoreality, is not in accordance with reality.

However, it is simply human nature that when a person becomes emotionally upset about something, others tend to assume that the thing causing the emotional disturbance is real, and not fake. They give the distressed person the benefit of the doubt and begin working to alleviate their distress. It is through such emotional assertions of paramorality that the Left makes people hostage to, or indoctrinates them into, pseudoreality. Perhaps the most obvious single instance of this was then-Senator Jeff Flake reversing his vote after being yelled at by a hysterical feminist activist with pseudoreal concerns—rape culture—in an elevator. This is the mechanism by which theater-kids inflict their tyranny.

It is possible to immunize people against paramoral assertions, and perhaps even begin to rescue hostages from pseudoreality, by unapologetically reasserting real morality and polarizing paramoral assertions as taboo. This should be pursued along similar information warfare lines that the Left employs: fix it through repetition, polarize it to encourage enforcement of the Overton Window to force it to the outside.

REMORALIZATION

Marcuse described how he would go about neutering the opposition such that the revolution could be completed relatively unopposed: through the colonization of the oppositional mind with cultural taboos that would effect a self-imposed pre-censorship of conservative thought. Eventually, he thought, it would become so discomforting to even think the strategies and words necessary to oppose the Marxists that the opposition would trip all over themselves coming up with indirect and ineffectual strategy, and eventually settle for the revolutionary position. He was largely right. This is how conservatism has come to conserve nothing at all: self-enforced censorship. Taboo is the most powerful force in the social universe. We have lost the ability to speak uncomfortable truths to the spirit of the age.

Consider how difficult it would be to tell a crowd of unknowns that "trans men are women." This is a biological reality. It is in accordance with everything we know to be true, yet many of us cannot summon a confident voice to utter it. It is these cultural taboos that are infecting our minds. We must learn to assert truth at all times to defeat this, both on a personal and on a cultural level. We must steel ourselves.

The actual solution is far simpler than magical alchemy, and alchemy can never achieve anything real. If it is true that we come to believe the things that we say, and that we write—and I believe we do—then remoralization is simply the process of speaking truth, writing truth, and believing it. It means that we come to believe what we act like we believe. To this end, I would encourage you to, quite literally, stand in front of a mirror and speak these prohibited truths aloud.

It will be uncomfortable. You have been trained that pain will follow as these unutterable things leave your lips. It is worth every bit of it and more. As you speak, check your posture, your projection, and your eye contact with yourself. Stand tall, hold your shoulders back, and permit yourself to tell yourself the truth without a single ounce of trepidation. Keep doing it until it becomes natural. Likewise, take a notepad, a pen, and write it down. Do it several times, then several times more. Repeat this process with each new forbidden truth that you uncover. Repeat this process until the pseudoreality melts away, you see things as they truly are, and you rediscover your moral capacity to get mad about being lied to. You ought to be mad about being lied to, and about the damage the lies are doing to the most vulnerable.

This anger becomes something you cannot help but to feel when confronted with a demand to conform to the pseudoreal. This righteous anger enacted in the world becomes the aesthetic by which others begin to question their own false ideological prison. It begins to polarize the lies and shift the Overton Window. Once the Overton Window comes to exclude the pseudoreal item, the process becomes a cascading, negative feedback mechanism by which culture begins to self-correct. This is how we win.

Currently yet another item is being actively tabooed before our eyes in real time: the burgeoning anti-white racism in America. We have no problems calling out anti-black racism. We regularly comment on the state of anti-Asian racism in America. But we are told we cannot mention that some ideology, or practice, or incident is anti-white.

The only consistent and moral position to hold against a white racial consciousness is to also be against black, or indeed any racial consciousness. It is, in fact, this glaring double standard among those seeking to quash any mention of anti-white racism that truly serves to create the type of backlash against hypocrisy that could see a movement for white racial consciousness gain further traction. I do not particularly wish to see this. I believe the proper Christian view is that *race* is not even the correct term for what is being described, and I cannot see a proper American ethnogenesis being anything but a multi-color one given the reality of several hundred years of history on these lands. Of course, if the enemies have their way we might just get a color-Balkanization with localized ethnogenesis leading to a semi-perpetual state of racial warfare. The oligarchs would not mind that at all.

The refusal to call out anti-white racism is an example of Marcuse's pre-censorship of words that threaten Leftism, as calling things by their proper name is at the heart of our overarching struggle. The pseudoreality cannot abide assertions of reality that do not accord with its dogma. So speak the truth. Do not self-censor. Speak truth with your chin up and your shoulders back. Speak it to yourself in a mirror until you can say it confidently. Speak truth that those who malign you for speaking truth are doing great evil. Say it out loud when it matters. Assert real morality and reclaim your ability to feel and project righteous anger. Get mad when you should, and let them know about it. Let people see your justified anger and they will feel it too, because real justice is contagious. Speak truth into the world until reality is reasserted—and we might just win this thing.

ON AGENCY

Before we proceed to the next major topic, we must stop and name something structural about who you are, and what you are responsible for, within the counter-revolutionary project. Everything in this chapter to this point has named the what and the why. What follows names the *you*.

Start with a proper definition of agency—the capacity for intentional action, undergirded in the Christian theological tradition from which American jurisprudence descends. Agency has several components: responsibility, capability, intentionality, and freedom from coercion. A person who possesses these is said to be a moral agent in the full sense of the term, and is answerable for everything evil they do and every good they decline to do.

Now draw the distinction our legal system has almost entirely lost the capacity to draw: between *diminished* agency and *abdicated* agency. Diminished agency is the condition of the small child flailing with a wayward knife, or the adult of profoundly reduced capacity. These persons lack such a degree of agency through no fault of their own, and legal system has always, rightly, treated them as bearing reduced liability. Abdicated agency is something else entirely. It is the condition of the adult who has chosen ignorance, allowed themselves to come under the spell of another, chosen to abandon the exercise of the agency they should be capable of wielding. These persons bear the responsibility for their actions and inactions. Allowing yourself to come under the spell of another is no excuse. Ignorance is no excuse. Our present system of injustice fails entirely to differentiate between genuinely diminished and abdicated agency, and in so failing it fails to uphold justice against the overwhelming majority of the populace who have surrendered the exercise of their own moral capacity, being given over to depravity in the process.

This matters because it lands on you, the reader. If you are reading this book, you are probably not suffering from diminished agency. You are a moral agent, answerable to yourself, your family, your posterity, your ancestors, and your God for the exercise of that agency. And the foundational claim of this section is the one our culture has most thoroughly suppressed: *sin is not merely the wicked acts one commits. It is also every good and proper thing one fails to do.* If you read this book, agree with it in substance, and then go home and do nothing, you have not escaped responsibility. You have exercised your agency toward the abdication of it.

We are, as a result, a society of friendly cowards. We were raised to be conflict-averse. We were taught that being *nice* was among the highest virtues. We were lied to. Niceness is not a virtue. It is the absence of a virtue. All that is required to achieve the false virtue of being nice is to be averse to conflict, and all that is required to avoid conflict is to allow evil to win uncontested. The cure is good men, not nice guys. The prophylactic is strong social institutions upholding properly ordered virtues that are willing to exclude, both physically and by taboo, the subversives. And the precondition for those institutions is a population of individuals who have recovered the agency they abdicated.

Our tongues have lost the sharpness of edge that represents the first sword in defense of goodness. It is the sword we must recover, else the material sword of government will be called upon to do work the tongue should have done first. *Open rebuke is better than secret love*, the Proverb says. *Faithful are the wounds of a friend; but the kisses of an enemy are deceitful.* This is a Christian foundation for what the preceding section has called taboo-making.

The personal protocol is simple and uncomfortable. There is no purely political solution to what ails us. There cannot be a political solution until there is a social solution for our politics. And the social solution is you, multiplied by thousands, refusing to tolerate the affect of evil in those around you, and *acting like you hate it*. The protocol proceeds in stages. First, identify the single moral failing in the present culture that irks you most—the one you cannot stop noticing. Perhaps it is the medical mutilation of children under the banner of gender-affirming care. Perhaps it is the normalization of casual blasphemy as the enemy misrepresents the Word of God, twisting it as Satan did. Perhaps it is the alignment of otherwise decent people with democratic faction, advancing their own interest in the spoils of theft over the future of America. Whatever it is for you, pick it. Second, spend time privately invoking disdain and revulsion toward it—several times a day, with intention—until your reaction to it becomes reflexive rather than suppressed. Third, when the circumstance arises, deliver the rebuke. Not a mealy-mouthed concession; not a qualified demurral. Immediate, animated, sharp enough to surprise the offender and induce self-reflection. Fourth, if the rebuke is dismissed, escalate—turn the outrage up and make sure the failure was not in your meekness. Fifth, if escalation also fails, adjust: perhaps the item was too obscure, too minor, or too major to be carried at this moment. Select a new target and begin again.

A word on scale. An ethically intact population of a more virtuous era would experience our present circumstances as a Weimar-America. The entirety of our present circumstances any serious moralist of yesteryear would find revolting. If you take equally maximal issue with every matter before us you will have little impact and you will rapidly wear down—becoming so demoralized that you might just lie down and die. Take the largest bite you can chew and swallow. If it feels small, it is not. *How do you eat an elephant? One bite at a time.*

The net effect of thousands of individuals undertaking this protocol across the varied moral failures in our midst is remoralization at population scale—not through deep moral philosophy delivered from a podium in a dusty lecture hall, but through the demonstrated enactment of an ethic publicly. That is how most people learn an ethic: not by logical argumentation, but by demonstration. Make the thing shameful, and the shameful thing will recede. Make it unshameful, and it will flourish. The Left has understood this for a century. We have not. This is the correction.

Chapter 24

✦ꜛ⊶────•••────⊷ꜛ✦

THEORY OF MIND

REASONING WITH THE WALL

That is, a working model for understanding how the Leftist mind operates, and why reasoned argument fails against it.

You have likely experienced the following: you present a Leftist with a well-reasoned, evidence-based argument. You defeat their position thoroughly. And then, without a moment's pause, they switch to an entirely different argument that flatly contradicts their first. Consistency is not required. You have not won anything. You have merely swiped at a vapid vapor.

This is not stupidity. It is the absence of the substrate from which consistent reasoning would proceed.

Conservatives tend to operate from a basis of ethics, and that ethical basis is typically transcendent—rooted in something above, beyond, and fundamental to the individual, the society, and the moment. Leftists tend to operate from shallow presuppositions: utilitarian, practically oriented, concerned with outcomes as defined by whatever the current social and strategic consensus holds to be desirable. Where the Leftist ethical basis is contemplated and well-formed—and it sometimes is—it is socially constructed and legitimized, not transcendent but immanent. It stands on the shifting sand of whatever the group currently affirms.

This is the foundational asymmetry. Reason does not produce ethics; it proceeds *from* ethics. Ethics are the first principle—the thing that exists before reason and informs experience. They do not exactly exist as "self-evident," as if holding up a speculum to ones own heart will reveal them with fidelity to the mind. They cannot be properly legitimized by an appeal to "common sense." As we established in our treatment of practical ethics, there are only three methods of ethical formation: assertion on one's own authority (which rests on the authority of the person, which is to say next to none), social mediation (which is inherently relativistic and therefore not truly an ethic at all, but an anti-ethic), and the transcendent (which alone provides an ideal against which actions can be measured). The Leftist operates, at best, from the second. The Right, when consistent, operates from the third.

Because the Leftist's ethical substrate is shallow, shifting, or absent, the reasoned argument has nothing stable to land on. Language for them is not a tool to describe reality; it is, per the alchemical tradition from which their entire project descends, a weapon to change it. You cannot argue someone out of a position they did not argue themselves into, but that was felt into. When the position rests not on reason but on social affirmation, emotionalism and shallow utility, your reason is simply irrelevant to the architecture of their belief.

THE PERSISTENCE OF CONSCIENCE

And yet something persists beneath the shallow presuppositions. The Leftist who operates against moral reality still *feels* it, even if they cannot name it. The moral law is written on every heart. The conscience registers violations of moral reality whether or not the person acknowledges the source of that reality.

For the reader who needs an account that does not rest on theological premise, the behavioral evidence makes the case. A purely social-constructivist account predicts that discomfort diminishes as social reinforcement of the in-group ethic increases—the more thoroughly embedded in an affirming ideological community, the less guilt the member should feel. The observable pattern runs precisely opposite. The doubling-down, the nihilistic self-injury, the intensifying need for social affirmation, the escalating suppression mechanisms—these deepen with ideological commitment rather than ease. The feedback loop tightens as the social endorsement grows. A model of suppressed conscience predicts exactly this: the harder you press against a functioning moral faculty, the harder it presses back, and the more energy must be expended in the pressing.

The secular materialist will object that cognitive dissonance theory explains the same data without requiring a transcendent moral faculty. The objection does not hold. Cognitive dissonance theory is itself a secular, incomplete reframing of the process inherent to conscience—it describes the symptom only. The theory predicts that dissonance diminishes as the contradiction is resolved through group affirmation and the adoption of a consistent in-group ethic. A person deeply embedded in an affirming ideological community should, under this model, experience decreasing discomfort as the community validates their beliefs. The observable pattern runs precisely opposite—and the in-group's tyrannical need to cancel, excise, and punish any pangs of conscience surfacing among its members is itself demonstrative of the unreality of socially constructed ethics. A social ethic that was actually functional, and foundational to the subject, would not require a perpetual suppression apparatus directed at its own adherents. The very acts of tyranny used to maintain the social construction point beyond the group itself—to a higher authority than the group consensus, one the group did not intend to point to, that must be the impetus for the escalating totalizing suppression and perpetual revolution of shifting targets. The cancel machinery is not just aimed outward at the enemy. It is aimed inward at the faithful. That fact alone testifies that something deeper than cognitive dissonance is at work.

Being given over is typically a slow process—progressive callousing rather than sudden conversion. The conscience does not extinguish cleanly. It protests, then more faintly, then requires greater stimulus to register at all. The person on that path experiences it as increasing self-assurance—the framework settling, the arguments feeling more natural—even as the underlying distress expresses itself in self-injury, nihilism, and an appetite for external affirmation that grows rather than satisfies. This is visible from outside. For those who have walked it and returned, it is recognizable from within. This is observable: watch the discomfort, the agitation, the need to constantly reaffirm their position through social ritual. People at peace with their convictions do not behave this way.

However, this persistence is not without limit. The conscience can be calloused. A person can be given over to depravity such that they take pleasure in evil—and in the Christian tradition, this would be understood as having been given over to possession—the searing of the conscience past the point of function. This calloused state represents the far end of the spectrum, not likely the majority of those who are Leftist-oriented. Most are somewhere on the continuum between a functioning conscience they cannot properly process and being given over completely.

For the majority—those whose conscience is still active but whose ethical framework is shallow—the experience is one of persistent, low-grade guilt and discomfort that they cannot identify or resolve. The transcendent ethical framework provides mechanisms for processing guilt: conviction, repentance, forgiveness, restoration in the covenant community. The socially constructed framework provides none of these. There is no one to repent to except in self-criticism of the Maoist sort, no fixed standard against which to measure the offense, no mechanism of forgiveness that resolves the underlying violation, and little assurance an honest moment will not be utilize by an ally to grandstand to increase their own social standing. The guilt therefore accumulates as unprocessed cognitive dissonance—a chronic psychic distress the person cannot name and cannot escape through the resources available within their worldview.

The Social Analgesic

Enter the thought-stopping cliche.

The bumper sticker. The yard sign. The chant. The social media declaration. The protest slogan. These are not arguments, and they often are entirely bereft of reason. They are sacraments of the socially constructed ethic. They provide temporary absolution through group affirmation: "I said the right thing, the group affirmed me, therefore I am good." The relief is observable in real time—watch what happens at a rally when the cliche lands and the crowd affirms. Watch the physical relaxation, the smiles, the sense of belonging. This is a liturgical moment.

But because the absolution is socially constructed rather than transcendent, it does not actually resolve the underlying guilt. It only suppresses it. The dose must be constantly re-administered. This is part of why Leftist political identity is so totalizing—it consumes the whole person because the maintenance regimen demands it.

This is where the weaponized concept of "empathy"—which we examined in detail earlier—does its most insidious work. "Have empathy" is not a request for compassion. Sympathy would accomplish that. It is a demand to project the oppressor-oppressed framework onto a situation and take the correct side. It functions as one of the most potent thought-stopping cliches in the system because it exploits the conscience's real capacity for genuine sympathy—that suffering-with that the conscience produces—and redirects it into the paramoral framework of overthrow of hierarchy. You feel the tug of real compassion, because the conscience is real and functioning. But the cliche of "empathy" channels that compassion into adopting the Leftist standpoint rather than exercising independent moral judgment from a grounded position, while that grounded position of sympathy is stigmatized as "uncaring."

THE COMPARATIVE MORAL IMPERATIVE

There is a further structural necessity built into this system that drives it toward perpetual escalation.

Because the Leftist moral paradigm is relativistic, goodness is not measured against a transcendent ideal but only in comparison to the designated enemy. There is no fixed standard against which they can measure themselves and be found good. The only way to be "good" in a relativistic moral system is to be *better than someone else*—and specifically, to be better than the designated enemy. Their goodness exists only as a delta between themselves and the people they oppose.

This has an inexorable escalation logic. If your moral status depends entirely on the gap between you and your enemy, and if your conscience is producing guilt that your shallow framework cannot process, you have two options: become genuinely better (which requires the transcendent framework you do not have without conversion) or make your enemy *worse*. The second option is the only one available within the systems logic.

So "conservative" becomes "reactionary" becomes "fascist" becomes "Nazi" becomes "existential threat to democracy." Each escalation is not primarily about describing the Right accurately. It is about maintaining the moral delta that constitutes the Leftist's entire claim to goodness. The worse the enemy, the better they are by comparison, and the more the conscience is temporarily quieted and the appetite for destruction whetted.

This also explains why victories never produce satisfaction. Every policy concession, every cultural win, every institution captured should, logically, reduce the urgency. But it intensifies it—because the victory removes a source of comparative moral distance. If the enemy concedes on one front, as the GOPe is wont to do, you can no longer define yourself as good relative to opposition on that front. You need a new frontier of accusation. The ratchet is not driven by genuine grievance; it is driven by the structural need for an ever-worse enemy to maintain the comparative moral position that is the only form of "goodness" the system can affirm.

THE FEEDBACK LOOP

These mechanisms combine into a self-reinforcing cycle—another ratchet that tightens with each turn.

Shallow ethics produce actions that violate the conscience. The conscience produces guilt. The guilt produces discomfort. The thought-stopping cliches temporarily suppress the discomfort. The suppression enables further conscience-violating action. More guilt requires stronger cliches and more aggressive policing of wrongthink to maintain suppression. The enemy must be made ever worse to sustain the moral delta. The system ratchets tighter with each cycle.

The chicken-and-egg objection—does the shallow framework cause the disorder, or does the disorder attract people to the shallow framework?—dissolves, because both directions are true and they reinforce each other. The shallow ethical framework attracts those with pre-existing tendencies toward narcissistic, borderline, or histrionic patterns, because it validates and socially rewards those tendencies. Simultaneously, it *produces* those patterns in otherwise healthy people through the sustained cognitive dissonance mechanism. The attracted bring intensity to the system. The system produces more of them. The pool grows. The culture shifts further.

THE "MENTAL HEALTH" CRISIS

What gets clinically categorized as anxiety, depression, borderline instability, narcissistic patterns, and histrionic behavior is, in significant part, the symptom of living in perpetual cognitive dissonance with a functioning conscience that has no effective means of quieting.

The field of "psychology"—and we must note the word itself, from the Greek *psyche*, meaning "soul"—was founded on esoteric metaphysics. Freud drew explicitly and implicitly from Greek metaphysics, carrying esoteric presuppositions into his mechanistic model of the mind—and his work proved so intellectually compatible with Marxist thought that the Frankfurt School synthesized the two into the psychoanalytic wing of critical theory. Jung was an explicit alchemist who framed the process of individuation as the alchemical *magnum opus*. The field was adopted according to Hermetic beliefs of spiritual evolution and enlightenment, and it carries those presuppositions to this day. This is a major contributing factor to the replication crisis in the field—the persistent failure of psychological studies to produce the same results when repeated: when psychological theories are subjected to empirical analysis via the scientific method, the results frequently cannot be replicated across multiple studies.

The field is built on a foundation of sand, even if some of its windows still provide a nice view. The descriptive observations—the cataloguing of behavioral patterns, the identification of symptom clusters, the mapping of observable phenomena—and the purposed mechanisms to affect certain changes make contact with reality and are often empirically valid. The symptoms are real. The suffering is real. But the explanatory and therapeutic framework sits on esoteric foundations that exclude the transcendent ethical dimension from consideration entirely. The establishment treats brain chemistry when the actual problem is often an ethical and spiritual void. And the therapeutic establishment is itself frequently captured by the same socially constructed ethical framework that produced the problem—the therapist trained to "empathize" in the critical-theory sense validates the pseudoreality rather than grounding the patient in actual reality. This is the medicalization of a foundationally ethical and spiritual issue, and it imports the deeply troubling Greek metaphysics inherent to a field of study built by men of occult orientation. We should not be surprised that its prescriptions fail to cure what ails.

Two Failure Modes

The feedback loop has a breaking point. When the ratchet tightens past what the cliches can manage—when the cognitive dissonance exceeds the system's capacity for suppression—there are observably two possible outcomes.

The first is conversion. The dam breaks. There is genuine psychological crisis—the depression, the disorientation, the collapse of a worldview that had been held together by social pressure and thought-stopping rituals. This is painful and disorienting. But on the other side of it is the possibility of reconstruction on a firm foundation and the cessation of ethical self injury. The guilt can finally be named as guilt, processed through repentance, and resolved through forgiveness.

The second is the pressure-vessel failure. The person who cannot break through to the other side—because they lack the intellectual or spiritual resources, or because the social cost is too high, or because the system has already calloused the conscience past the point of productive crisis—instead expresses the suppressed dissonance in violence. This is not calculated revolutionary action. It is detonation. It explains the observable pattern: the Left produces incidents of political violence observably linked to the ratcheting up of mainstream rhetoric, and when they occur they tend toward the extreme and seemingly irrational. The congressional baseball shooting. The Trump assassination attempts. The sustained rioting. These are not merely strategic operations by disciplined operators, though they are certainly that. They are pressure-vessel failures in people whose entire moral identity has been destabilized past the point of containment.

At the individual level, this is a snap—a person whose feedback loop ran amok. At the systemic level, however, the Leftist narrative complex deliberately escalates the tension. It ramps up the contradictions, intensifies the dissonance, and directs the energy toward designated targets to produce breakthrough violence as a political instrument (stochastic terrorism). The individual who snaps is both a victim of the feedback loop and a tool of the system that engineered it.

Returning to the beginning, a reader may object that this theory of mind cannot account for the union worker who votes blue because his father did, the suburban woman who holds a pro-choice position from libertarian premises, or the Black churchgoer whose communitarian politics flow from a deep Christian ethic rather than from Crenshaw. These people exist. The objection is that this theory only encompasses the terminally online or perpetually plugged-in. The theory accounts for them, too, however—and the account is not flattering.

A thick ethical substrate founded presuppositionally would, in fact, prohibit the elevation of personal or factional privileges over transcendent ethic in one's voting and association choices. The act of voting along factional lines for the delivery of spoils to one's *demos*, all at the expense of another's rights, is precisely the democratic behavior this book has identified as structurally designed for oligarchic management and regime change. A person whose ethical formation ran deep enough would recognize that behavior for what it is and refuse it—regardless of family tradition, personal circumstance, or communitarian sentiment. Whether the thinness arrived through initiate indoctrination in a college of education or through the slower social demoralization of a century's institutional capture, the criticism stands: their ethics exist at the level of utility and desire, not at the level of transcendent principle. The particulars differ. The depth does not. The system does not require that every participant be a true believer. It requires only that enough people operate at the level of faction and appetite to sustain the democratic infrastructure that the wizards manage – and a transition to a democratic form of government ensures every member of that body politic is incentivized toward democratic faction and away from virtue.

The Wizard, the Spellbound, and the Based

This theory of mind maps cleanly onto the tripartite model we established earlier.

The *wizards* are those who have been fully given over. The conscience is effectively extinguished. They take pleasure in evil, perhaps genuinely thinking it good. They wield the cliches and the escalation deliberately, as weapons, with clarity of purpose. In the Christian Scriptures, these would be understood as demonically possessed—not in the culturally distorted sense of involuntary seizure of the material body, but in the sense of volitional alignment with the demonic, a reprobate mind operating in service of wickedness. They are the operators of the system.

The *spellbound* are the majority. They are caught in the feedback loop at varying degrees of callousing. Their conscience is still functional but increasingly suppressed. They are dependent on the cliches. They are increasingly disordered. They are, in a very real sense, victims of the system—people operating in the world in a way that is not conducive to flourishing, because the ideas they have internalized are psychologically taxing and conducive to harm. Though, they are also undoubtedly villains. They are the target audience of the wizards and the raw material of the revolution.

The *based* are those who operate from a foundation grounded in reality—whether or not they have yet arrived at the fully transcendent. They have either never entered the feedback loop or have broken free of it. Among them are those who have survived the dam breaking and rebuilt on firmer ground. They know, from personal experience, what the spellbound are going through. That knowledge is both a burden and a weapon.

Implications for the Counter-Offensive

If this theory of mind is correct, several things follow for our counter-offensive strategy.

First, conventional reasoned argumentation against the spellbound is largely futile as a primary tactic. The substrate is not there. This does not mean reason is useless—it means reason must be subordinated to moral and emotional disruption of the pseudoreality. The cliches must be attacked, not the arguments that proceed from them, because the cliches are the load-bearing structure. Destroy the cliche, and the guilt it was suppressing floods back. Expose the religious nature of their own beliefs and they can no longer stand atop "science" to claim superiority. This is why taboo-making is the supreme weapon: it attacks the social analgesic directly.

Second, the comparative moral imperative means that any defensive posture—any attempt to prove we are "not fascists"—is structurally doomed. They *need* us to be fascists. Denying it does not reduce their need; it merely forces them to escalate the accusation further. The correct response is not defense but counter-accusation grounded in reality—forcing them to defend their own position against the actual moral standard, not the socially constructed one, as Socialists advancing murderous ideology, butchering children, robbing their neighbors, and grooming the young and impressionable.

Third, the spellbound are not the primary enemy. They are the captured population. The wizards are the enemy. The strategy must distinguish between the two: maximum pressure on the wizards, maximum opportunity for the spellbound to convert. This means creating conditions in which the dam can break safely—in which the person in crisis has somewhere to land, a community to receive them, a framework to rebuild on. Without this, we simply create more pressure-vessel failures.

Fourth, the field of psychology, as currently constituted, cannot be trusted to diagnose or treat the problem. This does not mean individual practitioners of discernment are useless—it means the institutional framework is captured, and the metaphysics are corrupted. Those seeking to help the spellbound must operate with clear eyes about what the therapeutic establishment actually is, and must be prepared to offer something it often does not: a transcendent ethical framework in which guilt can be named, processed, and resolved.

The path through exists. It is narrow, and it is painful. But it is real, and it leads somewhere better.

The spells are named. The counterspells are forged. Reality is the weapon, truth is the blade, and righteous anger is the arm that swings it. But a sword without a strategy is just a man flailing in the dark. What remains is the hardest question of all—not how to fight, but how to *win*. Win conditions, strategy, the threshold of victory, and the positive vision that must follow the destruction of the pseudoreal. That is the final chapter.

Chapter 25

The Counter-Revolution

Before we turn to what must be done, let us discuss plainly what is at stake. The American Republic has fallen. Not is falling. Not is at risk of falling. Fallen—and likely a long time ago. Probably a century ago. What sits where the Republic used to be is a managed regime animated by the religious system traced throughout this book. That is not prediction of where we are heading. That is a diagnosis for where we are at.

This is not a warning book. Every other author in this genre is writing to tell you the Republic is in peril, the hour is late, the danger is real. I am telling you that peril is no longer the accurate word. We are past peril. Of course, for us the peril remains, but for the Republic it has long since ceased to be relevant. The patient is in the ground. Everything that follows in this chapter proceeds from that starting point, and the reader who is still operating in the prospective register fails to account for what is observable and demonstrable.

This changes the register of the work ahead. If the Republic were merely in peril, "preservation" might be the appropriate verb. Because it has fallen, preservation is not on the menu. There is nothing to preserve. The scaffolding that remains is scaffolding of what replaced it—and much of what the reader has been trained to call "our institutions," "our norms," or "our democratic traditions" is in fact the machinery of the regime that displaced the Republic. You cannot preserve that. You must not preserve that. The task is restoration, and restoration of what has been overthrown is—by every definition that matters—counter-revolution.

That word is not a pose. It is a description of the position we occupy, whether we like it or not. What follows in this chapter is what the position requires.

What does victory look like?

The honest answer is that the win condition is a moving target—and acknowledging this is a requirement of strategic clarity, not a concession to defeatism. In a moment of imminent defeat, which is the moment this book addresses most directly, the win condition is survival. (The "defeat," here, is not of the Republic, but of the counter-revolution by total consolidation of power under the regime). The preservation of sufficient institutional and cultural space, sufficient community and distributed capability, sufficient transmission of this framework across a generation that can exploit the next more favorable moment. Deny the enemy complete capture. Keep the seed institutions alive. Keep the people who understand the nature of the fight connected and capable. Do not let the tradition go dark. That is "enough" in the present circumstances.

Mere survival is not the permanent win condition. In a more ascendant moment—which this work aims toward, however distant it presently seems—the win condition is the restoration of America's founding metaphysics across the spheres of family, Church, and civil government, and the increase in righteousness that follows from bringing our civilizational foundation back into alignment with the transcendent standard on which it was built. Such a restoration would require a social and spiritual revolution before a political one could follow—the population must come to want it before any political mechanism could deliver it. This is not an immediately actionable political program. It is the destination that gives meaning to the immediate task of survival and provides direction to every incremental victory along the way.

This is a question that we must be prepared to ask ourselves seriously, and we must also be prepared to adjust expectations as facts on the ground dictate. It is easy to get wrapped around an ideological axle on this question in demanding perfection, and thereby making the good the enemy of the perfect.

We must first accept that we are not going to, and we must not set out to, produce utopia. We are not going to perfect this world, nor the human condition. We must work within the fallen nature of this world and look to achieve what is possible. Our ideal should be high and lofty, but our strategy must be one of improvement.

In seriously evaluating what win conditions are acceptable in our current times, we must be honest—brutally so—in our evaluation of our present circumstances. The further we get down this current road, the less good victory looks, the less appealing the win conditions become, and the more difficult they become to achieve. That is a hard pill to swallow. It is doubly so given that justice dictates a far greater scope and severity the further we descend into tyranny, yet it becomes less and less likely to ever be sufficiently executed. This unfortunate fact is what contributes to the bloodiness of war, especially civil war.

As the trespasses of the enemy become greater, and one's personal suffering as a result likewise increases, it becomes ever harder to hit the brakes and extend that pro-civilization olive branch. Instead, often, it leads to cycles of retribution that build toward genocide. This is an example of the sunk-cost fallacy applied to the strategy of warfare—when in reality the expectations for resolution of hostilities must be diminished in order to facilitate a peace. We should, therefore, be willing to adjust for realistic expectations. As our anger surely grows at the crimes against us and our posterity, we must be capable of exercising temperance and even forgiveness in pursuit of achieving a win condition that we can all live with, rather than one that we will all die for.

That is not to say that we should be willing to accept continued tyranny. This is far from the point being made. After all, this is a discussion of win conditions, not surrender.

For a general outline of what such a win condition should look like, we should look to those rights enumerated in the American Constitution and Bill of Rights. These items have been identified historically within the Western tradition as being that minimum set of principles due a citizen. If these were to be respected to a large degree, that would represent a tolerable situation indeed.

American Caesar

In the interest of being realistic given our situation, it is substantially unreasonable to expect any benevolent strongman will arrive to save us and effect a victory on our behalf. There was one man in American history who might have been king—George Washington. This general and president had a command of the armed forces, the respect of the legislature, and the adoration of the citizenry. Yet, after winning the war for us, freeing us from the shackles of a foreign tyrannical monarchy, and overseeing the founding of our republic, he chose to instead step aside. George Washington was one in a million. A second roll of the dice likely starts badly and ends worse.

And yet. Ordinary polity has failed. The legislature is captured and feckless. The judiciary has become a revolutionary force, rewriting law through fiat and "living document" sorcery. The militia is neutered. Nullification is crushed in court if any have the gumption to enact it in the first place. Lower magistrates are isolated, infiltrated, or powerless. The republic faces existential threats on every front, and the revolutionary apparatus—both domestic and foreign—needs only one decisive victory while we must calculate every little move to avert disaster.

There remains one office with the unitary authority, the oath, and the constitutional tools to act decisively: the presidency. The highest magistrate in the land. The founders did not design the executive to be weak in crisis. Article II vests the executive power in a single president for a reason—swift, decisive action when the republic demands it. And the deepest warrant lies in Article IV, Section 4: "The United States shall guarantee to every State in this Union a Republican Form of Government." This is not a passive promise. It is an active, affirmative duty, and the founders would have balked at the suggestion that the executive ought to defer to the bureaucracy.

A strongman could, hypothetically, take control over the executive and wield it in the necessary fashion to right recent wrongs. The trouble should be obvious—in a time of near-universally better men, Washington was still a unicorn. Now, that may still be better than some potential outcomes. I would suggest it is absolutely better than Communist rule. But it would be nothing short of foolish to formulate our entire strategic planning on a low-probability outcome. Our bloated behemoth of the administrative state has already conducted a coup publicly with Nixon, probably removed JFK's head, and entirely negated the delegated powers of the Trump administration through perpetual resistance, lawfare and counter-state warfare. There is very little reason to believe that this beast can be tamed from the top alone.

So, we hold two truths simultaneously: America may well require an American Caesar, and it would be reckless to depend on one arriving. The wise course is to build the distributed, decentralized, dispersed centers of resistance that can function regardless—and that can, should such a figure emerge, provide the institutional infrastructure he would need to actually succeed where others have failed. A top-down reformation without a bottom-up foundation is a low-probability event layered on top of another low-probability event. We build from below, and we pray for the miracle from above.

The founders understood both modes of governance—the ordinary and the extraordinary. The Declaration of Independence is the extraordinary blueprint. It is the warrant for reformation. It begins with an appeal to "the Laws of Nature and of Nature's God." It declares that men are "endowed by their Creator" with certain unalienable rights. It subordinates every human magistrate to a higher, transcendent law – just as Washington's Appeal to Heaven flag declared. No king, no parliament, no court, no president stands above this law. When government becomes destructive of these ends, it is the right of the people to alter or to abolish it. The founders meant it. They spilled barrels of blood into this earth—not just for themselves, but that their posterity might not be unduly imposed upon. They pledged their lives, fortunes, and sacred honor to it.

The Constitution, by contrast, is the blueprint for ordinary polity. It sets up the mechanisms for day-to-day governance: elections, legislation, courts, checks and balances. But the founders also built in implicit and explicit warrants for appeal beyond the highest magistrates. The suspension clause in Article I, Section 9 allows habeas corpus to be suspended in cases of rebellion or invasion. The Second Amendment ensures that the people themselves remain armed and capable. Article IV contains a perpetual guarantee that the federal government will ensure a "republican form of government" in every state of the union.

It is not better, somehow, that this duty fall to the average gun-owning Rightist in America to accomplish this—Heaven forbid, no, this is an exercise of the principle of the lesser magistrate—the duty of lower authorities to check tyrants above them—, if a bit awkwardly exercised by the "greater magistrate," to save his country and his people, not to start a shooting war and enact vengeance. As ever, the objective is peace, but not "peace at all costs." Peace only under the ordered liberty prescribed by the Lord God.

Should such a figure arise—a man willing to wield the constitutional tools of the presidency for the reformation of the republic—that would be a blessing. It ought to be embraced. The insurrection powers—a constitutional item foundational to executive authorities to put down internal threats to the republic—are not a relic. The president's oath is to preserve, protect, and defend the Constitution—not a corrupted system, and not a damned "democracy," which we all know is not "ours," but "theirs." The so-called "Unitary Executive Theory" is nothing more than a plain reading of Article IV, uncorrupted by Progressive bureaucratic dogma. The full powers of the Executive are vested in but one man.

But embraced does not mean unmonitored. The founders' transcendent ethic governs always, and legitimizes what must be done to reform the republic in the image of the Constitution. The executive, as highest magistrate, remains subordinate to God's law. When lower tiers are captured and the republic faces existential threats on multiple fronts, the duty falls to him under God's Law to vindicate the rights of the people. He must act with whatever means are necessary for efficacy and justice. Old constraints, eroded by two centuries of revolutionary subversion, become mere foils. They cannot bind a magistrate fulfilling his oath against those who have already broken theirs – he who saves his country breaks no law.

The bottom-up infrastructure we must build serves both functions: it provides the institutional support such a figure would need to actually succeed where others have failed, and it provides the distributed, decentralized, armed citizenry due a constitutional republic that frustrates the oligarchy even now, so long after our transition away from that system of government. Build from below. Pray for the miracle from above. And keep your powder dry regardless.

NULLIFICATION AND INTERPOSITION

The founders of this nation built a very complicated model of government. They did this on purpose, and in no small part in order to frustrate the efforts of tyrants to do precisely what they currently are inflicting upon us. They divided the total powers of government between three branches and two sovereigns—executive, legislative, judicial, federal, and state.

Among the many what-if scenarios explored by the founders in debate was the question of how to deal with a federal government asserting powers far beyond those delegated. A response to this, found in the Federalist Papers as well as in Madison's Resolution of 1800, is the legal concept of nullification and interposition. This concept identifies the dual-sovereign nature of our government, whereby the federal government is not properly seen as hierarchically above the states, but rather lateral to them.

Surely, so far as the Supremacy Clause goes, federal law that comports with the Constitution and the narrow scope of authority and powers delegated to the federal government has primacy over state law. But, properly considered, state law and authorities have supremacy over their federal counterparts whenever that federal authority overreaches, asserts powers not delegated, or seeks to nullify the rights of citizens. In such cases, the doctrine of nullification and interposition—an extension of that very old theological doctrine of the lesser magistrate—not only authorizes but affirmatively requires those other authorities to exercise a check on arbitrary power.

The assertion of this doctrine should be strategic and judicious—where it can be applied in a manner likely to be overwhelmingly popular with the base and the people broadly, readily articulable and arguable as to its merits, and executable in a facts-on-the-ground sense. By choosing battles carefully, and hopefully recruiting numerous states to do likewise simultaneously, the movement might gain in popular sentiment while spreading the mid-range coercive mechanisms of the federal government too thinly to be effective.

It is through a long series of such well-chosen battles that ultimately the perceived legitimacy of the federal government—already rendered actually illegitimate through its own usurpation of powers not delegated—might be sapped. This may facilitate the possibility of a reformation of federal power and the state-federal relationship, forcibly, from the level of the states. And, no, the tragic ending of the lives of countless Americans in a bloody civil war did not "settle" that question. What kind of an ethic would appeal to the threat of mass-murder to legitimize its prescriptions? Seems a bit social constructivist to me.

THRESHOLD OF VICTORY

Victory is cumulative, and there exists a threshold below which no quantity of incremental wins amounts to anything final. A clever speech here, a viral hashtag there, a few state-level skirmishes that make the base feel good about the direction of travel—none of it registers if the increments do not stack up to breach the line. You can pile sandbags until your back gives out. The tsunami does not care.

The environment you are operating in has been engineered to keep you below that line. Excuses as to why the law cannot be enforced. Suggestions that the obviously correct course of action will not work. The odd bit of street chaos to monopolize your attention and resources. Social taboos manufactured to shame you out of winning moves. Controlled opposition nudging you toward defeat with a wink and a nod about respectability, or—my personal favorite—pushing such bonkers ideas that the whole fight looks like a farce and the serious people are tainted by association with the madness. All of it—a circus, orchestrated to exhaust you, distract you, and keep your strategies safely in the loser's bracket. The enemy crafts this environment with precision, and the function of the exercise is to inflict upon you strategic incomprehension—a fog of war so thick you cannot see where the threshold is, let alone what it takes to cross it.

They will swear up and down that the big plays—impeachment, enforcing laws against sedition or insurrection—are impossible. "We don't have the votes." "The Constitution—that dusty old thing—can't be done." That is the controlled opposition syncing up with the Left's sophist nonsense to make the right path seem radioactive. When both sides sneer at the plain text of your own laws, you are being played. Dead giveaway: if citing the Constitution or the black-and-white letter of the law gets you silence from one side and derision from the other, you are on to something. Those principles are inconvenient for those who would rather you not win, and to those more comfortable in managing decline than risking their neck for victory.

THE ITERATED GAME

The methodology of the Left is calculated. Through founding documents, transcendent ethics, and game theory, the pattern emerges plainly. The Left escalates incrementally—advances just below the threshold that would provoke a unified, decisive response from the Right that might shift the playing field in our favor. Even where the occasional overstep happens, such as we have now seen with the martyrdom of Charlie Kirk, just look at how many people who banked so much social capital over the years are now frothing to taint the whole situation publicly such that the unity it instilled in us is fractured. NGOs sustain internal subversion without direct challenge from authorities. Lawfare isolates targets. Alliances normalize revolutionary rhetoric without triggering backlash, as the sheer mass of persons undertaking these revolutionary activities acts to normalize it and prevent enforcement – how do we bring a hundred-thousand people up on seditious conspiracy charges?

At the same time, they provoke deliberately. Isolated incidents—engineered confrontations at enforcement sites, mob actions amplified as "resistance"—are memetically cemented as proof of "fascist violence." This justifies calls for further escalation: abolition of borders, defunding of police, silencing of dissent, and, eventually, calls to authorities to step down or be removed by force. The goal is to push the Overton Window leftward while portraying any effective counter as illegitimate.

Game theory clarifies the danger. This is an iterated contest—not a single battle but a long series of rounds in which the Left defects incrementally, escalating below the decisive threshold, while daring the Right to cooperate through perpetual restraint. Every round we fail to escalate above the victory threshold—fearing overreach, isolated backlash, or memetic traps—the Left accumulates gains toward ultimate victory. Over iterations, total defection wins when not met with equivelent defection. The republic collapses without a unifying counterstroke. If the optimal strategy is tit-for-tat, we must make certain, in iterated format, that the response is adequately calibrated to account for the thousands of tats unanswered to date.

Compounding this is profound demoralization. The Left is largely viewed as legitimate in all its undertakings because its actions are perceived as just under supplanted Marxist values—equity over equality, collective over individual, revolution over order. This is reinforced by virtually every cultural institution, long since captured, including media, academia, civil society, and religious. Information warfare has tarred true justice from the Right as illegitimate: enforcement of borders becomes "racism," defense of life, liberty, and property "extremism," adherence to transcendent law "theocracy." The violent-splinter ("peaceful protest" that leaves bodies in its wake) tactic accelerates this—the Left maintains non-violent mainstream lines while tolerating or directing violent splinters. The threat of violence normalizes radical demands—"give us policy concessions or the splinter acts"—while memetically framing the Right's responses as the real violence (arrest of rioters or illegal aliens), as per Marcuse's Repressive Tolerance—tolerate the Left's violence, repress the Right's response. This pushes the agenda forward, iteration by iteration.

The Counter-State

You have heard the term "deep state." It works, and it is popular, but it is also imperfect. It gives undue legitimacy to the thing by assigning it a role *in* the state, as if it were just another branch of government. It is not. The correct term is *counter-state*—a parallel structure formed through insurgency and political warfare to subvert and eventually replace the legitimate state. Credit is due Unconstrained Analytics for the background of this language.

Think of an iceberg. Above the waterline: protests, riots, the occasional Molotov cocktail. Below the surface, submerged and sprawling: networks of operatives, financiers, and ideologues—vast, unseen, and patient. That is the counter-state.

This counter-state is not merely domestic. It is international—a public-private hydra coiling through governments, looping into NGOs, civil society outfits, political parties, and supranational bodies like the European Union, which functions as something of a modern Comintern—the Communist International coordination body. The intelligence agencies are largely compromised, serving as the eyes, ears, and fingers of the Leviathan. The revolutionary NGO complex serves as the center of gravity for the shadow government while in official exile—fueled, in no small part, by American taxpayer money laundered through federal grantmaking pipelines back into the revolutionary apparatus.

The scope of this sedition is vast—far beyond isolated acts. It encompasses coordinated networks across government agencies, courts, NGOs, academia, media, and tech platforms. It utilizes the actionable, strategic language of "intersectionality," "peaceful protest," and "anti-fascism" to coordinate, signal, and target. Thousands of actors, from street agitators to high officials, advance the overthrow incrementally.

Insurgency is fundamentally about legitimacy—the real currency of government. The counter-state's game is to delegitimize the standing order, prop up the parallel structure, and merge the two when the time is ripe. Counter-hegemony leverages access to institutions to remake them from within, as a virus hijacks a cell. When one branch of government is captured, popular opinion—manufactured through information dominance across media, tech, and the whole psychological warfare apparatus—shields it from the others. Checks and balances are impossibly flawed under these conditions.

Political warfare is warfare. The actions of the counter-state are high crimes and forms of warfare against the Constitution and the people. The United States government should be on a war footing. We are not meant to be a democracy—we are meant to be a republic. And what they are doing at the strategic level is not "good trouble." It is a capital offense against the nation. Seditious conspiracy is about as normal as riding a bike it seems.

THE POSITIVE VISION

The positive vision is republicanism—the constitutional order we defined in detail in Chapter 2, grounded in transcendent ethics, sphere sovereignty, and the structural frustration of faction. That case has been made in brief:

the republic limits government to prevent theft and oppression, elevates God over government and individual rights as inalienable, divides powers to starve tyranny of its fuel, and stands as the exact opposite of the democratic form we have been taught to celebrate. What remains is not to restate the argument but to translate it into a fighting doctrine—a strategy that can recapture territory on two fronts simultaneously.

The ultimate goal must be to make doing the right thing first socially acceptable and then socially obligatory. It must come to be that doing the right thing is the social default and transgressions are met with social stigmatization and real social consequences. This means creating inertia of our own towards goodness and arresting the inertia of relativistic hedonism.

Of the government, the legislatures should be the easiest to effect, as the individuals wield the least power individually, are up for re-election with some frequency, and also wield the most power collectively—which makes them a logical place to focus efforts. The judiciary, by contrast, is a veritable fortified bunker. The path here should be clear to anyone with a working knowledge of Communist tactics—and yes, we are going to have to adopt some of those tactics for our own uses. In Gramscian hegemony or Maoist Long March strategies applied to the American landscape against the Left, the legislature should be the first target for institutional capture for Republicans. The great powers of that branch to be wielded against the more intransigent branches once effected. The starting point is the capture of your local GOP group, which often recruits and may have veto power over would-be legislators.

This needs naming directly. A counter-revolutionary movement that refuses on principle to study and adopt what actually works—that confuses fidelity to its ends with fidelity to a particular set of methods—is strategically disarmed from the outset against opponents who have no such compunction. The Left holds its nose and picks up whatever hammer drives the nail. The methods of the enemy are not contaminated by association with him. A hammer is a hammer. The question is not whether to pick it up but what you are going to drive with it. There is nothing inherently immoral to the Christian perspective to wield power as such. On the contrary, Christian tradition requires righteousness in the sword.

While efforts are underway to recapture the government on behalf of republicanism, those civil institutions capable of being retaken ought to be targeted smartly, and those intransigent institutions ought to be subject to rapid delegitimization. This means the creation of new republican parallel institutions from which the legitimacy of the Marxist institutions may be recouped—instead of capturing the intransigent institution itself, which in many cases is likely not possible. This should not be especially difficult conceptually, nor perhaps even in practice, as Marxist institutions are nothing if not self-delegitimizing. The simple creation of such an alternative republican institution would naturally attract and accumulate very much legitimacy by simply not being insane.

Specifically, we should seek, broadly: a return to pre-Marxist jurisprudence, a preference for significant federalism in opposition to pure nationalism including significant state-level authority, a recognition that constitutional natural rights exist to necessitate ordered liberty—not libertinism or liberationism—a general restriction of civil government to those items not reserved to other spheres of governance such as the family, church, or individual, and a significantly less tolerant civil society, buoyed by healthy institutions that can effect taboo-making around evil things that minimizes their prevalence without having to criminalize them.

Chapter 26

A Necropsy of the Republic

The vision for counter-revolution requires honest reckoning with the current state of the machinery that it will come into contact with. Let us consider the proper role of each branch of government, and how it was envisioned, versus how it is currently operating.

First, we take the Judiciary, famously said to be the "least dangerous branch" by Alexander Hamilton on account of its inherent inability to enforce its own decrees. The only court outlined in our Constitution is the Supreme Court. All other inferior courts are a creation of legislation.

It is the charge of the courts to uphold the protections on individual sovereignty and liberty both outlined, and not outlined within the Constitution, and Bill of Rights, as well as to enforce the specific prescriptions for government found therein through the offering of expert, educated opinion on founding doctrine. Here there is, obviously, an implied ability to "interpret" law, and to hold legislation against the Constitution to establish legitimacy in American virtues. Yet, there is likewise an assertion of "coequality" among the three branches that must rule out the court having sole authority in this regard. It was understood that all laws must be plainly stated and written such that a person of average intellect could understand and abide.

Early on in our American history, in Marbury vs. Madison, the court proved Hamilton wrong in a decision rendered by the court rendering the court the sole arbiter of the Constitution through the principle of *absolute judicial review*. This power grab went insufficiently challenged by the Executive—despite the quote "Marshall made his decision, now let him enforce it," being attributed to Jackson—and Legislative branches, and rendered, for practical purposes, our nation an oligarchy of a handful of lawyers.

Later SCOTUS would violate the very principle of federalism with their decisions of the New Deal era in dropping "direct effect," as applicable to the Commerce Clause, and replacing it with a Progressive *six degrees of Kevin Bacon* to find that virtually every single thing happening anywhere in this nation "effects" interstate commerce and is therefore within federal purview. This opened the door to the Progressive dream of a bureaucratic state of experts that would usher in the *perfected State*, and ultimate utopian vision.

In this early Progressive era, the court would begin shifting the entirety of the Constitution to the doctrine of a *living document* that could be reinterpreted at will to meet the needs of the Progressives. This had the effect of removing the most basic meaning from words of the document and replacing it with whatever was convenient and popular at the time within the movement. As it now stands our Supreme Court functions much like the Oracles of Sparta, looking into their tea leaves to find a path to a personally desired outcome—a Utopian State—and modifying meaning to fit that vision. It so happens that they are also overwhelmingly religiously oriented towards Progressivism, with even most of the conservatives being hostage to the paramoral assertions of Leftist dogma.

Taken together, the two correct understandings of "judicial capture" mean that the judiciary is both the most powerful seat of government, and the most corrupted. After all, most of the major historic and cultural shifts in America were portended by a major court decision, from the now overturned Roe "right" to kill the unborn, to the travesty for federalism of Wickard v. Filburn, to the upholding of the effective nationalization of the healthcare industry as a "tax" in Obamacare, to the slew of recent cases stripping Presidential authority to repel invasion and more. These items did not pass through The Peoples House, the Senate, and get signed by the President—a half-dozen supreme jurists decided these issues for the body politic as oracles of the esoteric Constitution.

These expansive powers claimed by the judiciary, having gone largely unchallenged from the Right for two centuries, now leaves the judges as a law unto themselves, fully capable of exercising both the powers of the

President and the Legislature, despite having no arms to speak of for their enforcement—which is truly a wonder to behold.

For these reasons it is imperative that the judiciary be placed back into its Constitutional restraints as rapidly and fully as possible—it represents an absolute obstacle to solving very many other existential threats, as it fundamentally represents an organ of The Revolution. The good news is that the founders provided ways to go about correcting this circumstance. The bad news is that the Legislature is considerably too feckless, and itself too Progressively oriented, to undertake the Constitutional remedy of impeachment and removal.

This requires a paradigm shift in the manner in which both the public and lawmakers view American republican government. The first order of business is to stop calling it a damned "democracy." It was never intended to be that and calling it that codifies the framework of the revolutionaries as legitimate. The Legislature must come to see themselves as more than mere middle-managers of bureaucracy, and instead as active agents of high office with a genuine responsibility to defeat The Revolution and uphold their oaths. Lawmakers are not there to be liked and enjoy social status. In times like these, when surrounded by enemies, to be liked ought to be a scarlet letter. They should learn to take pleasure in the idea that their enemies might celebrate their shuffling off this mortal coil, as their enemies' burden is lessened in their absence.

This requires of the body politic the demand for real, lawful, Constitutional accountability for misbehavior. Here, "lawful" and "Constitutional" is not meant as mitigating language against "unlawful" or "unconstitutional" remedies, but rather as a demand that the letter of the law and the Constitution be followed. We are surrounded by an active, open rebellion, insurrection, and revolution against Constitutional government. These are high crimes justifying impeachment and removal, and these remedies should be pursued.

Now, strategically, there is simply too many persons eligible to be pursued all at once—or even altogether at any point. If our republic was a game of Tetris, we have already racked up a full screen of colored shapes to the rafters. We, therefore, must be discerning and strategic in targeting. We should seek to effect accountability, such as impeachment, in a manner that firmly establishes disincentives to continued anti-Constitutional behavior. That probably means taking a bite of the biggest target we can chew—and chewing is important, as in these matters "momentum" is a real thing, and while wins beget wins, losses, too, beget losses.

In simple terms, judges at all levels must come to fear the repercussions of continuing on as they have been. They need to get used to hearing the word "no" from the magistrate fulfilling his duties before God to his people. The time for kid gloves and worries about delegitimizing the whole system are over—the system is already wholly delegitimized thanks, in large part, to the judiciary. Alas, we do not have a huge amount of time in which to accomplish this task. So many of the other solutions to outstanding existential threats run up against an intransigent judiciary that it must be among the first problems solved for if we are to avert catastrophe. (This is true at both the federal and state levels).

So, get to it. Flex every social muscle and leverage every last bit of yourself to make sure your representatives understand that you expect scalps—not theatre, but results, in the form of impeachment and removal of revolutionaries from the bench.

Now we take the Executive, the only branch to wield the ultimate authority of government: violence, through the ordering of the military, and federal police powers. This builds in an asymmetry that was ostensibly overcome by the constitutional provision of coequality of branches. The Executive was to be strong, yet dutifully subservient to the will of the people, and of the states, as exercised through the legislature writing good, necessary, and clear laws, and to the courts when upholding a correct reading of the Constitution as understood by the founders.

Today, the Executive under Democrat rule looks more a King than an administrator of just laws. Domestically, the Executive co-rules his fiefdom with the bureaucratic state of Progressive "experts," an inwardly focused police-state apparatus, and the (uncertainly, for any Republican) subservient intelligence and kinetic warfare divisions. These various co-rulers are the efficacious Progressive heart of the Executive ensuring fealty to Leftist doctrine, always forwarding the march towards the end of *History*, and perpetual revolution, regardless of who sits in the big office. In this manner the sole, unitary Executive has seemingly lost even more power to the bureaucrats than he has gained through usurpation from the legislature, courts, and states.

The permanent Progressive state resembles an immune system when faced with invading American traditionalist ideology. It abides not the slightest tinge of star-spangling, nor under-God-ing. The counter-state apparatus is bound up with private sector concerns from all major industries, and with them pulls the strings from behind the scenes manipulating the joints of the leviathan to block any efforts at reform.

This ever-growing, vigorous Progressive administrative State has slowly made the Judicial, but especially the Legislative branches vestigial organs of the decrepit, old body of American sovereignty.

The federal Legislative branch is seemingly wholly corrupted, and thoroughly weakened having ceded very much of its authority to the Executive and Judiciary in exchange for less voter accountability. The Judiciary is so backwards with indoctrination, and so easily captured due to the very limited personnel size of the branch and the amount of power vested in each person, that it will not even rule against an Executive directly censoring Americans online through its vast networks of NGOs, executive agencies, and regulatory oversight of Big Tech.

Well, if you ever found yourself in the unenviable position where your national government has become tyrannical and internally resistant to change it would be really nice if you happened to live in a system of dual-sovereigns, where power is rightfully shared between different forms of government, a decentralized system wherein power is not placed entirely in a single person, branch or party, and a system wherein the founders foresaw the inclinations towards tyranny and built in obstacles.

Guess what. We live in precisely that sort of system—one which was ideally setup from the beginning to be able to resist such a circumstance as we find ourselves in.

What Failure Looks Like in Practice

Consider what happened in New Hampshire—the state where "Live Free or Die" adorns every license plate and the right of revolution is enshrined in Article 10 of the state Constitution.

In 2023, a single superior court judge—David Ruoff—in the case of *Contoocook Valley School District et al. v. State of New Hampshire*, did willfully overstep the constitutional boundaries of the judiciary by imposing a specific and substantial financial expenditure mandate of over $537,55 0,970.95—a function that is reserved exclusively to "Acts and Resolves of the General Court" under Article 56 of the New Hampshire Constitution. He mandated that base adequacy aid funding must exceed $7,356.01 per pupil—over $3,200 more than the existing level—and he refused to stay his own decision pending Supreme Court review, creating significant disruption, uncertainty, and chaos in the implementation of state policies, budgetary allocations, and taxation. The judge himself acknowledged the implications, quoting from his own decision: "The short answer is that the Legislature should have the final word, but the base adequacy cost can be no less than $7356.01 per pupil per year and the true cost is likely much higher than that," and, "Moreover, the Court recognizes the significant implications of this Order, and the potential for political strain." He knew precisely what he was doing. He did it anyway.[31]

Possible impeachment articles were drafted. Five of them: abuse of judicial authority and violation of the separation of powers, judicial overreach and usurpation of legislative powers, undermining the legislative process and representative government, setting a dangerous precedent for judicial activism, and refusal to stay his decision pending Supreme Court review. Every article was grounded in the plain text of the New Hampshire Constitution. The resolution to undertake the necessary study towards impeachment was filed.

The legislature did not act.

And then the story got worse.

The decision went up to the New Hampshire Supreme Court. In 2025, the court ruled 3-2, upholding Ruoff's mandate. But look at who composed that majority. One justice—Anna Barbara Hantz Marconi—had been suspended from the bench in a manner that was procedurally irregular and arguably unconstitutional. Under the New Hampshire Constitution, Article 73, removal of a justice requires legislative impeachment, not unilateral court action. The Supreme Court's decision to place her on administrative leave bypassed this entirely. Any removal of official duties from a constitutional officer is tantamount to removal from office and is not within the court's delegated power. A resolution was brought to establish this principle—that the practice of "suspending" a Constitutional Officer is outside of the authorities delegated to the Judiciary, and that such authority is Constitutionally delegated to the Legislative branch under the provisions for impeachment and bills of address. That resolution, ultimately, failed. It failed in the same committee as the original impeachment investigation that failed prior.

With Hantz Marconi sidelined, the three-justice majority included two retired lower-court substitutes who had never been confirmed to the Supreme Court. A recusal and a suspension of questionable constitutionality produced the majority that imposed a 79% hike in base adequacy aid, translating to a commensurate 10-15% increase in property taxes if acted upon. This whole affair might just cost the state in excess of 5 billion dollars per decade going forward.

This is what the failure to impeach looks like in concrete terms. A lower-court judge usurps the legislature's power of the purse. The legislature does not impeach. The supreme court upholds the usurpation with a majority composed of substitute justices who were never confirmed to the bench—on a court whose composition was itself altered by a suspension that only the legislature had the constitutional authority to effect. And the taxpayers of New Hampshire might pay billions for the privilege. Every link in the chain of accountability was present. Every tool was available. None were used. The judiciary acted. The legislature watched. The people lost again.

This pattern is not unique to New Hampshire. It is the pattern everywhere. The judiciary acts as an organ of the revolution. The legislature wrings its hands. The people suffer. And the constitutional remedy of impeachment—sitting right there in the plain text, loaded and ready—gathers dust.

The Short Arm of the Law

What has been said of impeachment applies with greater force to prosecution for the high crimes that fall outside the judicial chamber. The revolution underway depends on a specific structural feature of modern governance: the decentralization of responsibility across politicians, bureaucrats, officers, agencies, and advisory bodies so thinly that no individual person can be held to the threshold required to enact punishment. The long arm of the law, in such a regime, is stunted. It flails about for purchase on the multitudes now queued for justice, and the responsible remain either just out of reach or turn to jelly upon being grasped. The revolutionaries have built the system this way on purpose. They understand that a crime distributed across forty hands is a crime never prosecuted, and that the very multiplicity of eligible defendants serves as its own defense.

This arrangement makes a mockery of the rule of law and invites every ambitious operator to join the queue, assured that no punishment will arrive before the next crisis supersedes the last. The trend must be broken, and it will only be broken by holding some specific person, or people, accountable to the fullest effect of law—preferably on charges such as sedition or treason, and ideally leading to capital punishment administered publicly.

Stated otherwise, the argument is not that every guilty party must be reached. The scale of present guilt is too vast; the scope of the Tetris board is already to the rafters. The argument is that when the law has a short arm, it must compensate with a strong bite. Find the single target most within reach and most conspicuously guilty of high crimes, prosecute that target with the full thorough completeness of the law, and carry the punishment through. That is how deterrence is restored. Not by broad prosecution of the very many—that is a capacity the present apparatus of justice does not possess—but by the exemplary, completed punishment of one, or of a few.

Imprisonment will not do the necessary work. In a functioning legal order with confidence that a sentence will be fully served, imprisonment might carry deterrent weight. We do not have that order. We have a sick justice system in which the oligarch class can expect special dispensations, selective pardons, quiet resentencing, and—where the stakes rise high enough—the prospect of a coup to free the guilty from prison. So long as any of those outcomes remain on the table, imprisonment is not sufficient deterrent, if it ever was. Only the irreversible sentence is.

Be clear about the stakes of naming this. Jefferson's remark about the tree of liberty being watered with the blood of patriots and tyrants was not entirely metaphor and was not restricted to war and rebellion. There will be blood. The question is not whether, but through what instrument and for what offense. The instrument is either the official, sanctioned, due-process administration of justice under the rule of law, or the mobs of tribalism, or the summary executions of counter-revolutionaries by the completed regime upon its consolidation of power, or the anarcho-tyranny that lets the streets run red with the blood of the innocent at the hands of criminals who receive official protection. Those are the four options actually on the menu — not the ones we wish were on it. A reader who recoils from the first but quietly accepts any of the other three is telling on themselves about where the repugnance actually lies, and should reconsider. Neither the criminal nor the regime is a force of nature lacking agency; both are chosen courses of action. Preferring them to official, lawful justice is preferring chaos or tyranny to order, and the preference ought to be examined rather than disguised.

This applies equally if you find yourself unable to countenance any lawful capital punishment at all. If you have not the stomach to see such official action carried out on your behalf, you are admitting you lack the seriousness of your own convictions. Serious people understand that blood is inseparable from liberty, as it is inseparable from every form of human existence east of Eden. Blood is a fact of life, and it is, rightly, sometimes an achievement of justice.

The ultimate purpose of the act is not soothing the bloodthirsty masses in vengeance. The purpose is the inculcation of deadly seriousness into a polity that has lost it. We are presently an unserious people in an unserious nation. Unserious people are not taken seriously by internal forces, and they are not taken seriously by external ones. Eventually, unserious people do not get to eat at will, sleep at will, or move at will. Will itself is a serious force outside the capacity of the unserious to exercise. Our current path makes sheep of men, and the would-be sheepdogs are trampled by the herd or put down by the authorities for daring to bare their teeth. The void left by men unwilling to act will be filled by serious men willing to act, and when it is filled, when that terrible day comes, the nation's sons and daughters and wives will be left to the disposition of the serious men.

The strategic principle reduces to a sentence. When the law has a short arm, give it a strong bite, and let the body politic see the fangs. If the first target proves gelatinous and slips the grip, move immediately to the next, with full effect, until the precedent is set. One completed, public execution of a genuinely seditious or treasonous actor will do more to restore deterrence against high crimes than a thousand prosecutions resulting in fines, a decade of stern speeches, and a library of unread op-eds combined. The law already possesses this authority. Our founders enshrined the punishment following from necessity. The Constitution permits it, and it always has. Every instrument required is already at hand.

Chapter 27

Reality Check

We have just spent a section on what must be wielded and what it must be wielded against. Before we proceed further into tactics, the chapter has to turn and look the other way. A reader who has absorbed the preceding argument and is now preparing to act on it needs to understand what the apparatus the counter-revolution will act against is built to do in response. Restoring deterrence works only if the counter-revolutionary is not first neutralized by the regime's own coercive machinery — and that machinery has been built, over many decades, precisely to neutralize what the preceding section has just argued for. What follows in this section is a sober inventory of what a serious counter-revolutionary should expect the regime to do, and why the strategic calculus cannot proceed without accounting for it.

How will the Regime Respond?

Before we go further into strategy, understand something structural. A counter-revolutionary effort to restore the Republic will be read, correctly, by the ruling order as an attempt to overthrow it. Because that is what it is.

Most books in this space make a mistake I will not make here. They pretend that the other side is confused about what the Right is doing—that with better messaging, sharper arguments, or a more "electable" candidate, the hostility on the other side will moderate. That is wrong. The hostility is not a misunderstanding. It is the ruling order of a post-Republic regime accurately identifying, in a serious restoration project, an existential threat to its continued existence. And when any competent regime identifies an existential threat, it responds with the full coercive apparatus available to it.

You already know what this looks like, because you have already watched it. The list writes itself. Show trials of political opponents dressed up as ordinary prosecutions. Open-ended investigations that exist to punish by process. Civil asset forfeiture turned on dissidents. Parents labeled as "domestic terrorists" by the Department of Justice for showing up to school board meetings. The January 6 prosecutions—the largest investigation in the history of the Department of Justice—aimed at a movement, provoked by radical regime actions, and resulting in what could reasonably be called the first gulag in America. Financial debanking of disfavored industries. The IRS targeting of tea party groups. Selectively-applied "hate speech" and "misinformation" enforcement and coordination via international intelligence bodies. Surveillance of traditional Catholics and politically active Protestants as radicalization risks. Grandmothers set to die in prison for protesting abortion. Wielding federal law enforcement tactical teams in a manner that looked an awful lot like summary executions of dissidents. And through it all, a press-information-media apparatus whose job is not reporting but delegitimization—making sure that the targets look like they deserved it, and giving fair warning to anyone else who might step out of line.

This is not an excess in the manner you might want to think. This is not the system breaking down, or a temporary departure that is now back on path. This is the system working exactly as designed—a regime defending itself against what it accurately identifies as a threat to its existence. This is the inexorable logic of trying to live as if in a republic under a democratic system.

Understand what follows from this.

Any strategy that does not account for the regime's response is naive. Any counter-revolutionary effort that proceeds as though it will be allowed to operate within the normal protections of due process and ordinary political contest is building its plans on a fiction. Some of our side will be prosecuted. Some will be surveilled. Some will be delegitimized, debanked, or otherwise punished through the administrative apparatus the regime has spent decades building for exactly this purpose. Some will not see the end of this battle. That is the price of a contest this side has not had to pay in living memory—and it is the price of citizenship under the conditions that actually exist, not the conditions we wish we had.

Plan accordingly. Anyone selling a strategy that pretends these costs do not exist is selling a fiction. And the side we are fighting eats people who build strategies on fictions.

THE BATTLESPACE

The necropsy prior establishes what we are fighting against. The theory of mind developed in Chapter 24 clarifies whom we are fighting and whom we are fighting for. Recall the tripartite model: wizards, spellbound, and based. Several strategic imperatives follow from that framework.

The *wizards* are the enemy. Maximum pressure. Against them, every constitutional tool must be brought to bear—impeachment, prosecution, exposure, delegitimization, and, where warranted, the full force of the magistrate's sword. There is no reasoning with them. There is no likelihood of converting them. They must be defeated.

The *spellbound* are not the primary enemy. They are the captured population. Maximum opportunity to convert. The strategy must create conditions in which the dam can break safely—in which the person in crisis has somewhere to land, a community to receive them, a framework to rebuild on. Without this, we simply create more pressure-vessel failures.

This distinction is not sentimentality. It is strategic precision. The relative handful of wizards—the cadre, the operators, the true believers who take pleasure in the destruction—are not the same threat as the hundred million spellbound who parrot the slogans because they have been taught nothing else. To treat them identically is to waste resources, alienate the persuadable, and hand the enemy a propaganda victory. The IFF doctrine—identify friend or foe—applies here with full force.

Central to all counter-strategies is the special place of truth as the primary mechanism for breaking the gnostic spells of esoteric Progressivism. When treated with utmost seriousness and deployed rigorously, truth resonates directly with observable sense perception, inherent logic, and heart-written ethics. This resonance possesses unique power to rapidly shift the Overton Window, awakening especially elites, or potential elites, to patterns previously concealed by sophistry. Success demands always advancing the most correct arguments, grounded firmly in traditional ethics and objective reality. Imperfect argumentation—flawed reasoning, significant exaggeration, or appeals lacking direct linkage to enduring moral frameworks—alienates the persuadable center, inculcates relativism by mirroring the Left's own ethical flexibility, and fails to distinguish the counter-position. Those susceptible to mere self-interest or expedient bad argumentation are already claimed by the Left's pragmatic vanguard; the decisive ground lies with hearts oriented toward truth, where uncompromising fidelity to the most accurate and ethically anchored claims alone secures lasting movement.

Chapter 28

Resolving the Paradox

Before we walk through the win conditions by domain, identifying what targets ought to be set, we state the logic plainly, so every tactic that follows is understood in its proper frame.

Everything that follows rests on two premises established earlier in this book. First, the Republic has already fallen; what sits in its place is an illegitimate regime. Second, the regime will respond to counter-revolution with the full coercive apparatus at its disposal. From those two premises, exactly two strategic postures are available, and they correspond to whether the Right holds lawful power or does not.

When the Right holds lawful power—governor's mansion, legislative majority, federal executive, county sheriff, any office—the imperative is maximal regime rollback. Every constitutional instrument of state authority available to us is to be wielded to dismantle the illegitimate structures of the post-Republic order: administrative, regulatory, judicial, and cultural. Half-measures preserve the regime. Norm-preservation preserves the regime—because the norms were established under the regime and function to sustain it. Neither norms nor the regime are *the good*, the people, their ordered liberty, and their traditional culture is. The window of lawful power is the window for restoration, and nothing less than the full use of that window answers the scale of what must be undone.

When the Left holds power, the imperative is maximal delegitimization. Not cooperation. Not moderation. Not compromise within the Left's framework—which is itself the framework of the regime that replaced the Republic. Delegitimization at every available opportunity, at every level. Treating the regime's governance as legitimate—even tacitly, through ordinary courtesies—reinforces the very order that must be overturned.

Here it is worth naming a specific asymmetry the reader must absorb before going further. The Left overthrew the Republic in part by exploiting its failure to solve for the paradox of toleration. The paradox, first named by Karl Popper in 1945[32] and since then weaponized almost exclusively against the Right, is simply this: a society that extends absolute toleration to all comers—including to actors who intend to destroy it—will eventually be conquered by the least tolerant force within it. A society with no mechanism to exclude the intolerant provides no defense against a takeover, and the takeover, once complete, ends the tolerance.

The dialectical inversion that followed Popper was ruthless. Marcuse's *Repressive Tolerance* argued that solving for the paradox required the active repression of Rightist movements and the active assistance of Leftist ones—tolerance redefined as one-way, as if the regime was already in their hands. Soros's Open Society Foundation operationalized the same logic at global scale. The argument was that the Right is the intolerant force against which the open society must defend itself. This is a lie, and it is a lie the reader should be equipped to refute at the level of definitions.

The truth is that toleration is a Rightist virtue, not a Leftist one. It descends from the classically liberal tradition of agreeing not to go to war over small differences, from the original American meaning of *secular* as the state refusing to arbitrate between Christian denominations, and from every civic tradition that proceeds from the presupposition of ordered liberty. Every historical test confirms this. The French revolutionaries of the Terror versus the French Catholic Right; the Bolsheviks under Lenin and Stalin versus the Russian monarchists and kulaks; the Woke versus the American traditionalist; America in 1996 versus America in 2026. In every case the Right is the more-tolerant party, and in every case the Left moves to censorship, eugenics, slander, and the seizure of children as soon as it acquires the power to do so. This is not an aberration. The Left's disposition to intolerance is structural. It descends from Plato, who demanded censorship of Homer, demanded the state manufacture a new faith, demanded children be seized from parents and raised communally in the state's ethic, and demanded the perpetual manufacture of noble lies.

These are not edge cases. They are the operating principles of every Platonic regime from Athens to the *Republic*-shaped institutions operating in America today.

Once the reader sees this clearly, the paradox resolves in the reverse of the direction the Left has been pointing it. The Left is not the party defending toleration against Rightist intolerance. The Left is the intolerant force to which toleration is always eventually lost. The Right's task—the counter-revolutionary task—is to solve for the paradox by identifying and excluding that tolerance that exceeds the threshold of allowing revolutionary victory, and doing so through the properly ordered mechanisms of government, civic institutions, and individual action that the following sections describe.

The playbook worked, in other words, because the Republic was built on the presumption of good-faith civic contest, and its institutions succumbed to subversion at scale. The early republic failed to be aggressive enough soon enough to prevent its own demise. Our leaders of the Progressive Era ran, not walked, hand in hand with agents of the Soviet Union, into the failure to solve for the paradox. Readers drawn to the symmetry of the situation may be tempted to imagine that the same playbook can be run in reverse—that patient infiltration of captured institutions will, over time, overthrow the new regime as the old one was overthrown.

It cannot. The regime that replaced the Republic is not vulnerable to that attack vector. It is an oligarchic democratic regime animated by the religious system this book has traced, and oligarchic regimes have no structural compunction about inflicting pain on their enemies. The Republic's tolerance was the very feature its enemies exploited; the regime has no such tolerance. It will not extend good faith. It will not treat infiltration as ordinary dissent to be answered with argument. It will identify infiltrators and crush them—and it will use the apparatus described in the preceding section to do it. The consequence is that the strategic register of the counter-revolution cannot be the mirror image of the revolution that preceded it. It cannot be the tortoise that wins the race by slow and steady means. The counter-revolution must operate through the maximal lawful wielding of power when power is held, and through delegitimization when it is not—not through patient infiltration hoping for eventual capture, because the regime will not sleep through the infiltration the way the Republic did. It must do so with little regard for manufactured public sentiments.

There is no neutral institutional ground to return to. Any strategy that behaves as if there were is operating on a fiction. The win conditions that follow are worked out on that understanding.

A final strategic distinction belongs here before we proceed to domain-by-domain tactics. Institutions are not uniformly vulnerable. The research on minority influence suggests it takes only a few percent of a group's membership, committed and intolerant of the dominant dogma, to bend the group as a whole. This is the mechanism by which the Left captured the institutions over the past century, and it is the mechanism available in reverse—but only against institutions that retain some degree of liberal operating firmware, some residual tolerance of internal dissent. Classically liberal institutions can be captured from within by a committed minority willing to be more intolerant than the surrounding culture. Totalitarian-dogmatic institutions cannot. Once an institution has locked onto the religious system of the Left as its operating code, and power is consolidated, it will not bend to an internal minority. It will purge that minority the moment it is recognized. For such institutions—and the reader should assume the major universities, the prestige media, and much of the federal bureaucracy fall into this category—the correct strategic posture is not counter-hegemonic capture but explicit replacement: the patient construction of parallel institutions built from the start on Rightist, traditionalist, transcendent-ethic foundations, and charter-level protection against recapture. Any new institution without such explicit foundations will be rapidly captured or externally battered into submission by the Leftist apparatus it was built to escape, and any founded on an unwillingness to be intolerant of Leftist internal attack are worse than useless – they are a money and time sink.

EDUCATION

The ethical factory described earlier in this book—the Prussian-imported, Dewey-corrupted, Blavatsky-to-CASEL pipeline that produces the spellbound at industrial scale—must be dismantled. This is not optional. It is the precondition for everything else. As long as the state retains a monopoly on the ethical formation of children, every other victory is temporary, because the factory will simply produce a new generation of spellbound to undo whatever gains we make.

The sphere-sovereignty principle is the key. Our Constitutions, SCOTUS precedents, and various legislation all serve to guarantee that most of education, and certainly the realm of ethical development, remains the sole domain of the parent and, if they so choose—and they should—the Church. These people are actively and with the most up-to-date scientific methods inculcating a totalizing ethical framework in your children that is, quite likely, oppositional to your own.

Victory in education means the restoration of parental authority over ethical formation as a matter of constitutional law and social expectation. It means legislation that breaks the Blavatsky-Bailey-Fetzer-CASEL pipeline at every joint—and the legislative toolkit for doing so was laid out in Chapter 8. The strategic keystone: a resolution declaring Marxism a religion under the Establishment Clause, reframing the entire legal battlespace such that every SEL module and "equity" training becomes the imposition of a state religion on captive children. The other sie of the same coin is legislative reform positively requiring a traditional American lens in public education. The tactical legislation: the CHARLIE Act prohibiting the pedagogy, the Science in Education Act attacking the pseudoscientific legitimation, the Anti-Communism Education Act mandating knowledge of the enemy, and targeted amendments cutting the data and money pipelines that fuel the apparatus. The full text of each bill appears in the endnotes. They are offered as proof of concept and as templates for any state legislature willing to wage this fight.

Each of these bills was filed. Each was fought over. Most were killed in committee by the very forces this book describes—Progressive legislators, captured education bureaucrats, and the NEA-affiliated lobbying apparatus that functions not as a union but as a political warfare machine. The point is not that they passed. The point is that they exist, that the arguments behind them are sound, that they can be adapted and filed in any state in the union, and that when enough legislatures begin filing them simultaneously the institutional resistance will be spread too thin to hold.

Next, those willing must be provided off-ramps from the government-run educational system. The total legalization of homeschooling, which simply recognizes a preexisting parental right, should occur everywhere. Where not all parents might have the luxury of being able to home-school while also putting food on the table, it can also be extremely helpful to offer scholarships, vouchers, freedom accounts, and the like to enable the selection of private education by everyday citizens. Further, legislation to mitigate risk to parents choosing home or private education, such as protections from using their own choice for education as predicate for investigations, can also be very helpful. These are, cumulatively, designed to give everyday citizens every opportunity to self-select out of the esoteric

This is what the counter-revolution looks like at the legislative level. It is not glamorous. It is not fast. It is, however, how you dismantle a factory—one bolt at a time.

GOVERNMENT

The necropsy above establishes the diagnosis. The remedy is impeachment—pursued strategically, with momentum, against the biggest targets we can chew. But the law domain extends beyond impeachment of individual judges. It encompasses:

A return to pre-Marxist jurisprudence. The abandonment of the "living document" sorcery that turned the Constitution into whatever Progressives needed it to be on any given Tuesday. The reassertion of coequality among the branches—which means the legislature must stop genuflecting to judicial supremacy and start wielding its own constitutional powers: impeachment, jurisdiction-stripping, dissolution of inferior courts, and the power of the purse.

The Executive Branch, through agencies like the Department of Justice and Federal Trade Commission, can independently initiate investigations and file antitrust lawsuits to break up collusive networks. One of the largest nongovernmental problems we face is the cartelization of seemingly every major industry. The Legislative Branch can act alone by drafting and passing bills to strengthen antitrust laws and target specific anticompetitive industries, particularly those involved with aufheben (cancel) campaigns, affecting impeachment of bad judges and executive officials, and conducting public investigations subpoenaing top-level revolutionaries. The Judicial Branch, through independent rulings, can uphold antitrust violations and order remedies—they could even utilize controversial "disparate impact" standards for these complaints, thereby souring the disparate impact doctrine used as a weapon against us for so long by finding discrimination against culturally disfavored groups by univariate analysis.[33]

CULTURE

The cultural win condition flows from the analysis in Chapter 9: anti-Communism is the coalition glue, but the transcendent ethic is the foundation stone. The Right's metaphysical fragmentation—libertarians, traditionalists, civic nationalists, and Christians converging on threats but diverging on why they matter—cannot be resolved by a negative vision alone. Revival, in the Church, family, and civil spheres, or bust. The cultural win condition is taboo-making around democracy, faction, and perversion. The ultimate goal must be to make doing the right thing first socially acceptable and then socially obligatory. This is the remoralization. It is the reversal of the aufheben der Kultur. And it begins with truth—deployed with precision, grounded in the transcendent, and wielded without apology.

THE REPUBLIC

The structural win condition is federalism—real, muscular, confrontational federalism and the restoration of the republic so ordered. Not the polite federalism of policy papers and think-tank luncheons, but the federalism of nullification, interposition, and lesser magistrates who understand that their oath is to the Constitution and to God, not to the federal leviathan. The dual-sovereign tools outlined earlier in this chapter—nullification, interposition, the doctrine of the lesser magistrate—must be exercised as practice, not admired as theory. States must nullify. Legislatures must impeach. Sheriffs must interpose. Citizens must organize. The infrastructure must be built from below so that when the opportunity comes—whether through an American Caesar or through the cumulative weight of a thousand well-chosen battles—the foundation is there to re-found America on stone.

CLOSING

We are no longer looking to conserve. The conservation of this remnant does not motivate us. It just cannot. We are on a path inexorably towards greater, not lesser, tyranny, and we know it. We are here for a refounding, a remoralization, and a political counter-revolution.

To advance this doctrine we must, for the moment, subordinate our own individual preferences to this broader goal. We must see the enemy clearly for what it is: a dogmatic and zealous cult of death bent on devouring our families and communities. That is not hyperbole. This is not simply for a better future, as politicians are known to say. We must do this to ensure *any* future at all. Everything is on the line now. We must hang together, or surely, we will hang separately.

There are no mulligans, no redoes, nobody coming to save us. This is what must be understood by those who contend that a good election result means that "we're winning." Even if it is true that "we're winning," in some respect, we're also very close to losing—just once. Once is all it takes. If they consolidate power completely its game over.

Incremental accommodation fails the iterated test. Provocation succeeds when met with restraint. Only decisive escalation—unified, transcendent in ethic, above the threshold—secures the republic.

There is no easy button. There are no shortcuts. There is no way out but through.

You have now read the anatomy of the spell. You know what the matrix is—the constructed pseudoreality in which you have been living. You know how it was built—from the mystery religions of Kemet through Plato's Academy, through Hegel and Marx and the Frankfurt School, through the Prussian import and Dewey's factory and the Blavatsky-to-CASEL pipeline, into your child's classroom and your state legislature. You know how the language was stolen, how the dialectic works, how the Church of Marx conducts its liturgy, how the Long March captured the institutions, how the ethical factory produces the spellbound at scale, how the Left-Right paradigm was engineered to keep you trapped, how the pseudoreality is maintained through paramoral enforcement, and how the theory of mind explains both the argumentative immunity of the indoctrinated and the psychological carnage left in their wake. You know the difference between the wizards who cast the spells and the spellbound who suffer under them.

The counterspells are forged. Reality is the weapon. Truth is the blade. Righteous anger is the arm that swings it.

I know the cost of this fight. I was raised on the Left, and the foremost orientation of that upbringing was not the goodness of Leftism but a hatred of—and an assuredness of the evil in—conservatism. I understood the effect of social mediation on beliefs quite strongly, as it was a very close family member who functioned as a perpetual link to Leftism, and whose opinions of me kept me constrained, mentally, outside of the realm of reality, unwilling to break free for fear of disappointment and relationship damage. Little did I realize at the time that the act of being disowned by my mother for my faith and politics would, though devastating emotionally, set me free both mentally and ethically to pursue truth and goodness. Since then I have been the subject of media hit pieces manufactured from whole cloth, slandered by small-time Progressive political warfare operators who bit off more than they could chew, and watched as colleagues I thought were allies folded under social pressure at critical moments. I am an effective opponent to the Leftist machine—as well as their GOPe allies—in my strategies, legislation, and my own political warfare on behalf of the good people I represent. That is why they come for me. It is also why I am still standing–because I must.

I tell you this not for sympathy—I chose this—but so you understand that the path through is not theoretical, nor is it rhetorical. It has been walked. It cost something real. It will cost you something too. It cost me relationships, comfort, and the ease of ignorance. It will cost you something too. But the alternative—the cost of doing nothing—is paid not by you alone, but by your children, and theirs, and the civilization that shelters them all.

How then do you move forward? What is the next step?

First: stop. You have recognized you are on a battlefield. Take cover and buy yourself space to think it through (again, turn off the television and stop doomscrolling). Take a moment to digest what you have read here, and consider the battlefield on which you now find yourself. When you put this book down, do not put it down for good—come back and pick it up again on occasion. You will find things the second time that you did not catch during the first go-round.

Then, once you have recovered a bit, and once you have decided to believe something is true, it is time to act like you believe it is true.

Nobody is coming to save us—unless you decide to. That does not mean putting on a cape and thrusting Communism into the sun. There is no one single thing I can tell you to do. You are unique. You have special talents. You have special circumstances. You have opportunities presented to you that nobody else does. Where do you fit in all of this? Maybe it is in raising up a strong family. Maybe it is taking what I have put together, doing ten-thousand hours of your own research, and releasing the next book that moves this fight down the road and exposes the areas that are still within the fog for me. Maybe it is having a conversation about what sacrifices are necessary to homeschool your child. Maybe it is operating a counter-hegemonic takeover of your local GOP entity to toss out the bums and recruit people who actually want to win to the political scene. Maybe it is stepping foot in a real Church for the first time in your life—or in a long time.

We must stop deluding ourselves. We must abandon relativism and nihilism. We must tear down those thorny hedgerows the enemy has built within our minds around those thoughts we must allow ourselves to think to defeat them. We must reconnect with our senses. We must find our way back to reality, and when we do we must purge our minds of the falsehoods that do not comport with it, and adjust our perspective to minimize our own errors going forward.

With what I have provided in this book I am confident you will come to think of dozens of things that never crossed my mind. I know you are going to take these next steps. I know it because I know you are beginning to understand the stakes. This is a fight for the existence of a civilization—it is not about marginal tax rates.

Find your footing. Be an anti-Communist. Do enough.

AFTERWORD

You have just finished a long book. The arguments were dense in places and the stakes were named at full weight, because the stakes are at full weight. But arguments and stakes do not, by themselves, change a single thing in the world. What changes things is a reader who closes the book and then does something on Monday morning.

What follows is not a summary. It is the version of this book you can carry in your pocket. Twelve plain lessons—no philosophy, no jargon, no footnotes—addressed to you as a person with a job and a family and only so many hours in the week. If you forget everything else and remember these, the book has done its work.

1. Call things by their proper name.

The lie that captures you first is the one you repeat uncritically. A man is a man. A woman is a woman. A lie is a lie. When the words are wrong, the thoughts that follow cannot be right. Most people who are losing the argument with the present culture lost it at the level of vocabulary before they ever reached the level of ideas. Fix the vocabulary and the rest becomes salvageable.

2. Niceness is not a virtue.

Conflict-aversion is not kindness, it is the absence of courage wearing kindness as a costume. Good men rebuke evil. Nice men let it pass and call their cowardice good manners. Do not be a nice man. Be a good one.

3. Ignorance is not an excuse, and neither is going along.

You are responsible for what you do and for what you fail to do. Abdicating your judgment to an authority—to an expert, to a party, to a pastor, to a commentator—does not transfer the moral weight of the decision. It just hides the weight from you. The weight is still there, still yours, still counted.

4. Pick one thing.

Do not try to correct the whole culture at once. You will exhaust yourself, alienate everyone near you, and accomplish nothing. Pick the one moral failing that offends you most—the one you cannot stop noticing—and practice being visibly, audibly intolerant of it. When you have made that one thing shameful in your corner of the world, or satisfactorily within yourself, pick the next one. How do you eat an elephant? One bite at a time.

5. Taboo is a tool. Use it.

The Left captured the culture by making its enemies' beliefs unspeakable. The same mechanism runs in reverse. Do not argue with every foolish claim; most foolish claims do not deserve argument. Make the foolish claim socially costly to hold. Shame is an underrated teacher. Most people will learn from the fact that the person next to them winced when they said something wrong.

6. A sharp tongue is the first sword.

Use it before the law has to. Open rebuke is a gift to the person being rebuked and to the community watching. Silence is complicity dressed up as manners. The people around you need to hear someone say the thing they are afraid to say. Be that person often enough and others will become that person too.

7. Do not trust anyone who tells you the fight is already won—or already lost.

Both are demobilization strategies. The first makes you comfortable while the ground shifts; the second makes you despair while the ground shifts. Neither is true, and anyone selling either is selling you a reason to go take a nap.

8. Raise your children yourself.

The people who wrote the curriculum for your child's ethical formation are the people this book has described. If you have handed that work over to the state, to a screen, to a peer group, or to whoever is trending this week, you have handed over the thing that matters most. Take it back. Eat dinner together. Read to them. Teach them what is true. Teach them what is beautiful. Teach them to pray. Teach them to work. Children sent to Caesar come back as Romans.

9. Build something.

The counter-revolution is not only a set of things to oppose. It is a set of things to build—families, churches, small institutions, friendships, businesses, neighborhoods, traditions. Every thing you build right is a brick pulled out of the regime's wall and set in the foundation of what replaces it.

10. Be useful to the people near you.

Grand political strategy is not for everyone. Today, be the person in your family, your church, and your street that the others can rely on. Be the one who shows up.

11. Keep your seriousness.

You are living through a time that rewards unseriousness and punishes the serious. Stay serious anyway. Stay serious about your work, your word, your marriage, your faith, your obligations, and the time you are living in.

12. Find a good local church, serve and be served.

This is the last lesson because it is the one that holds the other eleven together. You cannot do any of this on your own. You were not built to, and the project is not scaled for solo operators. Find a faithful local church—one that preaches the Word plainly, administers the sacraments rightly, and disciplines its members lovingly. Join it. Attend it every week. Give of your time and your money. Serve there. Bring your family there.

The counter-revolution is not going to be won by lone wolves with strong opinions. It is going to be won, if it is won at all, by reconstituted communities of serious, faithful people who have reordered their loves and their habits around something higher than the regime. The local church is where that happens. There is no substitute. Find one. Support it. Let it support you.

Acknowledgements

I would like to take a moment now to recognize and thank all the un-named influences that helped me to achieve the understanding of things I have now. That includes countless persons online, on social media, with podcasts and YouTube channels that I could not possibly recall for their individual contributions to my thoughts. It includes pastors and elders, both those I have been under, those I have only met briefly, and those whom I have only ever heard or read that influenced me greatly. It includes family and friends who have been patient with me in my younger years, and those who have been patient with me in my later years. Thank you all.

About the Author

Michael Belcher is a second-term Republican member of the New Hampshire House of Representatives, representing Carroll County District 4. He serves on the Education Policy and Administration Committee, the State-Federal Relations and Veterans Affairs Committee, and served on the Covid-19 Investigative Committee, where he was the primary author of the majority report. He is the author of the landmark resolution declaring Marxism a religion under the Establishment Clause (HR 15), the CHAR-LIE Act (HB 1792), and more than a dozen other bills and resolutions addressing education reform, judicial accountability, and the restoration of constitutional governance.

Born and raised in Portsmouth and Rye, New Hampshire, Belcher began his career in emergency medicine straight out of Portsmouth High School, serving as a Wilderness EMT and Paramedic, logging over a thousand volunteer hours with the Durham Ambulance Corps, and earning his Paramedic degree from Santa Fe College. He later taught emergency medicine at the college level. He went on to work in the trades at the Portsmouth Naval Shipyard, where he survived an industrial accident aboard a nuclear submarine.

Belcher lives in Wakefield, New Hampshire, with his wife, their daughter, and a stepson, along with a small flock of poultry. He is a Reformed Christian who attends church weekly in Wolfeboro. He gardens, shoots, and enjoys the New Hampshire outdoors.

He writes at apaththrough.substack.com and makes literally everyone mad on X @mikebelcher14.

BIBLIOGRAPHY

Aeschines. *Against Timarchus.*

American Academy of Pediatrics. "Policy Statement: Ensuring Comprehensive Care and Support for Transgender and Gender-Diverse Children and Adolescents." Authored by Jason Rafferty, Committee on Psychosocial Aspects of Child and Family Health, Committee on Adolescence, Section on Lesbian, Gay, Bisexual, and Transgender Health and Wellness. *Pediatrics* 142, no. 4 (October 2018).

Aristotle. *Metaphysics. Nicomachean Ethics. Politics.*

Bailey, Alice A. *Education in the New Age.* New York: Lucis Publishing Company, 1954.

Bernays, Edward. *Propaganda.* New York: Horace Liveright, 1928.

Blankenhorn, David. *Fatherless America: Confronting Our Most Urgent Social Problem.* New York: Basic Books, 1995.

Blankenhorn, David. *The Future of Marriage.* New York: Encounter Books, 2007.

Blankenhorn, David. "Clinton's Alinsky Problem—and Ours." *The American Interest,* October 11, 2016.

Blankenhorn, David. "How My View on Gay Marriage Changed." *New York Times,* June 22, 2012.

Cantor, James M. "Transgender and Gender Diverse Children and Adolescents: Fact-Checking of AAP Policy." *Journal of Sex & Marital Therapy* 46, no. 4 (2020): 307–313.

Cass, Hilary. *Independent Review of Gender Identity Services for Children and Young People: Final Report.* Commissioned by NHS England. London, April 2024. cass.independent-review.uk.

Coughlin, Stephen, and Rich Higgins. *Re-Remembering the Mis-Remembered Left.* Washington, DC: Unconstrained Analytics, 2018.

Crenshaw, Kimberlé, et al., eds. *Critical Race Theory: The Key Writings That Formed the Movement*. New York: New Press, 1995.

Crichton, Michael. "Aliens Cause Global Warming." Caltech Michelin Lecture, Pasadena, CA, January 17, 2003.

Dawkins, Richard. *The Selfish Gene*. Oxford: Oxford University Press, 1976. *The Extended Phenotype*. Oxford: Oxford University Press, 1982.

Dewey, John. *Democracy and Education*. New York: Macmillan, 1916.

DiAngelo, Robin. *White Fragility: Why It's So Hard for White People to Talk About Racism*. Boston: Beacon Press, 2018.

Dodd, Bella V. *School of Darkness*. New York: P.J. Kenedy and Sons, 1954.

Elias, Maurice J., et al. *Promoting Social and Emotional Learning: Guidelines for Educators*. Alexandria, VA: ASCD, 1997.

Fanon, Frantz. *The Wretched of the Earth*. New York: Grove Press, 1963.

Fauci, Anthony S. Interview on *Face the Nation*. CBS News, November 28, 2021.

Fichte, Johann Gottlieb. *Addresses to the German Nation*. 1808.

Food and Drug Administration, U.S. "Fact Sheet for Health Care Providers: Emergency Use Authorization (EUA) of Sotrovimab." Revisions in 2021 and 2022.

Freire, Paulo. *Pedagogy of the Oppressed*. Translated by Myra Bergman Ramos. New York: Herder and Herder, 1970.

Gallagher, Maggie. "Bigotry, David Blankenhorn, and the Future of Marriage." *Public Discourse* (Witherspoon Institute), June 25, 2012.

Gore, Al. Address to the COP15 climate conference. Copenhagen, December 14, 2009.

Gramsci, Antonio. *Prison Notebooks*. Written 1929–1935; published posthumously.

Green, Elliott. "What are the most-cited publications in the social sciences (according to Google Scholar)?" LSE Impact of Social Sciences Blog, May 12, 2016.

Hall, Manly P. *The Secret Teachings of All Ages*. San Francisco: H.S. Crocker, 1928.

Hegel, Georg Wilhelm Friedrich. *Phenomenology of Spirit*. 1807. *Philosophy of Right*. 1821. *Lectures on the Philosophy of Religion*. 1831.

Holliday, Derek E., et al. "Why depolarization is hard: Evaluating attempts to decrease partisan animosity in America." *Proceedings of the National Academy of Sciences*, 2025.

Kendi, Ibram X. *How to Be an Antiracist*. New York: One World, 2019.

Kengor, Paul, and Mary A. Nicholas. *The Devil and Bella Dodd: One Woman's Struggle Against Communism and Her Redemption*. Gastonia, NC: TAN Books, 2022.

Lewis, C.S. *Mere Christianity*. London: Geoffrey Bles, 1952.

Lukács, György. "The Old Culture and the New Culture." *Telos*, No. 5 (Spring 1970), pp. 21–30.

Magee, Glenn Alexander. *Hegel and the Hermetic Tradition*. Ithaca: Cornell University Press, 2001.

Marcuse, Herbert. *Eros and Civilization: A Philosophical Inquiry into Freud*. Boston: Beacon Press, 1955.

Marcuse, Herbert. "Repressive Tolerance." In Robert Paul Wolff, Barrington Moore Jr., and Herbert Marcuse, *A Critique of Pure Tolerance*. Boston: Beacon Press, 1965.

Marx, Karl, and Friedrich Engels. *The Communist Manifesto*. 1848.

Miroshnychenko, A., et al. "Puberty blockers for gender dysphoria in youth: A systematic review and meta-analysis." *Archives of Disease in Childhood*, published online January 24, 2025. DOI: 10.1136/archdischild-2024-327909.

Minnesota Department of Health. "Ethical Framework for the Allocation of Monoclonal Antibodies." December 2021.

New York State Department of Health. "Prioritization of Anti-SARS-CoV-2 Monoclonal Antibodies and Oral Antivirals for the Treatment of COVID-19 During Times of Resource Limitations." Memorandum, December 27, 2021.

Orwell, George. *1984*. London: Secker and Warburg, 1949.

Pieper, Josef. *Abuse of Language, Abuse of Power*. San Francisco: Ignatius Press, 1992.

Plato. *Republic. Symposium. Timaeus. Phaedrus. Charmides. Protagoras. Meno. Gorgias.*

Plato. *The Republic*. Edited by G.R.F. Ferrari, translated by Tom Griffith. Cambridge: Cambridge University Press, 2000.

Popper, Karl. *The Open Society and Its Enemies*. Vol. 1, *The Spell of Plato*. London: Routledge, 1945.

powell, john a. "Deepening Our Understanding of Structural Marginalization." *Poverty & Race* 22, no. 5 (2013).

Rubin, Gayle. "Thinking Sex: Notes for a Radical Theory of the Politics of Sexuality." 1984.

Ruuska, S.-M., K. Tuisku, T. Holttinen, and R. Kaltiala. "Psychiatric Morbidity Among Adolescents and Young Adults Who Contacted Specialised Gender Identity Services in Finland in 1996–2019: A Register Study." *Acta Paediatrica* (2026): 1–9. DOI: 10.1111/apa.70533. Published April 4, 2026.

Shapiro, Jeremy. "Dialectical Political Messaging: A Strategy for Democrats?" *Psychology Today*, December 1, 2020.

Sowell, Thomas. *Basic Economics: A Common Sense Guide to the Economy*. New York: Basic Books, 2000.

Steiner, David M., and Susan D. Rozen. "Preparing Tomorrow's Teachers." In *A Qualified Teacher in Every Classroom?*, edited by Frederick M. Hess et al. Cambridge, MA: Harvard Education Press, 2004.

Symonds, Kevin. "Communist Infiltration?" *Homiletic and Pastoral Review*, December 2021.

Utah Department of Health. "Crisis Standards of Care Monoclonal Antibody Allocation Guidelines." January 2022.

Westbrook, Robert B. *John Dewey and American Democracy*. Ithaca: Cornell University Press, 1991.

Xenophon. *Memorabilia. Symposium.*

Additional works referenced in the text include: *Active Measures*; Alinsky, Saul, *Rules for Radicals* (1971); *Beautiful Trouble*; the *Corpus Hermeticum*; the *Emerald Tablet*; the *Kybalion*; Sun Tzu, *The Art of War*; and *Unrestricted Warfare*. Works by Edward O. Wilson, Kant, Heidegger, and Crenshaw are referenced in context but not quoted at length. Frankfurt School and critical-theory works by Adorno, Horkheimer, Habermas, and Foucault are referenced throughout but cited primarily through secondary literature and through the *Coughlin and Higgins* volume noted above. Government and litigation records cited in the text—including *Jacobson v.*

Bassett (N.D.N.Y.) and *Roberts v. Bassett* (E.D.N.Y.)—are identified at the point of citation rather than indexed here.

1. The primary source is Mary A. Nicholas, MD, and Paul Kengor, PhD, *The Devil and Bella Dodd: One Woman's Struggle Against Communism and Her Redemption* (Gastonia, NC: TAN Books, 2022). ISBN: 978-1-5051-2918-2. The claim that Dodd helped place over a thousand Communist men into Catholic seminaries rests on the testimony of witnesses who attended her lectures in the 1960s, principally Alice von Hildebrand and Johnine and Paul Leininger (who signed a 2002 affidavit). The claim does not appear in Dodd's own autobiography, *School of Darkness* (1954), nor in her public congressional testimony before the Senate Internal Security Subcommittee (1952–53) or HUAC (1953). Kengor himself acknowledged in a Crisis Magazine interview that the number is "a pretty outlandish claim on its face" and speculated that of the claimed thousand, he would "be surprised if a hundred even got through." Researcher Kevin Symonds published the most thorough independent analysis in Homiletic and Pastoral Review (December 2021), concluding that the authority for the specific numbers rests not upon any documented statements from Dodd directly. The manuscript presents this claim as attributed to witnesses rather than as established fact.

2. Georgi Arbatov, quoted in Strobe Talbott and in contemporaneous reporting by Arnold Beichman (*Washington Times*) and Charles Paul Freund, "Where Did All Our Villains Go?" *Washington Post*, December 11, 1988.

3. Georgy Arbatov, memorandum to General Secretary Gorbachev, June 1988, describing the Moscow Summit as "the breaking of the enemy image" of the Soviet Union in Western perception. National Security Archive, George Washington University, declassified Soviet documents collection. Available at nsarchive.gwu.edu/document/22558-document-11-georgy-arbatov-memo-gorbachev.

4. Plato, The Republic, ed. G.R.F. Ferrari, trans. Tom Griffith (Cambridge University Press, 2000), Introduction.

274

5. Herbert Marcuse, *Eros and Civilization: A Philosophical Inquiry into Freud* (Boston: Beacon Press, 1955; reprinted with new preface 1966). The passage referencing Plato's *Symposium* and *orthos paiderastein*—the "road to higher culture" through the "true love of boys"—appears at p. 211 of the 1966 Beacon Press paperback edition, in the chapter "The Transformation of Sexuality into Eros." The passage is discussed and quoted by Stephen Coughlin and Richard Higgins in *Re-Remembering the Mis-Remembered Left* (Unconstrained Analytics, 2018/2019), which is where this book's attention to it originated. Mathematician and critical-theory analyst James Lindsay has publicly engaged with this passage and its context in joint discussion with Coughlin—see the December 9, 2022 Courtenay Turner Podcast episode "Platonic Roots of Marxism, Democracy & secret society references," in which Lindsay and Coughlin annotate *Eros and Civilization*, Plato's *Symposium*, and the *Republic* directly from the texts. Attempts to verify the passage against widely circulated digital editions of *Eros and Civilization* have encountered passages that appear incomplete relative to the physical text; whether this reflects editorial decisions by Beacon Press, idiosyncrasies of particular digital vendors, or something else remains unclear. Readers seeking to verify the passage at p. 211 are advised to consult physical library copies of the 1955 Beacon Press first edition or the 1966 Beacon Press paperback rather than relying on digital sources.

6. Glenn Alexander Magee, Hegel and the Hermetic Tradition (Ithaca: Cornell University Press, 2001; 2nd ed., 2008). ISBN: 978-0801438721 (hardcover); 978-0801474507 (paperback). 304 pp. Magee was Assistant Professor of Philosophy at the C.W. Post Campus of Long Island University. The book originated as a doctoral thesis and is the first book-length academic study of the subject. Magee's argument, sustained through painstaking textual and biographical analysis, is that Hegel was "decisively influenced by the Hermetic tradition, a body of thought with roots in Greco-Roman Egypt." The evidentiary record Magee assembles is extensive: Hegel's personal library included Hermetic writings by Agrippa, Böhme, Bruno, and Paracelsus; he read widely on Mesmerism, psychic phenomena, dowsing, precognition, and sorcery; he publicly associated himself with known occultists, including Franz von Baader; he structured his philosophy in a manner identical to the Hermetic use of Correspondences; he stated in his lectures more than once that the term "speculative" (the foundation of his speculative philosophy) means the same thing as "mystical"; he aligned himself informally with Hermetic societies including the Freemasons and Rosicrucians; his preface to the 1821 Philosophy of Right includes alchemical and Rosicrucian imagery; and his 1831 Lectures on the Philosophy of Religion show the structural influence of the mystic Joachim of Fiore and Jakob Böhme. The divisions of Hegel's philosophy follow the pattern typical of Hermetic philosophy: the Phenomenology as purification, the Logic as Hermetic ascent to Universal Mind. This was not a controversial claim in the decades immediately after Hegel's death. In the 1840s, Schelling publicly accused Hegel of borrowing from Jakob Böhme. A Hegel disciple, Friedrich Theodor Vischer, asked: "Have you forgotten that the new philosophy came forth from the school of the old mystics, especially from Jacob Boehme?" The suppression of this lineage was a later project of the secular academy—one this manuscript works to reverse. Specifically relevant to the Württemberg discussion: Magee documents that Hegel was raised in a Pietist tradition "deeply influenced by German mysticism, Boehmean theosophy, and Kabbalism"—naming Oetinger and Bengel as the specific Pietist figures whose mystical synthesis shaped the intellectual environment of Hegel's youth.

7. Blankenhorn biographical sources: Blankenhorn received an MA with distinction in Comparative Social History from the University of Warwick in 1978, as confirmed in his Perry v. Schwarzenegger trial testimony (Tr. 2717:24–2718:3) and his Encyclopedia.com entry (Contemporary Authors). E.P. Thompson, who founded the Centre for the Study of Social History at Warwick, resigned from the university in 1971—approximately six years before Blankenhorn's arrival. Blankenhorn studied in Thompson's program but not under Thompson personally. The Alinsky connection is documented in Blankenhorn's own words: in a 2012 interview with Connecticut Public ("David Blankenhorn And The Battle Over Same-Sex Marriage," ctpublic.org, June 22, 2012), he states "Alinsky was like our ultimate teacher for community organizing" and describes carrying Rules for Radicals "in our back pocket." His essay "Clinton's Alinsky Problem—and Ours" (The American Interest, October 11, 2016) confirms the "back pocket" phrasing verbatim. The same Connecticut Public interview confirms his visit to the Highlander Folk School during a 1985 bus tour. Perry v. Schwarzenegger, 704 F. Supp. 2d 921 (N.D. Cal. 2010). Under cross-examination, Blankenhorn conceded same-sex marriage would "be likely to improve the well-being of gay and lesbian households and their children" and identified twenty-two benefits from page 203 of his own book. Judge Walker ruled his testimony "unreliable and entitled to essentially no weight." Blankenhorn's op-ed, "How My View on Gay Marriage Changed," appeared in the New York Times, June 22, 2012. Maggie Gallagher's response, "Bigotry, David Blankenhorn, and the Future of Marriage," appeared on Public Discourse (Witherspoon Institute), June 25, 2012. Organizational data: Revenue and compensation from IRS Form 990 filings on ProPublica Nonprofit Explorer (EIN: 13-3400377). Revenue: $454,178 (FY Feb 2017) to $5,651,273 (FY Dec 2024). Blankenhorn base compensation: $245,466 (FY Dec 2024). The 60-40 funding split is self-reported (braverangels.org/our-financials/). Carnegie Corporation: $350,000 (2024 grants database). Hewlett Foundation: $75,000 seed funding (InfluenceWatch). Bill Doherty authored the "Citizen Therapist Manifesto Against Trumpism" in May 2016 (HuffPost; WNYC On the Media). Joan Blades co-founded MoveOn.org (1998) and Living Room Conversations (2010–11). Braver Angels (originally "Better Angels") was founded December 9, 2016 in South Lebanon, Ohio. Depolarization meta-analysis: Derek E. Holliday et al., "Why depolarization is hard: Evaluating attempts to decrease partisan animosity in America," Proceedings of the National Academy of Sciences, 2025. Average effect: 5.4-point shift on a 101-point scale, decaying within two weeks. Repeated exposure produced no cumulative benefits.

8. HR 15 (New Hampshire House, 2023)—Declaring Marxism a Religion. Prime sponsor: Rep. Belcher, Carr. 4; co-sponsor: Rep. Corcoran, Hills. 44. A resolution identifying the wholly religious nature of Marxism in order to begin building legal movement towards finding that the Progressive paradigm of government constitutes a violation of the Establishment Clause. The resolution defines religion as a faith system with accompanying metaphysics, theories of knowledge, presuppositions about existence and consciousness, ethical claims giving rise to duties of conscience, theories of history, and end-times mythology. It defines Marxism as any of the varied ideologies within the broader genus of dialectical Leftism, including communism, woke-ism, neo-Marxism, intersectionality, and fascism. Through fourteen whereas clauses, the resolution documents that Marxism presents fundamental metaphysical claims; asserts the oppressor-oppressed dialectic as the basis for understanding History; gives rise to duties of conscience to be "on the right side of history"; forwards a doctrine of scientism as religious faith; wields alchemically inspired "magic spells" of social construction; prophesies the immanentization of the eschaton; and seeks "equity," "diversity," "inclusion," and "justice" as religious concepts with specific esoteric meanings. The resolving clause finds that Marxism represents a religion and complete faith system, that this doctrine is in direct opposition and mutually exclusive to American founding ideology, that while citizens personally holding these views may be protected by First Amendment freedom of religion rights, this religious doctrine runs totally and disastrously afoul of the Establishment Clause insofar as its religious practices, doctrines, and eschatology have been implemented in or by government; and is violative of individuals' freedoms of religion, conscience, association, and speech insofar as mandated by any entity in America.

9. Antonio Gramsci, *Selections from the Prison Notebooks*, ed. and trans. Quintin Hoare and Geoffrey Nowell Smith (New York: International Publishers, 1971), 238.

10. György Lukács (1885–1971) theorized the dialectical destruction and revolutionary replacement of bourgeois culture in a lecture delivered on March 21, 1919—the day the Hungarian Soviet Republic was proclaimed—titled "The Old Culture and the New Culture" (Az régi kultúra és az új kultúra). The lecture was translated into English and published as "The Old Culture and the New Culture," Telos, No. 5 (Spring 1970), pp. 21–30. An introduction and contextual notes by Paul Breines appear in the same issue (pp. 1–20). In the lecture, Lukács argues that capitalism has destroyed the conditions for genuine culture by subordinating all human activity to production, and that communist society must therefore annihilate the old bourgeois cultural order entirely—not reform it—and replace it through a dialectical process of destruction and synthesis. The Hegelian aufheben—which simultaneously abolishes, preserves, and elevates—is the operative concept: culture is to be canceled in its present form precisely so that a higher cultural synthesis can emerge. Lukács's position was not merely theoretical. He served as Deputy Commissar for Culture and Education in the Hungarian Soviet Republic (March–August 1919), where he implemented sweeping cultural programs that contemporaries described as "cultural terrorism"—nationalizing theaters, restructuring education, and deploying state power against inherited cultural institutions. When the Republic fell, Lukács fled to Vienna; he spent subsequent decades elaborating the theory of cultural revolution that these weeks had enacted in practice. Antonio Gramsci's complementary concept of egemonia (hegemony) and the "war of position" through institutions, developed in his Prison Notebooks (written 1929–1935, published posthumously), provides the institutional capture dimension of the same strategy. Where Lukács theorized the cultural destruction, Gramsci theorized the patient institutional replacement.

11. Dewey enrolled at Johns Hopkins University in 1882 and received his Ph.D. in 1884. The Internet Encyclopedia of Philosophy (iep.utm.edu/john-dewey/) states: "George Sylvester Morris, a German-trained Hegelian philosopher, exposed Dewey to the organic model of nature characteristic of German idealism." The Stanford Encyclopedia of Philosophy (plato.stanford.edu/entries/dewey/) confirms that Dewey's graduate school influences were "Neo-Hegelian idealism, Darwinian biology, and Wundtian experimental psychology," and that his early work "aimed at merging experimental psychology with idealism." His first two books at the University of Michigan—Psychology (1887) and Leibniz's New Essays Concerning the Human Understanding (1888)—both expressed Dewey's early commitment to British neo-Hegelianism. Dewey's 1884 essay "The New Psychology" (Andover Review, vol. 2, pp. 278–289) and his 1887 Psychology are the primary texts of this early Hegelian period. In Psychology, Dewey attempted a synthesis of Hegelian idealism and experimental science—a project that mapped the Hegelian concept of spirit's self-realization onto the new empirical psychology. A note on terminology: The main text uses "Young Hegelian" as a descriptor for Dewey's formation. In the strict historical sense, the Young Hegelians were a specific mid-nineteenth-century German movement—the circle around Marx, Feuerbach, Bauer, and Strauss—that predated Dewey. The standard scholarly label for Dewey's early orientation is "neo-Hegelian" or "British neo-Hegelian idealist." The usage here is rhetorically apt—it places Dewey accurately within the Hegelian tradition as a committed inheritor of its structure—but readers familiar with European intellectual history may note the distinction. The most comprehensive scholarly biography is Robert B. Westbrook, John Dewey and American Democracy (Ithaca: Cornell University Press, 1991). For Dewey's educational philosophy and its Hegelian architecture, see Democracy and Education (New York: Macmillan, 1916) and Alan Ryan, John Dewey and the High Tide of American Liberalism (New York: W.W. Norton, 1995).

12. Third most cited in all social sciences: Elliott Green, "What are the most-cited publications in the social sciences (according to Google Scholar)?," LSE Impact of Social Sciences Blog, London School of Economics, May 12, 2016. Green surveyed all social science publications exceeding 20,000 Google Scholar citations and ranked Pedagogy of the Oppressed #3, behind only Thomas Kuhn's The Structure of Scientific Revolutions and Everett Rogers's Diffusion of Innovations. As of early 2026, Google Scholar shows approximately 133,000+ aggregated citations across editions. A Springer Nature encyclopedia entry states the book has been "cited more than 72,000 times—the most in the world in the education discipline," likely reflecting a different database or date-limited count. Among the most assigned in education schools: David M. Steiner and Susan D. Rozen, "Preparing Tomorrow's Teachers: An Analysis of Syllabi from a Sample of America's Schools of Education," in Hess, Rotherham, and Walsh, eds., A Qualified Teacher in Every Classroom? (Cambridge, MA: Harvard Education Press, 2004), pp. 119–148. Analysis of 45 foundations-of-education syllabi from 16 schools of education (14 ranked in the U.S. News top 30) found Freire among the top four most frequently assigned authors, and among the top two or three excluding standard textbook authors. For contrast, E.D. Hirsch appeared on only 2 of the 45 syllabi and Diane Ravitch on just 1. The Open Syllabus Project, analyzing 27.6 million syllabi across 140 countries, places Pedagogy of the Oppressed in the top 100 most assigned texts across all university disciplines worldwide—the only Brazilian-authored book on the list. Full citation: Paulo Freire, Pedagogy of the Oppressed, trans. Myra Bergman Ramos (New York: Herder and Herder, 1970; 30th anniversary ed., New York: Continuum, 2000). Over 1 million copies sold worldwide.

13. The organizational history of the Lucis Trust is documented on the organization's own website and requires no inference. The Lucis Trust History page (lucistrust.org/about_us/history) states: "A publishing company, initially named Lucifer Publishing Company, was established by Alice and Foster Bailey in the State of New Jersey, USA, in May 1922 to publish the book, Initiation Human and Solar. The ancient myth of Lucifer refers to the angel who brought light to the world, and it is assumed that the name was applied to the publishing company in honour of a journal, which had been edited for a number of years by theosophical founder, HP Blavatsky. The company's name was changed in 1924 to Lucis Publishing Company." A separate Lucis Trust article on "The Esoteric Meaning of Lucifer" elaborates: "For a brief period of two or three years in the early 1920's, when Alice and Foster Bailey were beginning to publish the books published under her name, they named their fledgling publishing company 'Lucifer Publishing Company'. . . the name was changed to Lucis Publishing Company." The organization thus acknowledges the original name on its own website while explaining its interpretation of the symbolism. UN address and consultative status: The Lucis Trust's New York office is located at 866 United Nations Plaza, Suite 482, New York, NY 10017—a building adjacent to the United Nations headquarters. The UN's own ECOSOC database (esango.un.org, Profile Code 945) confirms that the Lucis Trust holds Roster Consultative Status with the UN Economic and Social Council (ECOSOC), granted in 1989. The Lucis Trust's own page (lucistrust.org/about_us/support_un) states: "The Lucis Trust has Consultative Status with the Economic and Social Council of the United Nations (ECOSOC) and World Goodwill is recognized by the Department of Global Communications at the United Nations as a Non-Governmental Organisation (NGO)." A note on "publishing UN materials": The Lucis Trust publishes its own materials in support of UN goals and programs, and distributes them through channels adjacent to the UN. It is not an official publisher or contractor of UN documents—that function belongs to the UN's own publishing operations. The more precise characterization is that the Lucis Trust produces and disseminates advocacy material aligned with UN educational and spiritual programs, and that Alice Bailey's Education in the New Age appears in the UNESCO document library. The organizational relationship is one of aligned mission and mutual recognition, not contractual publishing.

14. Alice A. Bailey, Education in the New Age (New York: Lucis Publishing Company, 1954; posthumous). Full text publicly available at bailey.it/files/Education-in-the-New-Age.pdf. The following quotations are confirmed verbatim from the sections on parenthood trends and the new racial type: "The need of an increasing birthrate will be eventually regarded as erroneous"; "The science of eugenics and of sex hygiene and the development of mentally controlled relationships will steadily grow" (enumerated point 3 in the same section); "millions of souls have been brought into incarnation who were never intended at this time to incarnate... War has consequently been the inevitable result of this undue and unlimited propagation of the human species" (in the context of Theosophical evolutionary soul doctrine, wherein insufficiently evolved souls inhabiting human bodies produce civilizational degradation); and the new race emerging "primarily in those lands where the fifth or Caucasian races are to be found." Bailey's caveat—"I speak not in terms of the Aryan race as it is generally understood today or in its Nordic implications"—does not alter the substance of the racial hierarchy she describes. Scholars Victor Shnirelman and Isaac Lubelsky have both documented the racist dimensions of Bailey's Theosophical racial theories.

15. The founding of CASEL at the Fetzer Institute is not a matter of inference. It is stated plainly in the peer-reviewed academic literature, in CASEL's own published history, and in the Fetzer Institute's own communications. The most authoritative academic account appears in Nicole A. Elbertson, Marc A. Brackett, and Roger P. Weissberg, "School-Based Social and Emotional Learning (SEL) Programming: Current Perspectives," in Andy Hargreaves et al., eds., Second International Handbook of Educational Change (Springer, 2010), pp. 1017–1032. Weissberg was a CASEL co-founder and served as its executive director for decades; the account is effectively primary. The text reads: "In 1994, the Fetzer Institute hosted a conference to address concerns about the various, disjointed school-based efforts that had surfaced over the years. In attendance were a range of researchers, educators, and advocates. . . these issues were discussed, and the term social and emotional learning (SEL) was introduced. . . Out of this 1994 meeting, the Collaborative for Academic, Social, and Emotional Learning (CASEL) was formed." CASEL's own website (casel.org/about-us/our-history/) lists seven founders, one of whom is identified as David J. Sluyter, Senior Advisor of the Fetzer Institute—confirming that the Institute was not merely a venue but an organizational participant. The site describes the founding location as "a small conference in Kalamazoo"—the city where the Fetzer Institute is headquartered. The Fetzer Institute's own website (fetzer.org/news/sel-numbers/, December 1, 2022) states: "The Fetzer Institute's commitment to whole child development dates to the 1990s when we played a significant funding and organizing role in what would become social and emotional learning." A Fetzer historical timeline entry additionally references "Support of Dan Goleman on early stage of what has become known as emotional intelligence. This work also helps establish the Collaborative for the Advancement of Social and Emotional Learning at Yale Child Study Center." The foundational published volume of the CASEL framework is: Maurice J. Elias et al., Promoting Social and Emotional Learning: Guidelines for Educators (Alexandria, VA: Association for Supervision and Curriculum Development, 1997), co-authored by nine CASEL collaborators. The term "social and emotional learning" itself was coined at the 1994 meeting. CASEL's original name was the "Collaborative to Advance Social and Emotional Learning," changed in 2001 to the "Collaborative for Academic, Social, and Emotional Learning." For a forensic examination of the Fetzer Institute's esoteric orientation and its role in establishing the SEL apparatus, see James Lindsay, "WTF is SEL?," New Discourses podcast, Episode 103, December 19, 2022 (newdiscourses.com/2022/12/wtf-is-sel/).

16. The Robert Muller School's World Core Curriculum Manual (Arlington, TX: Robert Muller School, ©1986; OCLC #17345643) states in its preface: "The underlying philosophy upon which The Robert Muller School is based will be found in the teachings set forth in the books of Alice A. Bailey by the Tibetan teacher, Djwhal Khul (published by Lucis Publishing Company, 113 University Place, 11th floor, New York, N.Y. USA 10083)." This is not inference or implication—it is the school's own statement of its philosophical foundation. The World Core Curriculum Journal Volume I lists ten references under "References for Curriculum Philosophy," all drawn from Alice Bailey's published works. Robert Muller himself endorsed the school bearing his name. His personal website records his response upon learning a school in Texas wished to adopt his curriculum: "I was overwhelmed to see a school named after me before I was dead!" The school was a service branch of the School of Ageless Wisdom, founded by Gloria Crook, who was herself an active participant in Lucis Trust's World Goodwill program and whose booklet The Fires of Group Work is sold through the Lucis Trust Store to this day. Crook presented the World Core Curriculum at a World Goodwill Seminar at which Robert Muller also spoke.

17. Lyndsey Layton, "How Bill Gates pulled off the swift Common Core revolution," *Washington Post*, January 6, 2015. Documents the Gates Foundation's approximately $5.2 million in grants to Jeb Bush's Foundation for Excellence in Education during the Common Core adoption push, alongside parallel funding to the National Governors Association, the Council of Chief State School Officers, and Achieve Inc.

18. HB 1792 (New Hampshire House, 2026)—The Countering Hate And Revolutionary Leftist Indoctrination in Education (CHARLIE) Act. Prime sponsor: Rep. Belcher, Carr. 4; co-sponsors: Rep. Noble, Hills. 2; Rep. Osborne, Rock. 2; Rep. Corcoran, Hills. 28; Rep. Sabourin dit Choiniere, Rock. 30. The bill's statement of findings establishes that certain pedagogical practices derived from Hegelian or Marxist dialectical analysis, Paulo Freire's critical pedagogy, Crenshaw's intersectionality framework, critical race theory, critical legal theory, and LGBTQ+ ideology as prescriptive worldview promote purposeful division by framing society through lenses of inherent oppression and liberation narratives. It finds that government-run education should not infringe on the sovereign spheres reserved to the family or religion, and that "culturally relevant" pedagogies build barriers to a unifying American culture by establishing permanent, balkanized subcultures exploited by demagogues. The operative section prohibits public schools and employees from engaging in the pedagogy, praxis, or inculcation of critical theories that promote division, dialectical worldviews, critical consciousness, or anti-constitutional indoctrination—including teaching that American structures are inherently illegitimate, compelling students to identify "oppressors" and "oppressed" through Marxist lenses, implementing culturally relevant pedagogy that prioritizes identity-based division, inculcating LGBTQ+ ideology as normative, or using dialectical analysis to frame events primarily as identity-based conflicts. The act preserves factual, neutral instruction on historical events and permits instruction on critical race theory only if presented objectively as Marxian theory contrary to American tradition. Violations constitute unprofessional conduct and may result in certification revocation. A private right of action permits civil suits with compensatory damages up to $10,000 per violation plus attorney fees. The act does not apply to higher education, private schools, or homeschools.

19. HB 129 (New Hampshire House, 2025)—The Science in Education Act. Prime sponsor: Rep. Belcher, Carr. 4; co-sponsors: Rep. Corcoran, Hills. 28; Rep. Drye, Sull. 7; Rep. Noble, Hills. 2; Rep. Peternel, Carr. 6; Rep. Sabourin, Rock. 30. Designed specifically to target the replication crisis in the education field brought about by the alignment of education with religious Leftism. The act seeks to prohibit pedagogical methods that utilize bad science to uphold their own legitimacy, defining "evidence-based" according to the actual scientific method—falsifiability, reproducibility, and resistance to falsification—rather than institutional consensus or peer review alone. Legislative findings: The scientific method relies on the concept of falsifiability and testing of theorems in properly designed experimentation to test truth claims. The paramount metric and standard for evaluation of theorems is resistance to falsification by achieving repeatedly consistent results over multiple experiments. While peer review of studies has uses, including evaluating the proper design of studies, peer review alone has no weight in evaluating or falsifying truth claims. A rigorously scientific approach to education will give substantial weight to repeatability of studies confirming theorems of educational praxis while affording relatively little weight to peer review alone. Operative provisions: All methods of delivering public education shall be evidence-based, including educator training, policies, and any pedagogical methods attached to or accompanying curriculum. "Evidence-based" shall exclude surveys and other self-reported data sets, and other subjective measurements such as reports of student progress and learning. "Evidence-based" means methods or techniques that meet at least one of the following requirements, without regard to peer review status: (a) reproducibility in multiple, well-designed studies within a single discipline; (b) independent confirmation by well-designed studies across multiple disciplines. The department and all local school districts shall make publicly available the scientific studies on which they relied to assure the methods meet the definition of "evidence-based."

20. Anthony S. Fauci, interview on *Face the Nation*, CBS News, November 28, 2021. The full quote: "So if they get up and criticize science, nobody's going to know what they're talking about. But if they get up and really aim their bullets at Tony Fauci, well, people can recognize there's a person there. So it's easy to criticize, but they're really criticizing science because I represent science." The remarkable feature of this statement is not its arrogance but its precision: Dr. Fauci had become *incapable* of distinguishing between his institutional position and the scientific method itself, and he said so on national television. The conflation is the diagnosis.

21. Jason Rafferty et al., "Ensuring Comprehensive Care and Support for Transgender and Gender-Diverse Children and Adolescents," *Pediatrics* 142, no. 4 (October 2018). The policy statement endorses the so-called "affirming care" model and was authored by a single committee whose composition reflected the prior ideological commitments of the participants. James M. Cantor's subsequent fact-check, "Transgender and Gender Diverse Children and Adolescents: Fact-Checking of AAP Policy," *Journal of Sex & Marital Therapy* 46, no. 4 (2020): 307–313, documented that the AAP policy statement systematically misrepresented every cited study, in each case in the direction of the affirming-care conclusion, and that the underlying evidence base did not support the position the AAP took. The AAP has not retracted the statement.

22. U.S. Food and Drug Administration, "Fact Sheet for Health Care Providers: Emergency Use Authorization (EUA) of Sotrovimab," revisions in 2021 and 2022, p. 3, which authorized clinicians to consider "race or ethnicity" as a factor that "may also place individual patients at high risk for progression to severe COVID-19." Operationally, this language gave state health departments cover to introduce racial weighting into rationing schemes for scarce monoclonal antibodies and oral antivirals during the Omicron period. Three states implemented explicit scoring frameworks: New York State Department of Health Memorandum, "Prioritization of Anti-SARS-CoV-2 Monoclonal Antibodies and Oral Antivirals for the Treatment of COVID-19 During Times of Resource Limitations," December 27, 2021, which classified "non-white race or Hispanic/Latino ethnicity" as an independent risk factor; Utah Department of Health, "Crisis Standards of Care Monoclonal Antibody Allocation Guidelines," January 2022, which assigned non-white race a 2-point weight on a 25-point clinical-risk scale—identical in weight to congestive heart failure, and double the weight of diabetes; and Minnesota Department of Health, "Ethical Framework for the Allocation of Monoclonal Antibodies," December 2021. Utah and Minnesota withdrew the racial criterion in early 2022 following litigation threats; the New York policy was challenged in *Jacobson v. Bassett* (N.D.N.Y.) and *Roberts v. Bassett* (E.D.N.Y.). The point for the present argument is not the legal disposition but the operational fact: the medical priesthood, given a scarce drug and a patient at the bedside, judged that race-as-class-membership should outrank congestive heart failure in determining who lived and who did not. That is not medicine. That is the doctrine.

23. The substitution of *equity* for *equality* in late-twentieth-century progressive jurisprudence and rhetoric is not a synonym swap. The two terms refer to incompatible regimes. *Equality* in the American constitutional tradition is procedural and applies to persons: the Fourteenth Amendment's Equal Protection Clause guarantees that the state will treat each person under the same rules. *Equity*, as the term is now deployed, is statistical and applies to demographic aggregates: the regime is judged by whether outcomes across groups are proportional, and the state is licensed to administer differential treatment of individuals to engineer that proportionality. The shift is operationalized by Ibram X. Kendi, *How to Be an Antiracist* (New York: One World, 2019), Chapter 1: "The only remedy to racist discrimination is antiracist discrimination. The only remedy to past discrimination is present discrimination. The only remedy to present discrimination is future discrimination." See also john a. powell, "Deepening Our Understanding of Structural Marginalization," *Poverty & Race* 22, no. 5 (2013), and the Othering & Belonging Institute's ongoing distinction between "formal equality" (rejected) and "targeted universalism" (endorsed). The clearest popular illustration is the cartoon, widely deployed in DEI training, of three figures of unequal height watching a baseball game over a fence: under "equality" each receives an identical box to stand on; under "equity" the boxes are reapportioned so each can see over the fence. The cartoon is sentimental but the operational point it conceals is severe: equity, in the regime that wields the term, requires a central authority to measure each person, classify her, and reapportion accordingly. Equality requires nothing of the kind. The replacement of one with the other transforms the entire constitutional logic of the American order.

24. On Marcuse's rehabilitation of pederasty as the "road to higher culture" in *Eros and Civilization*, see the extended treatment in the chapter on the Esoteric Lineage above, including the verification questions surrounding p. 211 of the 1966 Beacon Press paperback. The point for the present chapter is narrower: Marcuse and his successors operationalized the rehabilitation through the doctrine of *repressive tolerance*—see Herbert Marcuse, "Repressive Tolerance," in Robert Paul Wolff, Barrington Moore Jr., and Herbert Marcuse, *A Critique of Pure Tolerance* (Boston: Beacon Press, 1965)—which holds that "genuine" tolerance requires the active suppression of right-coded speech and the active promotion of left-coded speech. This is the operational doctrine that authorizes the censorship apparatus around every laundered claim discussed in this chapter.

25. On the failure of the gender-affirming care evidence base under serious methodological scrutiny, see the extended discussion later in this book, with full citation to the Cass Review (NHS England, April 2024), the Miroshnychenko et al. McMaster meta-analysis (*Archives of Disease in Childhood*, January 2025), and the Ruuska et al. Finnish national-register cohort (*Acta Paediatrica*, April 2026). Three independent authoritative reviews, three separate national contexts, one conclusion. The American medical establishment's continued endorsement of the affirming-care model in the face of this evidence is not a scientific finding. It is a confessional commitment.

26. Al Gore, address to the COP15 climate conference, Copenhagen, December 14, 2009, citing then-recent projections by Wieslaw Maslowski and colleagues for an ice-free Arctic within 5–7 years. Gore: "The entire North polar ice cap may well be completely gone in 5 years." The North Pole has retained ice every year since. Earlier deadlines failed earlier: the 2007 IPCC AR4 projected significant Arctic ice persistence into the 2050s; activist amplification compressed those timelines repeatedly across two decades; none of the predicted catastrophes occurred on the predicted schedule; no major activist or institutional figure has retracted any of them. The pattern—serial confident prophecy followed by serial silent failure followed by serial new confident prophecy—is diagnostic of religious eschatology, not of empirical science. As I argue in the dialectic chapter, science answers to falsification; prophecy answers to the imperative of the eschaton.

27. Robin DiAngelo, *White Fragility: Why It's So Hard for White People to Talk About Racism* (Boston: Beacon Press, 2018); Ibram X. Kendi, *How to Be an Antiracist* (New York: One World, 2019). DiAngelo's consulting practice charges institutional clients in the tens of thousands of dollars per engagement; Kendi's Boston University Center for Antiracist Research received approximately $43 million in pledges following the summer of 2020 and was the subject of internal restructuring and layoffs within three years. The financial dependency of the priesthood on the perpetuity of the diagnosis is the empirical answer to the question "why will this never end?" Both authors' frameworks are unfalsifiable by design: the absence of observed racism is interpreted as evidence of more sophisticated racism, in precisely the structure of the medieval witch test.

28. Michael Crichton, "Aliens Cause Global Warming," Caltech Michelin Lecture, Pasadena, CA, January 17, 2003. Crichton's exact formulation: "Let's be clear: the work of science has nothing whatever to do with consensus. Consensus is the business of politics. Science, on the contrary, requires only one investigator who happens to be right, which means that he or she has results that are verifiable by reference to the real world. In science consensus is irrelevant. What is relevant is reproducible results." Crichton, an MD trained at Harvard Medical School and a working scientist before becoming a novelist, was, in 2003, ahead of nearly every credentialed academic in identifying the precise mechanism by which *consensus* was being weaponized to terminate inquiry. He died in 2008; the lecture is preserved at the Stephen H. Schneider archive at Stanford and is widely reprinted.

29. Willi Münzenberg, quoted in Stephen Koch, *Double Lives: Stalin, Willi Münzenberg, and the Seduction of the Intellectuals* (New York: Free Press, 1994), 14–15. See also Babette Gross, *Willi Münzenberg: A Political Biography*, trans. Marian Jackson (East Lansing: Michigan State University Press, 1974).

30. Good Start, Grow Smart: The Bush Administration's Early Childhood Initiative. White House Office of the Press Secretary, announcement and fact sheet, April 2, 2002. Archived at georgewbush-whitehouse.archives.gov/infocus/earlychild hood/earlychildhood.html. The initiative established federal guidance on "early learning" standards, including social-emotional development benchmarks from birth through age five, and provided the federal architecture later extended into K–12 through the SEL apparatus.

31. HR 7 (New Hampshire House, 2025)—Resolution to Investigate Impeachment of Judge David Ruoff. Prime sponsor: Rep. Belcher, Carr. 4; co-sponsors: Rep. Bernardy, Rock. 36; Rep. Weyler, Rock. 14. A resolution instructing the House to investigate whether grounds exist to impeach Judge David Ruoff for his decision in Contoocook Valley School District et al. v. State of New Hampshire. The resolution documents that Ruoff demanded the allocation of over $500,000,000 of state funds in excess of those allocated by the legislature—powers delegated exclusively to the legislature under the state constitution, Part 2, Articles 5 and 56—and that Ruoff himself acknowledged the legislature's exclusive budgetary authority even as he attempted to exercise it. The resolution further charges that Ruoff refused to stay his own order pending Supreme Court review, throwing the government into chaos. It directs the House to investigate and submit a report by November 1, 2025.

32. Karl Popper, *The Open Society and Its Enemies*, vol. 1, *The Spell of Plato* (London: Routledge, 1945), note 4 to Chapter 7. Popper's formulation, in full: "Unlimited tolerance must lead to the disappearance of tolerance. If we extend unlimited tolerance even to those who are intolerant, if we are not prepared to defend a tolerant society against the onslaught of the intolerant, then the tolerant will be destroyed, and tolerance with them." The note was a footnote to Popper's broader argument that Plato's *Republic* represented not the foundation of open-society thought but its philosophical enemy—a closed, totalitarian social order dressed in philosophical garb. The irony of Popper's formulation being weaponized, over the subsequent eighty years, almost exclusively against the Right by descendants of the Platonic tradition Popper himself identified as totalitarian is itself instructive about the inversion mechanism this chapter describes. For the dialectical inversion proper, see Herbert Marcuse, "Repressive Tolerance," in Robert Paul Wolff, Barrington Moore Jr., and Herbert Marcuse, *A Critique of Pure Tolerance* (Boston: Beacon Press, 1965), which argues that genuine tolerance requires repression of Rightist movements and active promotion of Leftist ones. Marcuse's essay is the operational doctrine that has animated the one-directional application of the paradox ever since.

33. HR 6 (New Hampshire House, 2025)—Condemning the Judicial Doctrine of Disparate Impact. Prime sponsor: Rep. Belcher, Carr. 4; co-sponsor: Rep. Perez, Rock. 16. Condemns the judicial doctrine of disparate impact as unscientific nonsense—reliant on univariate analysis of complex phenomena—good only for rationalizing discrimination and effecting Leftist activism from the bench based on phenomenological critical legal theory that has no limiting principles. Whereas, the practice of univariate analysis for complex, real-world phenomena is illegitimate and unscientific, rendering such nonsensical conclusions as "thing one happened, then thing two happened, therefore the first thing was causative of the second thing"; and whereas, the judicial doctrine of "disparate impact" is reliant upon univariate analysis of complex, real-world phenomena to assign causation and legal responsibility; and whereas, this judicial doctrine has served to legitimize the wholly illegitimate, anti-constitutional practices of "critical legal theory," with the attendant holistic, phenomenological approach to legal interpretation; whereas, holistic phenomenology, as critical legal theory, has no limiting principles, thereby rendering all conceivable connections, second, third, and further order factors as "causative," and therefore legally implicated, eligible for regulatory actions, and imposing liability; resolved by the House of Representatives that the judicial doctrine of "disparate impact" must be overturned as a necessary restraint on government and to secure the liberty of the people, the exercise of federalism, and the powers delegated to the several states.

www.ingramcontent.com/pod-product-compliance
Lightning Source LLC
Chambersburg PA
CBHW051217130726
47988CB00001B/117